Just for the Middle Level SSAT

- **Test Prep Works materials are developed for a specific test and level, making it easier for students to focus on relevant content**

- **The Middle Level SSAT is for students applying for admission to grades 6-8 – see table at the end of this book for materials for other grades**

- **Two books are available from Test Prep Works to help students prepare for the Middle Level SSAT**

Success on the Middle Level SSAT: A Complete Course

- Strategies for each section of the test

- Reading and vocabulary drills

- In-depth math content instruction with practice sets

- 1 full-length practice test

The Best Unofficial Practice Tests for the Middle Level SSAT

- 2 full-length practice tests

 W9-AZI-663

Are you an educator?

Incorporate materials from Test Prep Works into your test prep program

- Use the materials developed specifically for the test and level your students are taking

- Customize our books to fit your program

    - Choose content modules from any of our books – even from multiple books

    - Add your branding to the cover and title page

    - Greet your students with an introductory message

    - Create custom books with a one-time setup fee[1], then order copies at list price[2] with no minimum quantities

- Volume discounts available for bulk orders of 50+ copies

You provide the expertise – let us provide the materials

Contact *sales@testprepworks.com* for more info

1 - Setup fees start at $199 per title, which includes branding of the cover and title page and a customer-provided introductory message. Additional customization will incur additional setup fees.

2 - The list price for custom books is the same as the list price of the corresponding title available for retail sale. If the content of a book is modified so that it no longer corresponds to a book available for retail sale, then Test Prep Works will set the list price prior to assessing any setup fees.

SUCCESS

on the
Middle Level SSAT®
a Complete Course

2019-2020

Christa Abbott, M.Ed.

Published by:
Test Prep Works
PO Box 100572
Arlington, VA 22210

For information about buying this title in bulk, or for editions with customized covers or content, please contact us in writing at sales@testprepworks.com, by phone at (703) 944-6727, or visit our website at www.AbbottLearning.com.

The SSAT is a registered trademark of The Enrollment Management Association, which has neither endorsed nor associated itself in any way with this book.

Neither the author nor the publisher of this book claims responsibility for the accuracy of this book or the outcome of students who use these materials.

ISBN: 978-1-68059-000-5

Contents

———

———

Notes for Parents

What is the SSAT?

The SSAT is a standardized admissions test. It is used by many of the top independent schools in the United States. You may have heard of another test, the ISEE (Independent School Entrance Exam). The schools that your student is applying to may accept either the SSAT or the ISEE, or they may exclusively use one test or the other. It can also depend upon what grade your child is applying for. Contact each school that your child will apply to in order to be sure that he or she is taking the correct test.

- Contact schools so that your child takes the correct test

Which Level Should I Register My Child For?

This book is designed to help students who are taking the Middle Level SSAT. If students are currently in grades 5-7, applying for grades 6-8, then they should be taking the Middle Level SSAT.

- Middle Level is for students currently in grades 5-7, applying for grades 6-8

Just How Important is the SSAT to the Admissions Process?

Every school uses the test differently. In general, the more competitive the school, the more that test scores are going to matter, but there are certainly exceptions to that rule. Reading through a school's literature is a great way to figure out whether or not a school emphasizes or deemphasizes testing. Also, call the admissions office where your child will be applying. Admissions officers are often quite candid about what the testing profile of their admitted students tends to be.

- Talk to the schools that your child is applying to in order to get a sense of the scores they look for

How Can I Help My Student?

Keep your own cool. Never once has a student gotten a higher score because mom or dad freaked out. Approach this as a project. Good test taking skills can be learned and by working through the process with your child in a constructive manner, you are providing them with a roadmap for how to approach challenges in the future. We want them to be confident, but to earn that confidence through analysis, self-monitoring, and practice.

- Keep a positive attitude

What are the key elements of successful test preparation?

Analysis

It is important that students don't just do practice problem after practice problem without figuring out what they missed, and most importantly WHY they missed those problems. Is there a particular type of problem that they keep missing? One issue that many students have is categorizing problems. When you go through a problem that they are stuck on, be sure to point out the words in the problem that pointed you in the correct direction.

- Teach your child to analyze why he or she missed a question

Self-monitoring

Students should develop a sense of their strengths and weaknesses so that they can best focus preparation time. This book provides many practice opportunities for each section, but your child may not need that. For example, if they are acing the average problems, they shouldn't keep spending valuable time doing more of those problems. Maybe their time would be better spent on vocabulary. This is a great opportunity, and your student is at the perfect age, to be learning how to prioritize.

- Help your student prioritize material to work on

Practice

While it is important that a student understand WHY he is doing what he is doing, at a certain point it just needs to become automatic. This is a timed test and you want the strategies to spring to mind without having to reinvent the wheel every time. Practice will make this process fast and easy. On test day all that practice will kick in to make this a positive and affirming experience for your student.

- Teach your child that he or she needs to practice what they have learned so that it is automatic on test day

What Do Parents Need to Know About Registration?

Registration is done through The Enrollment Management Association. Their website is www.ssat.org. When you register for the test, be sure to also order the official SSAT book, *The Official Guide to the Middle Level SSAT*. You can also sign up for their online practice portal for additional practice questions. Nothing can replace the practice tests in this book because they are written by the people who write the actual test that your student will be taking.

- Order the practice book from www.ssat.org and sign up for their online practice portal

There are a few other things you should know about registration options:

You can choose from either a national test date or a flex test date

On the national test dates, the SSAT is given in a group setting. It is a similar experience to what you might remember when you took the SAT or ACT. The flex test can be given in the office of an educational consultant in a small group, or even a one-on-one, setting.

There are many advantages of the flex testing

You can generally pick a day and time. If your child doesn't do well in the morning, schedule it for the afternoon. If you really want to get the test out of the way before the holidays and are away when the national test is given in December, then you can choose another day. Also, fewer students means fewer distractions. Flex testing is more expensive than national testing, but given the investment that you are making in independent school, it can be well worth it.

To find consultants in your area, visit www.ssat.org, go to the "About SSAT" link at the top of the page, and hover over "Registration" from the drop-down menu. From the sub-menu, choose "Find a Test Center." On that page, click on the "Flex Test w/ Consultant" tab and look for a consultant close to you. (This information is current as of August 4, 2019 – if you cannot find this document then the SSAT website may have changed!)

One big disadvantage of the flex testing is that you can only do it once per testing (or academic) year

Only one flex test form of the SSAT is developed each year, so a student can only do flex testing once each year. However, students can take the test on a flex test date and then one of the national dates (or vice versa) if they want to retake the test.

The SSAT does offer score choice

What this means is that you can take the test as many times as you want and then choose the test date (or dates) that you wish to send. Don't make your student anxious by having him or her take the test a bunch of times, but for some students it reduces stress to know that they can have another shot at the test.

You must request accommodations if your child needs them

If your child has an IEP or receives accommodations in school, then start the paperwork with the SSAT promptly. Don't wait until the last minute, because accommodations must be approved before you register. Spots for students with accommodations may be limited at a testing site and fill early. If your child is going to get extended time, he or she should also know that as he or she works through practice tests.

Above all else, remember that your student will look to you to see how you approach this challenge. If you become anxious, they will too. If you are confident about developing a game plan and building confidence through practice, this experience will stay with them in a profoundly positive way.

National testing dates for 2019-2020

Registration for national testing dates began on August 1, 2019. The dates and associated deadlines for the Middle Level SSAT are listed in the table below – again, don't wait until the deadline if you are requesting accommodations. Go to www.ssat.org to register.

Test Date	Regular Deadline (no added late fee)	Last Possible Day to Register	$45 Late Fee Added	$85 Rush Fee Added
Oct 19, 2019	Sep 28, 2019	Oct 16, 2019	Sep 29 - Oct 5	Oct 6 - Oct 16
Nov 16, 2019	Oct 26, 2019	Nov 13, 2019	Oct 28 - Nov 2	Nov 3 - Nov 13
Dec 14, 2019	Nov 23, 2019	Dec 11, 2019	Nov 24 - Nov 30	Dec 1 - Dec 11
Jan 4, 2020	Dec 14, 2019	Jan 1, 2020	Dec 15 - Dec 21	Dec 22 - Jan 1
Feb 8, 2020	Jan 18, 2020	Feb 5, 2020	Jan 19 - Jan 25	Jan 26 - Feb 5
Mar 7, 2020	Feb 15, 2020	Mar 4, 2020	Feb 16 - Feb 22	Feb 23 - Mar 4
Apr 25, 2020	Apr 4, 2020	Apr 22, 2020	Apr 5 - Apr 11	Apr 12 - Apr 22
Jun 13, 2020	May 23, 2020	Jun 10, 2020	May 24 - May 30	May 31 - Jun 10

This table reflects the information available on www.ssat.org as of August 4, 2019. Please visit www.ssat.org to ensure you have the latest information as you make plans for your student.

———

How To Use This Book

This book is designed to teach you what you need to know in order to maximize your Middle Level SSAT performance.

There are strategies for each of the four multiple-choice sections as well as advice on the writing section. This book also includes a lot of content practice. There is a complete vocabulary section and detailed instruction for the math concepts that are tested on the SSAT.

You may find that you don't need to complete all of the content instruction. It is important to prioritize your time! If vocabulary is a weakness for you, then spend your time working through the vocabulary lessons. If some of the math concepts are challenging, then you should spend your study time working through the math sections.

There is also a full-length practice exam at the end of this book.

I have spent years studying the test and analyzing the different question types, content, and types of answers that the test writers prefer. Now you can benefit from my hard work! I will show you how to approach questions so that you can raise your score significantly.

Let's get started!

———

The Format of the Middle Level SSAT

You can expect to see four scored sections *plus* a writing sample *plus* an experimental section on the Middle Level SSAT.

The Four Scored Sections

- ✓ Quantitative (there will be two of these sections on your test)
  - A variety of math problems
  - Each section has 25 problems, for a total of 50 math problems
  - 30 minutes to complete each section, or a little more than a minute per problem

- ✓ Verbal
  - 30 synonym questions and 30 analogy questions
  - 30 minutes to complete the section, or about 30 seconds per question

- ✓ Reading Comprehension
  - Passages and questions
  - Passages can be fiction, non-fiction, and poetry
  - A total of 40 questions
  - Generally 6-8 passages, each passage having 4-8 questions, but this is not carved in stone so you may see some variation
  - 40 minutes to complete section

The four above sections are all multiple choice. Each question has five answer choices.

There are two other sections that you will see on the SSAT:

The Experimental Section

- ✓ 15 minutes to complete
- ✓ Will NOT contribute to your score – the SSAT is just trying out new problems for future tests
- ✓ You may not even see this section (if you have extended time, you probably will not)

The Writing Sample

- ✓ Will NOT be scored, but a copy will be sent to all of the schools that you apply to
- ✓ Choice of two writing prompts – both are the beginning sentence of a story and you can choose which story you wish to finish
- ✓ 25 minutes to write, and you will be given two pages to write on

Now, on to the strategies and content! The strategies covered in this book will focus on the multiple-choice sections since those are what is used to determine your percentile score. Please also see the section near the back with tips on the writing sample.

What Students Need To Know for the SSAT - Just the Basics

Here is what you really need to know to do well on the Middle Level SSAT:

How the Scoring Works

On the Middle Level SSAT, if you answer a question correctly, then you are given one point. If you answer a question incorrectly, then you lose a quarter point. If you don't answer a question, then a point isn't added to your raw score, but you don't lose a quarter point either.

- If you answer a question correctly, you get one point

- If you answer a question incorrectly, you lose $\dfrac{1}{4}$ point

- If you don't answer the question at all, you don't get a point but you don't lose $\dfrac{1}{4}$ point either

You might be asking why they use this crazy system. The thinking behind it is that on a regular test, you would get ahead by guessing. You would answer some of the questions that you guessed on correctly, and therefore your score would be higher for blindly guessing. Chances are you would answer $\dfrac{1}{5}$ of the questions correctly if you blindly guessed, because there are five answer choices for each question. By taking off $\dfrac{1}{4}$ point for the $\dfrac{4}{5}$ of the questions that you miss, the test writers are making sure that you don't get ahead for blindly guessing.

- Example: You guess on five questions, answering one correctly.

1 correct answer $\times 1 = +1$ point

4 incorrect answers $\times \left(-\dfrac{1}{4} \right) = -1$ point
_____
0 points gained or lost

When to Guess

With this scoring policy, you should guess if you can rule out one or more answer choices.

What Schools are Looking for and the Beauty of the Percentile Score

You will get a raw score for the SSAT based upon how many questions you answer correctly or incorrectly. This raw score will then be converted into a scaled score. Neither of these scores is what schools are really evaluating. They are looking for your percentile scores that compare you to other students applying to independent schools.

- Percentile score is what schools are really looking at

The percentile score compares you to other students that are in your grade. For example, let's say that you are in eighth grade and you scored in the 70th percentile. What this means is that out of 100 students in your grade, you would have scored higher than 70 of them.

Keep in mind that the Middle Level SSAT is given to students through the 7th grade. That means that if you are taking the test in 5th grade, there could very well be material on the test that you simply have not yet covered. You may miss some of these questions, but as long as the other students your age also miss them, then it won't affect your percentile score.

- Your percentile score compares you only to other students in your grade

Many students applying to independent schools are used to answering almost every question correctly on a test. You will probably miss more questions on this test than you are used to missing, but because the percentile score is what schools are looking at, don't let it get to you.

- You may miss more questions than you are used to, but that is OK as long as other students your age also miss those questions

Learn to Rule Out Answer Choices

Use the Process of Elimination, or "Ruling Out"

If you remember nothing else on test day, remember to use the process of elimination. This is a multiple-choice test, and there are often answers that don't even make sense.

After you read a question, you should read all of the answer choices before selecting one. You need to keep in mind that the test will ask you to choose the answer choice that "best" answers the question. "Best" is a relative word, so how can you know which answer choice best answers the question if you don't read them all?

- After you read the question, read ALL of the answer choices
- Look for the "best" answer, which may just be the least wrong answer choice

After you have read all of the answer choices, rule them out in order from most wrong to least wrong. Sometimes the "best" answer choice is not a great fit, but it is better than the others. This process will also clarify your thinking so that by the time you get down to only two answer choices, you have a better idea of what makes choices right or wrong.

- Rule out in order from most wrong to least wrong

Above all else, remember that you are playing the odds on this test. To increase your score, you need to answer questions even when you are not positive what the correct answer is.

Let's say that you rule out three answer choices on four questions. You then guess on those questions. If you answer two of those questions correctly (which is the most likely outcome), then the scoring would look like this:

$$2 \text{ correct answers} \times 1 = +2 \text{ points}$$

$$2 \text{ incorrect answers} \times \left(-\frac{1}{4}\right) = -\frac{1}{2} \text{ point}$$

$$\overline{\text{Total change to score} = +1\frac{1}{2} \text{ points}}$$

Now let's say that you only answer 1 question correctly out of those 4 questions. The scoring would look like this:

$$1 \text{ correct answer} \times 1 = +1 \text{ point}$$

$$3 \text{ incorrect answers} \times \left(-\frac{1}{4}\right) = -\frac{3}{4} \text{ point}$$

$$\text{Total change to score} = +\frac{1}{4} \text{ point}$$

As you can see, if you missed three questions and only answered one question correctly, you would still come out ahead.

- Ruling out allows you to play the odds, and that is how you will come out ahead of your peers

Verbal Section — Basic Strategies

In the verbal section you will see two question types:

- Synonyms
- Analogies

On the synonym questions, you will be given one question word and be asked to choose the answer choice that has the word that comes closest in meaning to the question word.

Synonym questions look something like this:

1. JOYOUS:
    - (A) loud
    - (B) crying
    - (C) happy
    - (D) shy
    - (E) lame

Out of all the answer choice words, *happy* comes closest in meaning to *joyous*. Choice C is correct.

The synonym questions probably won't be quite this easy, but you get the idea.

The analogy questions generally give you two words, and you have to figure out the relationship between them and then choose the answer choice that has the same relationship.

The analogy questions usually look something like this:

2. Panther is to cat as
    - (A) lion is to jungle
    - (B) wolf is to dog
    - (C) chick is to blue jay
    - (D) mouse is to guinea pig
    - (E) horse is to cow

In this case, a *panther* is a wild cat. A *wolf* is a wild dog, so choice B is correct.

Sometimes, you will be given the first word in the answer relationship and you will have to choose the second word.

These questions look like this:

3. Tall is to short as narrow is to

    (A) long
    (B) square
    (C) wide
    (D) measured
    (E) lax

Tall and *short* are opposites, so we are looking for the answer choice that is the opposite of *narrow*. *Wide* is the opposite of *narrow*, so choice C is correct.

Since synonym and analogy questions are very different, we use different strategies for them.

Synonym Strategies

There are several strategies that we can use on the synonym section. Which strategy you use for an individual question is highly variable. It depends on the word roots you know, whether or not you have heard the word before, and your gut sense about a word.

Think of these strategies as being your toolbox. Several tools can get the job done.

One thing that you should note is that the synonym questions tend to go in order from easiest to most difficult. The difficulty of the question will affect which strategy you use.

Here are the strategies:

*   Come up with your own word
*   Is it positive or negative?
*   Can you think of a sentence or phrase in which you have heard the word?
*   Are there any roots or word parts that you recognize?
*   If you have to guess, see if there is an answer choice that has the same prefix, suffix or root as the question word

Strategy #1: Come up with your own word

Use this strategy when you read through a question and a word just pops into your head. Don't force yourself to try to come up with your own definition when you aren't sure what the word means.

*   Use this strategy when a definition pops into your head

If you read a question word and a synonym pops into your head, go ahead and jot it down. It is important that you write down the word because otherwise you may try to talk yourself into an answer choice that "seems to come close." One of your biggest enemies on any standardized test is doubt. Doubt leads to talking yourself into the wrong answer. Writing down the word gives you the confidence you need when you go through the answer choices.

- Physically write down the definition – don't hold it in your head

After you write down the word, start by crossing out answer choices that are not synonyms for your word. By the time you get down to two choices, you will have a much better idea of what you are looking for.

- Cross out words that don't work

The following drill contains words that you may be able think of a definition for. These are the types of words that you are likely to see at the beginning of the synonym section. You should focus on creating good habits with these questions.

What are good habits?

- Jot down the definition – this will actually save time in the long run
- Use ruling out – physically cross out answer choices that you know are incorrect

1. RAPID:

   (A) marvelous
   (B) exhausted
   (C) swift
   (D) professional
   (E) icy

2. STEADY:

   (A) constant
   (B) nervous
   (C) friendly
   (D) hollow
   (E) cozy

3. DEBRIS:

   (A) whim
   (B) trash
   (C) core
   (D) knapsack
   (E) humor

4. PLAYFUL:

   (A) loud
   (B) careful
   (C) honest
   (D) fun
   (E) respectful

5. SEQUENCE:

   (A) nation
   (B) resource
   (C) bid
   (D) farce
   (E) order

(Answers to this drill are found on page 33.)

Strategy #2: Using positive or negative

Sometimes you see a word, and you couldn't define that word, but you have a "gut feeling" that it is either something good or something bad. Maybe you don't know what that word means, but you know you would be mad if someone called you that!

- You have to have a gut feeling about a word to use this strategy

To use this strategy, when you get that feeling that a word is either positive or negative, then write in a "+" or a "–" next to the word. Then go to your answer choices and rule out anything that is opposite, i.e., positive when your question word is negative or negative when your question word is positive.

- Physically write a "+" or "–" after the question word

To really make this strategy work for you, you also need to rule out any words that are neutral, or neither positive nor negative. For example, let's say the question word is DISTRESS. *Distress* is clearly a negative word. So we could rule out a positive answer choice, such as *friendly*, but we can also rule out a neutral word, such as *sleepy*. At night, it is good to be sleepy, during the day it is not. *Sleepy* is not clearly a negative word, so it goes.

- Rule out words that are opposite from your question word
- Also rule out neutral words

To summarize, here are the basic steps to using this strategy:

1. If you have a gut negative or positive feeling about a word, write a "+" or "–" next to the question word
2. Rule out any words that are opposite
3. Also rule out any NEUTRAL words
4. Pick from what is left

Here is an example of a question where you may be able to use the positive/negative strategy:

4. CONDEMN:
   (A) arrive
   (B) blame
   (C) tint
   (D) favor
   (E) laugh

Let's say that you know that *condemn* is bad, but you can't think of a definition. We write a "–" next to it and then rule out anything that is positive. That means that choices D and E can go because they are both positive. Now we can also rule out neutral words because we know *condemn* has to be negative. *Arrive* and *tint* are neither positive nor negative, so choices A and C are out. We are left with choice B, which is correct.

On the following drill, write a "+" or "–" next to each question word. Then rule out answer choices that are opposite or neutral. Pick from what is left. Even if you aren't sure if the question word is positive or negative, take a guess at it! You may get more right than you would have imagined.

Drill #2

1. ALLURE:

   (A) attraction
   (B) color
   (C) disgrace
   (D) wilderness
   (E) confidence

2. SERENE:

   (A) confusing
   (B) musical
   (C) dark
   (D) tall
   (E) calm

3. HUMANE:

   (A) invalid
   (B) compassionate
   (C) portable
   (D) restricted
   (E) bashful

4. DEJECTED:

   (A) resourceful
   (B) humid
   (C) depressed
   (D) proper
   (E) cheery

5. REEK:

   (A) express
   (B) qualify
   (C) thrill
   (D) stink
   (E) flavor

(Answers to this drill are found on page 33.)

Strategy #3: Use context – Think of where you have heard the word before

Use this strategy when you can't define a word, but you can think of a sentence or phrase where you have heard the word before.

- This strategy only works when you have heard the word before

To apply this strategy, think of a sentence or phrase where you have heard the question word before. Then try plugging the answer choices into your phrase to see which one has the same meaning within that sentence or phrase.

- Think of a sentence or phrase where you have heard the word before
- Plug question words into that sentence or phrase

Here is an example:

5. SHIRK:

    (A) rush
    (B) send
    (C) learn
    (D) avoid
    (E) clutter

Now let's say you have heard the word *shirk* but can't define it. You remember your mom telling you "don't shirk your responsibilities" when you tried to watch TV before your chores were done. So we plug in the answer choices for the word *shirk* in your sentence. Does it make sense to say "don't rush your responsibilities?" It might make sense, but it wouldn't have the same meaning as your context. You weren't in trouble for rushing your chores, you were in trouble for not doing them at all, so we can rule out choice A. Does it make sense to say "don't send your responsibilities?" Not at all. Choice B is out. Does "don't learn your responsibilities" work? Nope, choice C is out. Would your mom say "don't avoid your responsibilities?" You bet. Choice D is correct. We would also plug in choice E to make sure it wasn't a better fit, but in this case it is not, and choice D is correct.

Sometimes the only word or phrase that you can think of uses a different form of the word. That is fine as long as you change the answer choices when you plug them in.

- You can use a different form of the word, just change answer choices as well

Here is an example:

6. CHERISH:

    (A) treasure
    (B) enforce
    (C) utter
    (D) concern
    (E) calm

Maybe you have heard your English teacher talk about *Little Women* as "one of my most cherished books." We can use that context, we just have to add the "-ed" to the answer choices when we plug them in. Does it make sense to say "one of my most treasured books?" Yes, it does, so we will keep choice A. Would "one of my most enforced books" work? No, so we can rule out choice B. What about "one of my most uttered books," or "one of my most concerned books," or "one of my most calmed books?" No, no, and no, so we rule out choices C, D, and E. Choice A is correct.

In the following drill, if you have heard the word before, then come up with a sentence or phrase and practice our strategy. If you have not heard the word before, you can't use the strategy of thinking where you have heard the word before! Use another strategy and ruling out to answer the question anyways. You may not answer every question correctly, but remember, nothing ventured, nothing gained.

Drill #3

1. WILY:

   (A) serious
   (B) flattering
   (C) tough
   (D) cunning
   (E) powerful

2. PROPHESY:

   (A) quiver
   (B) copy
   (C) mystify
   (D) predict
   (E) advance

3. ABOLISH:

   (A) end
   (B) salute
   (C) liberate
   (D) manage
   (E) baffle

4. APPALLING:

   (A) worthy
   (B) horrifying
   (C) available
   (D) omitted
   (E) various

5. CONSENT:

   (A) worry
   (B) knowledge
   (C) approval
   (D) draft
   (E) requirement

(Answers to this drill are found on page 33.)

Strategy #4: Look for roots or word parts that you know

This strategy works when you recognize that a word looks like another word that you know or when you recognize one of the roots that you have studied in school or in this book.

If you see something familiar in the question word, underline the roots or word parts that you recognize. If you can think of the meaning of the root, then look for answer choices that would go with that meaning. If you can't think of a specific meaning, think of other words that have that root and look for answer choices that are similar in meaning to those other words.

- Underline word parts that you recognize
- Think of the meaning of that word part
- If you can't think of a meaning, think of other words with that word part

Here is an example of a question that uses a word with recognizable word parts:

7. EXCLUDE:

   (A) prohibit
   (B) feel
   (C) rest
   (D) drift
   (E) rejoice

There are two word parts in the word *exclude* that can help us out. First, we have the prefix "ex" which means out (think of the word *exit*). Secondly, "clu" is a word root that means to shut (think of the word *include*). Using these word parts, we can see that *exclude* has something to do with shutting out. Choice A comes closest to this meaning, so it is correct.

For the following drill, try to use word parts to come up with the correct answer choice. If you can't think of what the word root, prefix, or suffix means, then think of other words that have the same root, prefix, or suffix.

1. MAGNANIMOUS:

   (A) possible
   (B) generous
   (C) cruel
   (D) restrained
   (E) barren

2. POSTPONE:

   (A) allow
   (B) recruit
   (C) delay
   (D) stifle
   (E) label

3. SUBTERRANEAN:

   (A) partial
   (B) tragic
   (C) appreciative
   (D) hectic
   (E) underground

4. ERR:

   (A) stumble
   (B) fix
   (C) expand
   (D) gasp
   (E) laugh

5. NONDESCRIPT:

   (A) wise
   (B) occasional
   (C) dreadful
   (D) vague
   (E) lazy

(Answers to this drill are found on page 33.)

_____

Strategy #5: Guess an answer choice with the same prefix, suffix, or word root as the question word

If nothing else, if you have no idea what the word means but you see an answer choice that has the same root, prefix, or suffix, then guess that answer choice! You would be amazed how many correct answers have the same root as the question word. What if there are two answer choices with the same root? Guess one of them. Remember, if we can rule out even one answer choice, we should guess.

Let's look at the following example:

8. PERMISSIBLE:

(A) edible
(B) crazy
(C) strong
(D) allowable
(E) gentle

Even if you don't know what _permissible_ means, the "–ible" ending tells us that it must mean "able to do something." The "–ible" and "–able" suffixes have the same meaning, so we could guess between choices A and D. _Edible_ means "able to be eaten," but _allowable_ is a synonym for _permissible_, so choice D is correct.

Complete the following drill by looking for answer choices that repeat roots, prefixes, or suffixes.

Drill #5

1. CONGEAL:

(A) bury
(B) habituate
(C) coagulate
(D) reimburse
(E) limit

2. DISPARAGE:

(A) resurrect
(B) discredit
(C) deceive
(D) praise
(E) label

3. COMPREHENSIBLE:

(A) laudable
(B) independent
(C) remorseful
(D) authentic
(E) understandable

(Answers to this drill are found on page 33.)

Now you have the strategies that you need to succeed on the synonym section! To keep improving your score, keep studying that vocabulary.

_____

Strategies for the Analogy Section

The analogy section tests not only your vocabulary, but also your ability to see how words are related.

We have two main strategies for the analogy section:

- If you know the question words, make a sentence

- If you don't know one of the question words, head to the answer choices

Strategy #1: Make a sentence from the question words

In order to use this strategy, you have to at least have a vague sense of what both question words mean. Basically, you make a sentence from the question words and then plug answer choices into that sentence to see which answer choice has the same relationship.

Here is an example of a question with words that we know and can make a sentence from:

9. Water is to ocean as

    (A) cloud is to sky
    (B) mountain is to hill
    (C) paint is to watercolor
    (D) ice is to glaciers
    (E) sneaker is to marathon

If we make a sentence from the question words, we might say "water fills the ocean." Now we plug in our answer choices, subbing in the answer words for the question words. Does it make sense to say "cloud fills the sky?" Sometimes that is true, but if we have to use the word sometimes, then it is not a strong relationship so we can rule out choice A. Does a "mountain fill a hill?" No, so choice B is gone. Does "paint fill a watercolor?" Not in the same way that water fills an ocean, so we can rule out choice C. Does "ice fill glaciers?" Yes. Choice D is correct. We would keep going and plug in choice E just to make sure that it wasn't a better fit, but choice D is correct.

The general steps to use this strategy are:

1. Make a sentence with question words

2. Plug answers into that sentence

3. Do NOT use the words *could*, *maybe*, *can*, or *sometimes* – if you have to use those words then the relationship is not strong enough

There are several relationships that show up frequently on the SSAT. If you become familiar with them, it makes it much easier to make up your own sentences quickly.

They are:

#1   Occupation – one word is a job related to the other word
      example: Architect is to building

#2   Part of – one word is a part of the other word
      example: Kitchen is to house

#3   Type of – one word is a type of the other word, which is a broader category
      example: Whale is to mammal

#4   Means without – one word means without the other word
      example: Poor is to money

#5   Used for – one word is used to do the other word
      example: Shovel is to dig

#6   Degree – the words have roughly the same meaning, only one is more extreme
      example: Hungry is to starving

#7   Characteristic of – one word is a characteristic of the other
      example: Massive is to elephant

#8   Synonyms – the words have roughly the same meaning
      example: Deceitful is to dishonest

#9   Antonyms – the words are opposite in meaning
      example: Friendly is to rude

#10   Sequence – there is a distinct order that the words go in (months, time, etc.)
      example: March is to July

#11   Found in – one word is found in the other
      example: Shark is to ocean

Keep in mind that every single analogy on this test is not going to have one of these relationships. But the vast majority of the questions will.

For the following drill, provide the number of the relationship from above that the words use.

Drill #6

1. Instruct is to teacher – uses relationship # _____

2. Sonnet is to poem – uses relationship # _____

3. Seahorse is to ocean – uses relationship # _____

4. Flat is to plains – uses relationship # _____

5. Wrench is to tightening – uses relationship # _____

6. Processor is to computer – uses relationship # _____

7. Bleak is to hopeful – uses relationship # _____

8. Audacious is to bold – uses relationship # _____

9. Daybreak is to noon – uses relationship # _____

10. Camera is to picture – uses relationship # _____

(Answers to this drill are found on page 33.)

Strategy #2: If you don't know one of the question words, go to the answer choices

If you read through the question words and don't know what one (or both) of the question words mean, all is not lost. Sometimes there are answer choices with words that are not even related. Rule these out. Then make sentences from the words in the remaining answer choices, plug in the question words, and see if it could work. Rule out any that don't. Guess from what you have left.

Here are the steps to this strategy:

1. Rule out answer choices that have unrelated words

2. Make a sentence with the remaining answer choices

3. Plug your question words into those sentences and see what could work

4. Remember to guess if you can rule out even one answer choice

Keep in mind that if you find yourself using *could*, *maybe*, *can*, or *sometimes*, it is not a strong relationship so you should rule it out. If you hear yourself using those words, you are talking yourself into a wrong answer choice!

- If you have to use *could*, *maybe*, *can*, or *sometimes*, then it is not a strong relationship and you should rule out that answer choice

_____

Here is an example:

10. (Weird word) is to ship as

    (A) luck is to delay
    (B) fun is to laughter
    (C) helmet is to football
    (D) mansion is to house
    (E) first is to last

Since we don't know one question word, we go to the answers. If we try to make a sentence from choice A, we can see that *luck* and *delay* just don't have a strong relationship. You could say that if you are lucky, you might not have a delay. However, that would be talking yourself into a relationship isn't strong at all (if you have to use *sometimes*, *might*, *may*, or *could*, it is not a good relationship). Choice A is out. For choice B, you could say that *laughter* is the result of *fun*. However, if we plug the question words back into that sentence, is there anything that *ship* is a result of? Not really, so we can rule out choice B. If we look at choice C, you could say that a *helmet* is worn to play *football*. But if we plug our question words into that sentence, is there anything that is worn to play ship? No. Choice C is out. On to choice D. A mansion is a type of house. Could something be a type of ship? Absolutely, so we keep choice D. Finally, choice E. *First* and *last* are opposites. But is there a word that means the opposite of *ship*? No, so choice E is out. We were able to narrow it down to one choice (choice D) without even knowing one of the question words.

For the following drill, you may not know one (or both!) of the question words. Rule out any answer choices that have words that are not related. From what is left, plug the question words into the sentence that you made from the answer choice. Rule out any answer choices that don't work. Remember, if you can rule out even one answer choice, then you should guess.

Drill #7

1. Contempt is to respect as

    (A) clever is to lazy
    (B) fast is to afraid
    (C) doubt is to delay
    (D) defined is to uncertainty
    (E) funny is to crowded

2. Nefarious is to villain

    (A) beneficent is to hero
    (B) crazy is to rock star
    (C) funny is to politician
    (D) loud is to nun
    (E) fast is to cast

3. Obliterate is to destroy

    (A) overlook is to film
    (B) build is to correct
    (C) horrify is to upset
    (D) ease is to worsen
    (E) ask is to function

4. Fortress is to stronghold

    (A) tiger is to lion
    (B) mansion is to shack
    (C) cuff is to shirt
    (D) criminal is to juvenile
    (E) car is to automobile

5. Cordial is to rude as

    (A) baffling is to strict
    (B) devoted is to mild
    (C) luxurious is to energetic
    (D) quaint is to sophisticated
    (E) cherished is to tough

(Answers to this drill are found on page 33.)

Answers to Synonyms and Analogies Drills

Drill #1

1. C
2. A
3. B
4. D
5. E

Drill #2

1. A
2. E
3. B
4. C
5. D

Drill #3

1. D
2. D
3. A
4. B
5. C

Drill #4

1. B
2. C
3. E
4. A
5. D

Drill #5

1. C
2. B
3. E

Drill #6

1. #1
2. #3
3. #11
4. #7
5. #5
6. #2
7. #9
8. #8
9. #10
10. #5

Drill #7

1. D
2. A
3. C
4. E
5. D

———

Additional Analogies Practice

Many students find the analogies to be particularly challenging. The following are drills that will give you more practice with the skills that you learned in the strategy section. You may not need this extra practice, but many students find it very helpful.

Drills #1-5 (p. 36-40) give you practice with making sentences from two words or determining if two words are not related. You can use these skills for making sentences from question words/answer choices and ruling out answer choices that have unrelated words.

It is important that you do the drills one at a time and check your answers between drills. We want you to figure out WHY you missed questions so that you can apply that knowledge to the next drill. You won't learn as you go if you just do all the drills in a row without checking answers.

- Check your answers after each drill
- Figure out what to do differently before you move on to the next drill

Drills #6-8 (p. 44-46) give you practice with figuring out answer choices when you don't know the meaning of one of the question words. Again, check your answers and read the explanations before moving onto the next drill.

Now onto the drills!

Drills #1-5

For these drills, you will be given two words in the format of an analogy question or answer choice. On the blank next to each word, write a sentence that relates the two words. If the words are NOT related at all, write NR on the blank.

- Write a sentence relating the two words if they are related
- If the words are not related, write NR on the blank

Be sure to check your answers and read explanations for any questions that you missed before you move onto the next drill. Your sentences will not be exactly like the answers given, but they should get at the same meaning.

- Check your answers and read explanations before moving onto the next drill

———

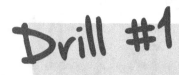

1.   Doctor is to prescription _____

2.   Tardy is to people _____

3.   Trickle is to deluge _____

4.   Untidy is to sarcastic _____

5.   Barn is to building _____

6.   Key is to lock _____

7.   Mast is to sail _____

8.   Concrete is to board _____

9.   Albino is to pigment _____

10. Bat is to cave _____

Now, check your answers. Answers to drills #1-5 begin on page 41.

Which questions did you miss?

What is one thing that you learned from the questions that you missed?

Drill #2

1. Creep is to crept _____

2. Pen is for painting _____

3. Industrious is to lazy _____

4. Introduction is to conclusion _____

5. Jar is to paper _____

6. Dog is to wolf _____

7. Placemat is to tray _____

8. Peel is to orange _____

9. Uniform is to soldier _____

10. Boisterous is to loud _____

Now, check your answers. Answers to drills #1-5 begin on page 41.

Which questions did you miss?

What is one thing that you learned from the questions that you missed?

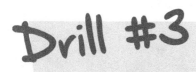
Drill #3

1.   Possible is to definite _____

2.   Regal is to queen _____

3.   Pond is to mountain _____

4.   Watercolor is to painting _____

5.   Pole is to firehouse _____

6.   Idea is to occupation _____

7.   Foggy is to hot _____

8.   Uniqueness is to conformity _____

9.   Fertile is to flattering _____

10. Stethoscope is to doctor _____

Now, check your answers. Answers to drills #1-5 begin on page 41.

Which questions did you miss?

What is one thing that you learned from the questions that you missed?

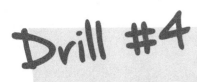

1. Mansion is to shack _____

2. Archipelago is to island _____

3. Meager is to overabundant _____

4. Request is to command _____

5. Lamp is to mirror _____

6. Cougar is to cat _____

7. Broom is to disinfect _____

8. Sill is to window _____

9. Satiated is to hungry _____

10. Violin is to piccolo _____

Now, check your answers. Answers to drills #1-5 begin on page 41.

Which questions did you miss?

What is one thing that you learned from the questions that you missed?

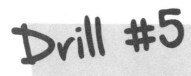

1. Decibel is to volume _____

2. Electricity is to coal _____

3. Treaty is to countries _____

4. Chemistry is to physics _____

5. Monkey is to tundra _____

6. Steel is to girder _____

7. Sport is to soccer _____

8. Limber is to flexible _____

9. Orange is to grass _____

10. Lavish is to Spartan _____

Now, check your answers. Answers to drills #1-5 begin on page 41.

Which questions did you miss?

What is one thing that you learned from the questions that you missed?

Answers to Drills 1-5

Drill #1

1. A doctor's job is to write prescriptions.
2. NR – A person could be tardy, but "could" tells us that it is not a strong relationship.
3. A deluge is a really big trickle. This is a degree relationship where one word is just more extreme than the other. It is OK to reverse the order of the words when we make a sentence as long as we then reverse the order of the answer choice words when we plug them into the sentence to see if the meaning is the same.
4. NR – These two words aren't related.
5. A barn is a type of building.
6. A key is used to open a lock.
7. A mast is used to hold up a sail.
8. NR – Concrete and board seem to go together because they are both used in construction, but there is not a strong relationship between the two words. Words that are part of the same larger category are not necessarily related to each other.
9. A characteristic of albino is a lack of pigment.
10. A bat is found in a cave, or a bat lives in a cave.

Drill #2

1. Crept is the past-tense form of creep. (Remember that we can reverse the order of the question words as long as we reverse the order in the answer choices as well.)
2. NR – even though these words "seem to go together", they are not related. A pen is used for writing and not for painting.
3. Industrious is the opposite of lazy.
4. An introduction comes before a conclusion or an introduction is the opposite of a conclusion.
5. NR – jar and paper are not related. Jars are not made of paper and do not hold paper. If you used one of these relationships, you were probably trying too hard. On this test the relationships don't require stretching the meaning of the word.
6. A wolf is a wild dog. We can switch the order of the question words as long as we switch the order of the words when we plug answer choices into the same sentence.
7. NR – a tray could be placed on a placemat, but if we find ourselves using the word "could", we know that the relationship is not strong enough for this test.
8. A peel is found on the outside of an orange or a peel is used to protect an orange.
9. A uniform is worn by a soldier.
10. Boisterous is another word for loud (they are synonyms).

Answers to Drills 1-5 continued

Drill #3

1. This is a degree relationship that is hard to make an exact sentence for. Possible is not the opposite of definite. Rather, if we think of a spectrum running from never happening to definite, possible falls about in the middle. We would look for an answer choice with the same type of relationship.
2. Regal is a characteristic of a queen.
3. NR – A pond and a mountain are both land features, but just because two words are part of the same larger category does not mean that they have a strong relationship with one another.
4. A watercolor is a type of painting.
5. A pole is used in a firehouse to go downstairs.
6. NR – Occupation is another word for job, which is not directly related to an idea.
7. NR – Foggy and hot are both types of weather, but they are not necessarily related to one another.
8. Uniqueness means without conformity or uniqueness is the opposite of conformity. Either sentence would get the job done.
9. NR – Fertile describes land that grows plants easily, which is not related to whether or not something is flattering.
10. A stethoscope is used by a doctor.

Drill #4

1. A mansion is a much nicer shack. This is a degree relationship. They are both houses, just at opposite ends of the spectrum of how nice a house can be.
2. An archipelago is a group of islands. We can change island to islands as long as we also make the second word in the answer choices plural when we plug them into our sentence.
3. Meager is the opposite of overabundant.
4. Request is to ask someone to do something nicely and command is to order someone to do something. This is a degree relationship.
5. NR – A lamp and a mirror might both be found in a home, but they are not related to one another directly.
6. A cougar is a type of cat.
7. NR – A broom is not used to disinfect.
8. A sill is the bottom part of a window (it is the piece of wood just under the window).
9. Satiated is the opposite of hungry.
10. NR – A violin and a piccolo are both types of instruments, but belonging to the same larger category is not a relationship on the SSAT.

Answers to Drills 1-5 continued

Drill #5

1. A decibel is used to measure volume (how loud something is).
2. Electricity is made from coal.
3. A treaty is an agreement between countries.
4. NR – They are both sciences but that doesn't mean there is a strong relationship between the two.
5. NR – A monkey does not live in the tundra.
6. A girder is made from steel. A girder is one of those big beams that is used when large buildings are constructed.
7. Soccer is a type of sport. We can change the order of the words as long as we change the order of the words in the answer choices when we plug into our sentence.
8. Limber and flexible are synonyms.
9. NR – Orange is not the color of grass.
10. Lavish and Spartan are antonyms.

Drills #6-8

In these drills, you will be given a question with one word that is just ???????????s. This represents a word that you do not know the meaning of.

- The ?????????????s represent a word that you do not know

To answer these questions, first rule out answer choices that are not related. Then make sentences from the remaining answer choices. Plug the question word that you do know into each answer choice sentence and then rule out answer choices that wouldn't work given the question word that you do know. Finally, we can rule out answer choices that have the same relationship. For example, let's say choices A and D both have words that are synonyms. Since there can only be one right answer choice, we can rule out both choices A and D because otherwise there would be more than one correct answer. You may not be able to rule out down to one answer choice. On the real test, you would guess from what you have left. The answers for this drill will let you know which answer choices are possibilities.

- First rule out answer choices that are not related
- Make sentences from remaining answer choices and rule out any that would not work with the word that you do know
- If there is more than one answer choice with the same relationship, rule out all the answer choices that have the same relationship
- If you have more than one answer choice left, just guess from what you have left

Be sure to check your answers and read explanations for any questions that you missed before you move on to the next drill.

- Check your answers and read explanations before moving onto the next drill
- Remember that you may wind up with more than one answer choice that works – the answer key will let you know all the answer choices that are possibilities

1. ??????????????????? is to obese

    (A) fast is to loud
    (B) corrupted is to rejected
    (C) plain is to ornate
    (D) dreary is to tired
    (E) brave is to courageous

2. House is to ???????????????????? as

    (A) fleet is to ship
    (B) boat is to raft
    (C) shovel is to digging
    (D) knee is to elbow
    (E) voter is to candidate

3. Confusing is to ????????? as mocking is to

    (A) poetry
    (B) prose
    (C) letters
    (D) satire
    (E) song

4. Villain is to ????????? as

    (A) guardian is to protective
    (B) principal is to stern
    (C) teacher is to punctual
    (D) nurse is to sleepy
    (E) architect is to eloquent

5. ?????????? is to leather as

    (A) neighborhood is to homes
    (B) blanket is to wool
    (C) barge is to canoe
    (D) sparkle is to downpour
    (E) chapter is to book

Now, check your answers. Answers to drills #6-8 begin on page 47.

Which questions did you miss?

What is one thing that you learned from the questions that you missed?

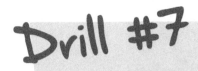

1. ????????? is to somber

    (A) lazy is to smug
    (B) harmonious is to cacopho-
        nous
    (C) hasty is to patient
    (D) frank is to direct
    (E) lame is to green

2. Manageable is to ?????????? as
    obedient is to

    (A) unruly
    (B) kind
    (C) submissive
    (D) painful
    (E) ravenous

3. ???????? is to cutting

    (A) hammer is to sawing
    (B) leg is to table
    (C) dimmer is to brightness
    (D) whisk is to mixing
    (E) mourn is to funeral

4. ??????? is to adaptable as

    (A) indifferent is to zealous
    (B) vivid is to bright
    (C) startled is to humid
    (D) parched is to sated
    (E) wise is to visible

5. ????????? is to opinion as exhaus-
    tion is to

    (A) humor
    (B) youth
    (C) luck
    (D) comfort
    (E) energy

Now, check your answers. Answers to drills #6-8 begin on page 47.

Which questions did you miss?

What is one thing that you learned from the questions that you missed?

Drill #8

1. ???????? is to limousine as

   (A) shack is to mansion
   (B) cab is to truck
   (C) bicycle is to tricycle
   (D) spaceship is to barge
   (E) airplane is to jet

2. ??????? is to knight as

   (A) top is to table
   (B) shell is to mussel
   (C) plow is to sheep
   (D) instrument is to musician
   (E) novice is to expert

3. ????????? is to resist as push is to

   (A) crank
   (B) loosen
   (C) pull
   (D) deflate
   (E) curtail

4. ???????? is to possible as

   (A) grotesque is to beautiful
   (B) hardworking is to happy
   (C) revolutionary is to compla-
       cent
   (D) humane is to compassionate
   (E) hostile is to sincere

5. Mammal is to ?????????????? as

   (A) plant is to fish
   (B) carnivore is to cow
   (C) marsupial is to opossum
   (D) goldfish is to tadpole
   (E) canine is to horse

Now, check your answers. Answers to drills #6-8 begin on page 47.

Which questions did you miss?

What is one thing that you learned from the questions that you missed?

Answers to Drills 6-8

Drill #6

1. C or E could be correct. Answer choices A and B have clearly unrelated words so we can rule them out. Answer choice D is a little trickier since the words "seem to go together". While dreary weather could make you feel tired, the word "could" means that it isn't a strong relationship. Answer choice D can be eliminated. We would then guess from what we have left. If the ?????? was a word that was opposite in meaning from obese, such as the word emaciated, then answer choice C would be correct. If the ??????? was a word that was similar to obese, such as the word corpulent, then answer choice E would be correct. Even if we can't rule out down to one choice, remember that if we can rule out even one answer choice, we should guess.

2. B is the correct answer. First we can rule out answer choice D since knee and elbow are not directly related. Then we make sentences from the remaining answer choices. In choice A, a fleet is a group of ships that travel together. Is a house a group of objects that travels together? No, so we can rule out choice A. With choice B, a raft is a type of boat. Is there a word that could be a type of house? Absolutely, so we leave choice B. Now we look at choice C. A shovel is a tool used for digging. Is a house a tool used for something? No. We can rule out choice C. Now let's look at choice E. A voter chooses a candidate. Does a house choose something? No, so we can also eliminate choice E. We are left with only choice B.

3. D is the correct answer. For these types of questions, we have to find a word that is related to the last word in the question. Although we don't know what the ?????????s represent, it is a good guess that confusing is a characteristic of the ?????????s. We are looking for the answer choice that has mocking as a characteristic. Poetry, prose, letters, and songs all could be mocking in tone, but they don't have to be. Even if we don't know what "satire" means, we know that the others can be eliminated, so we choose answer choice D. A satire is a piece of writing that is meant to mock.

4. A is the correct answer. Our first step is to rule out any answer choices that are unrelated. If we look at answer choice A, it is a guardian's job to be protective, so those two words are related. If we look at answer choice B, a principal can be stern but the word "can" tells us that it is not a strong relationship. Answer choice B is eliminated. If we look at answer choice C, you would hope that a teacher is punctual (on time), but this is not true by definition so we can rule out choice C. If we look at choice D, a lot of nurses are probably sleepy from working the night shift, but not all nurses are sleepy and not all sleepy people are nurses. We can rule out choice D. Finally, we have choice E. Eloquent means well-spoken, which has nothing to do with designing buildings, so we can eliminate choice E. We are left with choice A.

_____

Answers to Drills 6-8 continued

5. B is the correct answer choice. First we should rule out any answer choices that have unrelated words. Choice D can be eliminated because sparkle has nothing to do with downpour. Now we make sentences from the remaining answer choices. A neighborhood is a group of homes. Is there a word that means a group of leather? No, so answer choice A can be ruled out. For answer choice B, blankets are commonly made from wool. Could ?????? be something that is commonly made from leather? Sure, so we will leave choice B. If we look at choice C, a barge is a much larger form of a boat than a canoe. Is there a word that means a larger form of leather? That doesn't make sense so choice C is out. Finally, we have choice E. We divide a book into sections called chapters. Can we divide leather into sections called ??????? No, so answer choice E is eliminated. We are left with choice B.

Drill #7

1. D is the correct answer choice. First we have to rule out answer choices that have unrelated words. Lazy is not related to smug and lame is not related to green, so we can eliminate choices A and E. Now we have to make sentences from the remaining answer choices. If we look at choice B, we can make the sentence that harmonious is the opposite of cacophonous. Could somber be the opposite of some word? Sure, so we keep answer choice B. Now we move on to answer choice C. We could make the sentence hasty is the opposite of patient. We know that somber could be the opposite of some word but the problem is that if the relationship being tested was antonyms there would be more than one correct answer. We can rule out both choices B and C since they have the same relationship. Now we have ruled out every choice except for choice D. Frank and direct are synonyms and there could very well be a word that is a synonym for somber (the word somber means serious).

2. A or C could both be correct. We know that we need to choose an answer that is related to the word obedient. We can rule out choices B, D, and E since those words are not related to being obedient (ravenous means really hungry, by the way). The word unruly is the opposite of obedient and the word submissive is a synonym for obedient. Since we don't know the second word in the question, we can't be sure what the correct answer is, but keep in mind that if we answer the question correctly we get plus one point and if we answer the question incorrectly we only lose a quarter point.

3. D is the correct answer. First we rule out choice A because a hammer and sawing are unrelated. If we look at answer choice B, a leg is part of a table. Is something part of cutting? Not in the same way, so we can rule out choice B. Now we move on to choice C. A dimmer is used to lessen brightness. Is there a word that means something that lessens cutting? No, you can't

_____

Answers to Drills 6-8 continued

really lessen cutting. You either cut or you don't. Answer choice C is out. Let's look at choice D. A whisk is used for mixing. Could ??????? be a word that means something used for cutting? Absolutely, so we leave choice D. Finally, we have choice E. Mourning is done at a funeral. Is something done at a cutting? No. Choice E is gone. We are left with choice D.

4. B is the correct answer choice. First we have to rule out any answer choices with unrelated words. Startled is not related to humid and wise is not related to visible, so we can eliminate choices C and E. Now we make sentences from the remaining choices. In answer choice A, indifferent is the opposite of zealous (indifferent means to not care and zealous means to be fanatical). Since a word could be the opposite of adaptable, we keep answer choice A. In answer choice B, vivid is a synonym for bright. The ???????s could represent a word that is a synonym for adaptable, so we keep answer choice B. If we look at answer choice D, parched is the opposite of sated (parched means extremely thirsty). Now we can see that answer choices A and D have the same relationship, so we can rule out both of them. We are left with choice B as the correct answer.

5. E is the correct answer. For this question, we just have to find a word that is related to exhaustion. Of the answer choices, only the word energy has a relationship to exhaustion – exhaustion means without energy.

Drill #8

1. A or E could be correct. Let's start by ruling out any answer choices that have unrelated words. Spaceship and barge are unrelated (a barge is a really big boat), so answer choice D can be eliminated. Now we look at the remaining choices. In choice A, we have a degree relationship. The words shack and mansion are on opposite ends of the spectrum describing houses. Could the same relationship work with limousine? You bet, so we keep A. Now we look at B. A cab is the front part of the truck where the driver sits. Is there a word for the front part of the limousine where the driver sits? Not really. We can rule out B. With choice C, a tricycle is just a bicycle with one more wheel. Is there a vehicle that we add one wheel to in order to get a limousine? No, so we eliminate choice C. Now we look at choice E (we already ruled out D). A jet is a type of airplane. Could a limousine be a type of something? Yes, it could. We are left with both choice A and choice E, so we would guess one of them and move on.

2. B is the correct answer. First we rule out any answer choices that are not related. Plow and sheep are not related (sheep do not pull plows), so answer choice C is gone. Now we look at what we have left. In choice A, a top goes on top of a table. Is there something that goes on top of a knight? Not really in the same way, so choice A is ruled out. In choice B, a shell protects a

Answers to Drills 6-8 continued

mussel. Is there a word for something that protects a knight? Yes, so we keep choice B. If we look at choice D (we already eliminated C), an instrument is played by a musician. Is there anything that a knight plays? Not really. Choice D is eliminated. Finally we have choice E. A novice is the opposite of an expert. Is there a word that could the opposite of a knight? Not really. We are left with just choice B.

3. C is the correct answer. To answer this question, we just have to find a word related to push. Push and pull are opposites, so choice C is correct.

4. D is the correct answer. First we rule out any answer choices that do not have related words. Hardworking is not necessarily related to happy and hostile is not related to sincere, so we can eliminate choices B and E. Now we look at what we have left. In choice A, grotesque and beautiful are opposites. Could a word mean the opposite of possible? Yes, so we keep answer choice A. Now we look at choice C. Revolutionary and complacent are also opposites, so we can eliminate both choices A and C since there can't be two correct answer choices. We are left with choice D. Humane and compassionate are synonyms and there could be a word that means the same thing as possible.

5. C is the correct answer choice. First we eliminate answer choices with unrelated words. Plant and fish are not related, so we can rule out choice A. If we look at choice B, a cow is not a carnivore, so we can rule out choice B. If we look at choice D, a goldfish does not develop from a tadpole, so we can eliminate choice D. Finally, a horse is not a canine, so we can rule out choice E. We have eliminated everything but choice C. An opossum is a type of marsupial, and there could definitely be something that is a type of mammal. By the way, you may not have known some of these relationships. That is OK. Just rule out what you can on the real test and then guess from what you have left.

———

Vocabulary Review

A key component of improving your verbal score is increasing your vocabulary. Following are ten lessons that will help you do just that.

Each lesson has twenty new words for you to learn. There are good words, there are bad words, and there are even words with roots. Exciting, eh?

After you learn the words, complete the activities for each lesson. The best way to learn new words is to think of them in categories and to evaluate how the words relate to one another. The activities will help you do this.

The activities also give you practice with synonyms and analogies. You will be working on strategy while you are learning new words – think of it as a two for one!

If there are words that you have trouble remembering as you work through the lessons, go ahead and make flashcards for them. Continue to review these flashcards until the words stick. There may also be words that you run across in the analogies or synonyms practice that you do not know the meaning of. Make flashcards for these words as well.

After each lesson are the answers. Be sure to check your work.

Now, on to the lessons!

Lesson One

Words to Learn

Below are the twenty words used in Lesson One; refer back to this list as needed as you move through the lesson.

Marina:	dock
Trivial:	unimportant
Terrain:	ground
Apathetic:	disinterested
Calamity:	disaster
Devastate:	destroy
Sentient:	aware
Mariner:	sailor
Grapple:	struggle
Inter:	bury
Cognizant:	informed
Ameliorate:	improve
Prosperity:	good fortune
Aloof:	withdrawn
Perceptive:	sensitive
Adversity:	misfortune
Subterranean:	underground
Crucial:	important
Submarine:	underwater
Oblivious:	unaware

Word List Practice

Use the words from the preceding list to complete the following activities.

List three words that describe a person who doesn't know or doesn't care.

1.

2.

3.

_____

List three words that could describe a person who knows what is going on.

4.

5.

6.

List three words that have a decidedly negative meaning.

7.

8.

9.

Analogies Practice

One of the common relationships used in the analogy part of the test is the antonym relationship. In this relationship, words are used that are opposite in meaning.

To complete the questions below, use the following word bank:

Sentient
Adversity
Trivial
Oblivious

Use the antonym relationship and the list of words above to complete the following questions.

1. Happy is to sad as prosperity is to _____.
2. Fearless is to scared as cognizant is to _____.
3. Good is to bad as crucial is to _____.
4. Joy is to pain as aloof is to _____.

Roots Practice

For questions 1-2, write the definitions for the words on the lines provided. Based on their meanings, define the common root.

Marina _____
Mariner _____
Submarine _____

1. The root _mar_ means

Inter _____
Subterranean _____
Terrain _____

2. The root _terr/ter_ means:

_____

3. If *aqu/a* is the root meaning water, what do you think the word *aquamarine* means?

4. Based on the roots *terr/ter* and *aqu/a*, what does the word *terraqueous* mean?

5. Based on the words *submarine* and *subterranean*, can you figure out the meaning of the root *sub*?

Synonyms Practice

1. CALAMITY:

   (A) laughter
   (B) disaster
   (C) heaven
   (D) species
   (E) morale

2. DEVASTATE:

   (A) help
   (B) forgive
   (C) glow
   (D) destroy
   (E) break

3. AMELIORATE:

   (A) improve
   (B) cook
   (C) construct
   (D) relax
   (E) defy

4. GRAPPLE:

   (A) release
   (B) remember
   (C) struggle
   (D) blend
   (E) incorporate

5. PERCEPTIVE:

   (A) ignorant
   (B) convivial
   (C) incompatible
   (D) dense
   (E) sensitive

6. APATHETIC:

   (A) enthusiastic
   (B) overjoyed
   (C) hyper
   (D) disinterested
   (E) tired

7. CRUCIAL:

   (A) loud
   (B) miniature
   (C) important
   (D) late
   (E) crunchy

Answers to Lesson One

Word List Practice

1. apathetic
2. aloof
3. oblivious

4. sentient
5. cognizant
6. perceptive

7. calamity
8. devastate
9. adversity

Analogies Practice

1. adversity
2. oblivious
3. trivial
4. sentient

Roots Practice

1. sea
2. earth
3. color of sea water
4. formed of land and water
5. under/beneath

Synonyms Practice

1. B
2. D
3. A
4. C
5. E
6. D
7. C

Lesson Two

Words to Learn

Below are the twenty words used in Lesson Two; refer back to this list as needed as you move through the lesson.

Enunciate:	pronounce
Procrastinate:	delay
Inscribe:	write
Cleave:	split
Magnitude:	importance
Abashed:	embarrassed
Indescribable:	beyond words
Denigrate:	criticize
Hew:	cut
Figurative:	symbolic
Grotesque:	ugly
Proscribe:	forbid
Corpulent:	fat
Eminence:	superiority
Incorporate:	include
Metaphorical:	figurative (not literal)
Repugnant:	loathsome (nasty)
Exhilarated:	elated (thrilled)
Manifest:	demonstrate
Corporeal:	bodily

Word List Practice

Use the words from the preceding list to complete the following activities.

List three words that describe something you could do to someone.

1.

2.

3.

4. If you called someone "corpulent," they might think that you are _____.

5. If you realized at school that your pants were cleaved in two, you would probably feel

   _____.

Analogies Practice

One of the common relationships used in the analogies part of the test is the synonym relationship. This relationship uses words that have the same meaning.

To complete the questions below, use the following word bank:

Metaphorical
Procrastinate
Hew
Repugnant

Use the synonym relationship and the list of words above to complete the following questions.

1. Mock is to tease as cleave is to _____.
2. Clear is to translucent as figurative is to _____.
3. Jump is to hop as delay is to _____.
4. Calm is to placid as grotesque is to _____.

Roots Practice

For questions 1-2, write the definitions for the words on the lines provided. Based on their meanings, define the common root.

Inscribe _____
Proscribe _____
Indescribable _____

1. The root *scribe* means:

Corpulent _____
Incorporate _____
Corporeal _____

2. The root *corp* means:

3. Based on the meaning of *corp*, what popular term for business also means "body of men?"
   (This is not a word from our lesson, but rather one you might know from another place.)

   _____

4. A doctor has to _____ many drugs before you can take them (this word is similar to one of the words in this lesson, but it is NOT that word!).

5. Based on one of the roots above, can you think of a term meaning "one who writes?"

   _____

_____

Synonyms Practice

Since you practiced with synonyms in the analogy section, use the crossword below to spend more time with the words from this lesson.

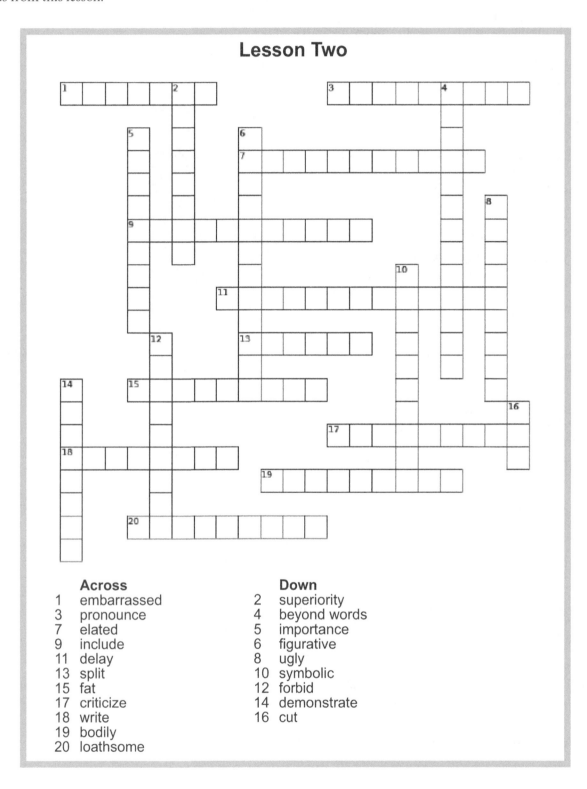

Lesson Two

Across

1 embarrassed
3 pronounce
7 elated
9 include
11 delay
13 split
15 fat
17 criticize
18 write
19 bodily
20 loathsome

Down

2 superiority
4 beyond words
5 importance
6 figurative
8 ugly
10 symbolic
12 forbid
14 demonstrate
16 cut

Answers to Lesson Two

Word List Practice

1. proscribe
2. denigrate
3. incorporate
4. repugnant
5. abashed

Analogies Practice

1. hew
2. metaphorical
3. procrastinate
4. repugnant

Roots Practice

1. to write
2. body
3. corporation
4. prescribe
5. scribe

Synonyms Practice

1. abashed
2. eminence
3. enunciate
4. indescribable
5. magnitude
6. metaphorical
7. exhilarated
8. grotesque
9. incorporate
10. figurative
11. procrastinate
12. proscribe
13. cleave
14. manifest
15. corpulent
16. hew
17. denigrate
18. inscribe
19. corporeal
20. repugnant

_____

Lesson Three

Words to Learn

Below are the twenty words used in Lesson Three; refer back to this list as needed as you move through the lesson.

Animate:	enliven (bring to life)
Boisterous:	noisy
Paraphrase:	summarize
Irate:	angry
Rejuvenate:	refresh
Surfeit:	excess
Circumvent:	go around
Magnanimous:	generous
Vitality:	energy
Fractious:	bad-tempered
Ravenous:	starving
Equanimity:	composure (calmness)
Intimidate:	frighten
Miscreant:	villain
Satiated:	satisfied
Vivacious:	lively
Craving:	hunger or desire
Incensed:	enraged
Convivial:	friendly
Culprit:	wrongdoer

Word List Practice

Use the words from the preceding list to complete the following activities.

1. Would you rather spend time with someone who is fractious or convivial? _____

2. If you were rejuvenated, you would have more _____.

List three words that can be related to eating and/or being hungry:

3.

4.

5.

_____

_____

Analogies Practice

One of the common relationships used in the analogies part of the test is the degree relationship. In this relationship, the words have roughly the same meaning, only one word is more extreme than the other word.

To complete the questions below, use the following word bank:

Miscreant
Incensed
Surfeit
Ravenous

Use the degree relationship and the list of words above to complete the following questions.

1. Happy is to exhilarated as craving is to _____.

2. Sadness is to depression as culprit is to _____.

3. Cold is to icy as irate is to _____.

4. Lack is to dearth as plenty is to _____.

Roots Practice

For questions 1-2, write the definitions for the words on the lines provided. Based on their meanings, define the common root.

Animate _____
Equanimity _____
Magnanimous _____

1. The root *anim* means:

Vivacious _____
Vitality _____
Convivial _____

2. The root *vi/viv* means:

3. Based on the meaning of the root *anim*, why do you think cartoons are called *animation*?

4. The root *magna* means large. What is an alternate definition of *magnanimous*, using its two roots?

5. If *oviparous* means producing young in eggs, based on one of the roots above, what do you think the word *viviparous* means?

_____

Synonyms Practice

1. BOISTEROUS:

   (A) happy
   (B) uncoordinated
   (C) noisy
   (D) silly
   (E) sad

2. PARAPHRASE:

   (A) forget
   (B) give away
   (C) release
   (D) summarize
   (E) take

3. CIRCUMVENT:

   (A) frighten
   (B) go around
   (C) jump
   (D) drive
   (E) cross

4. FRACTIOUS:

   (A) bad-tempered
   (B) overjoyed
   (C) despondent
   (D) crucial
   (E) hardworking

5. INTIMIDATE:

   (A) alleviate
   (B) resist
   (C) boil
   (D) conspire
   (E) frighten

6. REJUVENATE:

   (A) drain
   (B) refresh
   (C) assist
   (D) wash
   (E) create

Answers to Lesson Three

Word List Practice

1. convivial
2. vitality
3. craving
4. ravenous
5. satiated

Analogies Practice

1. ravenous
2. miscreant
3. incensed
4. surfeit

Roots Practice

1. life, spirit
2. life
3. cartoons bring drawings or still images to life
4. large spirit
5. producing live young

Synonyms Practice

1. C
2. D
3. B
4. A
5. E
6. B

Lesson Four

Words to Learn

Below are the twenty words used in Lesson Four; refer back to this list as needed as you move through the lesson.

Pandemonium:	uproar
Hierarchy:	ranked system
Subsist:	exist (barely get by)
Eulogy:	speech in praise
Unwittingly:	unknowingly
Paraphernalia:	belongings
Desist:	cease (stop)
Cadaverous:	ghastly (ghost-like)
Imminent:	impending (about to happen)
Agitator:	troublemaker
Wrangle:	dispute
Deciduous:	falling off
Prevalent:	widespread
Stagnant:	sluggish (not moving)
Decadence:	decline
Epiphany:	insight
Accolades:	praise
Serf:	slave
Pilgrimage:	journey
Reimburse:	pay back

Word List Practice

Use the words from the preceding list to complete the following activities.

1. Your parents probably give you this for bringing home good grades.

2. Trees with leaves that turn colors each fall are called deciduous. Why?

3. A speech written for a funeral is called a _____.

4. Though often used to describe rich desserts and other food or pleasure, this word actually means something negative:

_____

Analogies Practice

One of the common relationships used in the analogy part of the SSAT is the "found in" relationship. In this relationship, one word is found in the other, such as "fish is to sea."

To complete the questions below, use the following word bank:

Serf
Paraphernalia
Eulogy
Pandemonium

Use the "found in" relationship and the list of words above to complete the following questions.

1. Animal is to zoo as agitator is to _____.

2. Beans are to burrito as accolades are to _____.

3. Jail is to prisoner as farm is to _____.

4. Suitcase is to clothes as a bag is to _____.

Roots Practice

For questions 1-2, write the definitions for the words on the lines provided. Based on their meanings, define the common root.

Subsist _____
Desist _____
Stagnant _____

1. The root *sist/sta* means:

Cadaverous _____
Decadence _____
Deciduous _____

2. The root *cad/cid* means:

3. Based on *desist*, *decadence*, and *deciduous*, what do you think the root *de* means?

4. Based on the meaning of *cadaverous*, what does the word *cadaver* mean?

5. If the root *cad* means "to fall," what did a *cadaver* fall from?

6. What makes water *stagnant*?

Synonyms Practice

To spend some more time with the words from this lesson, complete the crossword below.

Lesson Four

Across

3. pay back
4. sluggish
5. ranked system
7. slave
8. cease
9. decline
11. belongings
14. journey
15. falling off
17. unknowingly
19. exist
20. troublemaker

Down

1. widespread
2. dispute
6. ghastly
10. uproar
12. praise
13. insight
16. speech in praise
18. impending

Answers to Lesson Four

Word List Practice

1. accolades
2. because the leaves fall off
3. eulogy
4. decadence

Analogies Practice

1. pandemonium
2. eulogy
3. serf
4. paraphernalia

Roots Practice

1. stand
2. to fall
3. opposite or away from
4. corpse
5. life
6. If water is standing or not moving, it becomes stagnant.

Synonyms Practice

1. prevalent
2. wrangle
3. reimburse
4. stagnant
5. hierarchy
6. cadaverous
7. serf
8. desist
9. decadence
10. pandemonium
11. paraphernalia
12. accolades
13. epiphany
14. pilgrimage
15. deciduous
16. eulogy
17. unwittingly
18. imminent
19. subsist
20. agitator

Lesson Five

Words to Learn

Below are the twenty words used in Lesson Five; refer back to this list as needed as you move through the lesson.

Pragmatic:	sensible
Mercurial:	temperamental (moody)
Morose:	depressed
Frustrate:	disappoint
Serene:	calm
Carnivorous:	meat-eating
Ostentatious:	flashy
Insolent:	disrespectful
Omniscient:	all-knowing
Effervescent:	bubbly
Stupendous:	wonderful
Incarnation:	embodiment (a spirit being born into a body)
Omnivorous:	eats everything
Impetuous:	impulsive
Mediocre:	unexceptional
Grovel:	beg
Reincarnation:	rebirth
Omnipotent:	all-powerful
Interminable:	boring
Fraudulent:	deceptive

Word List Practice

Use the words from the preceding list to complete the following activities.

1. Would you rather have a mediocre meal or a stupendous meal?

2. It would be _____ for the bank to tell you that your account had $100 in it, when you had actually deposited $500.

3. _____ people think through decisions. Those who are _____ often do not.

Analogies Practice

One of the common relationships used in the analogy part of the test is the "characteristic of " relationship. In this relationship, one word is a characteristic of the other word, such as "tiny is to ant."

To complete the questions below, use the following word bank:

> Serene
> Ostentatious
> Interminable
> Effervescent
> Mercurial

Use the "characteristic of" relationship and the list of words above to complete the following questions.

> Elephant is to massive as long lines is to _____.
> Ice is to freezing as Las Vegas is to _____.
> Silk is to smooth as pacifist is to _____.
> Sugar is to sweet as carbonated beverages is to _____.
> Hero is to brave as toddler is to _____.

Roots Practice

For questions 1-2, write the definitions for the words on the lines provided. Based on their meanings, define the common root.

> Carnivorous _____
> Incarnation _____
> Reincarnation _____

1. The root *carn* means:

> Omniscient _____
> Omnipotent _____
> Omnivorous _____

2. The root *omni* means:

3. If an *herbivore* eats plants, what does a *carnivore* eat?

4. What, then, does an *omnivore* eat?

5. Based on the meaning of the root, for whom does an *omnibus* provide transportation?

6. Based on the meanings of *incarnation* and *reincarnation*, what do you think the root *re* means?

Synonyms Practice

1. INSOLENT:
   (A) happy
   (B) frightened
   (C) disrespectful
   (D) furious
   (E) timid

2. IMPETUOUS:
   (A) disillusioned
   (B) impulsive
   (C) curious
   (D) smooth
   (E) beautiful

3. MOROSE:
   (A) gleeful
   (B) conciliatory
   (C) jaded
   (D) depressed
   (E) sleepy

4. GROVEL:
   (A) beg
   (B) answer
   (C) touch
   (D) flee
   (E) forgive

5. FRUSTRATE:
   (A) assist
   (B) locate
   (C) endure
   (D) master
   (E) disappoint

6. MEDIOCRE:
   (A) grand
   (B) unexceptional
   (C) easy
   (D) constricted
   (E) forgotten

Answers to Lesson Five

Word List Practice

1. stupendous
2. fraudulent
3. pragmatic; impetuous

Analogies Practice

1. interminable
2. ostentatious
3. serene
4. effervescent
5. mercurial

Roots Practice

1. flesh
2. all, every
3. flesh (meat)
4. everything
5. everyone (many people)
6. back, again

Synonyms Practice

1. C
2. B
3. D
4. A
5. E
6. B

Lesson Six

Words to Learn

Below are the twenty words used in Lesson Six; refer back to this list as needed as you move through the lesson.

Disdain:	scorn
Prognosis:	forecast
Bias:	prejudice
Lenient:	permissive
Jaded:	indifferent (not easily impressed)
Philanthropy:	humanitarianism (giving to people in need)
Limpid:	clear
Confound:	confuse
Diagnose:	identify
Arrogant:	proud
Arduous:	difficult
Philosophy:	beliefs
Bellicose:	belligerent (looking for a fight)
Compassion:	pity
Consensus:	agreement
Bibliophile:	book lover
Humility:	modesty
Gnostic:	wise
Distort:	warp
Haphazard:	disorganized

Word List Practice

Use the words from the preceding list to complete the following activities.

1. What word found in the word list is an antonym for *humble* (the adjective form of the word *humility*)?

2. Most people want their parents to be more _____ when it comes to curfews and house rules.

3. It can be hard for _____ people to reach a consensus with people that they disagree with.

4. It is easy to become confounded when instructions are _____.

5. Studying for exams like the SSAT is an _____ process.

_____

Analogies Practice

One of the common relationships used in the analogy part of the test is the "means without" relationship. In this relationship, one word means without the other word, such as "freedom is to prison."

To complete the questions below, use the following word bank:

Disdain
Jaded
Arduousness
Bellicose
Arrogance

Use the "means without" relationship and the list of words above to complete the following questions.

1. Hearing is to deaf as naivety is to_____ .

2. Food is to starving as peace is to _____.

3. Poor is to money as compassion is to _____.

4. Naked is to clothing as humble is to _____ .

5. Blind is to sight as ease is to _____.

Roots Practice

For questions 1-2, write the definitions for the words on the lines provided. Based on their meanings, define the common root.

Philanthropy _____
Philosophy _____
Bibliophile _____

1. The root *phil* means:

Prognosis _____
Diagnose _____
Gnostic _____

2. The root *gnos* means:

3. If the root *soph* means wise, what is a meaning of *philosophy* derived directly from its two roots?

4. Based on the meaning of *prognosis*, what does someone who *prognosticates* do?

5. If the root *anthro* means man, what is a meaning of *philanthropy* derived directly from its two roots?

Synonyms Practice

Use the crossword below to spend more time with the words in this lesson.

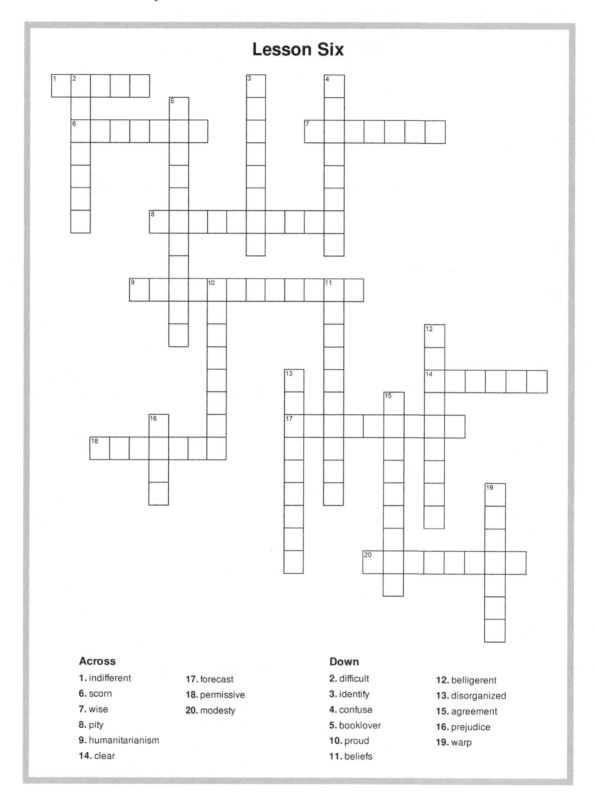

Lesson Six

Across

1. indifferent
6. scorn
7. wise
8. pity
9. humanitarianism
14. clear
17. forecast
18. permissive
20. modesty

Down

2. difficult
3. identify
4. confuse
5. booklover
10. proud
11. beliefs
12. belligerent
13. disorganized
15. agreement
16. prejudice
19. warp

Answers to Lesson Six

Word List Practice

1. arrogant
2. lenient
3. bellicose
4. haphazard
5. arduous

Analogies Practice

1. jaded
2. bellicose
3. disdain
4. arrogance
5. arduousness

Roots Practice

1. love of
2. know
3. love of wisdom
4. they foretell or prophesy
5. love of man(kind)

Synonyms Practice

1. jaded
2. arduous
3. diagnose
4. confound
5. bibliophile
6. disdain
7. gnostic
8. compassion
9. philanthropy
10. arrogant
11. philosophy
12. bellicose
13. haphazard
14. limpid
15. consensus
16. bias
17. prognosis
18. lenient
19. distort
20. humility

_____

Lesson Seven

Words to Learn

Below are the twenty words used in Lesson Seven; refer back to this list as needed as you move through the lesson.

Mediator:	negotiator
Allege:	claim
Deficient:	lacking
Eloquent:	expressive
Exasperate:	irritate
Facile:	easy
Artifice:	hoax (deceptive trick)
Frivolous:	light-minded
Ecstasy:	rapture (extreme happiness)
Proletariat:	workers
Mortician:	undertaker (funeral home worker)
Facilitate:	help
Confection:	candy
Notary:	public official (who verifies signatures)
Dynamic:	energetic
Facsimile:	copy
Psychiatrist:	therapist
Absolution:	forgiveness
Cursory:	brief
Lobbyist:	advocate

Word List Practice

Use the words from the preceding list to complete the following activities.

List the five words that describe a job or occupation:

1.

2.

3.

4.

5.

6. It's best not to take a _____ look at these words, but rather to spend some time with them.

_____

Analogies Practice

One of the common relationships used in the analogy section of the test is the "occupation" relationship. In this relationship, one word means the job of the other word, such as "architect is to building."

To complete the questions below, use the following word bank:

Notary
Mediator
Lobbyist
Proletariat
Psychiatrist

Use the "occupation" relationship and the list of words above to complete the following questions.

1. Legality is to lawyer as mental health is to _____.
2. Build is to contractor as advocate is to _____.
3. Article is to journalist as document is _____.
4. Ceramics is to potter as agreement is to _____.
5. Surgery is to doctor as manual labor is to _____.

Roots Practice

For questions 1-2, write the definitions for the words on the lines provided. Based on their meanings, define the common root.

Facsimile _____
Facile _____
Facilitate _____

1. The root *fac* means:

Artifice _____
Deficient _____
Confection _____

2. The root *fic/fect* means:

3. Give an alternate definition for *facilitate*, using the root and the definition of *facile*:   to _____.

4. Based on one of the roots above, what do you think happens in a factory?

5. If the root *magni* means great, using one of the roots above, what could the definition of *magnificent* be?

6. If something is *artificial*, do you think it is created by man or does it occur in nature?

Synonyms Practice

1. FRIVOLOUS:

   (A) serious
   (B) active
   (C) light-minded
   (D) bashful
   (E) ornery

2. ELOQUENT:

   (A) expressive
   (B) certain
   (C) terrified
   (D) rapacious
   (E) chatty

3. ALLEGE:

   (A) lie
   (B) frighten
   (C) leap
   (D) sigh
   (E) claim

4. DYNAMIC:

   (A) goofy
   (B) energetic
   (C) distinguished
   (D) hopeful
   (E) happy

5. ECSTASY:

   (A) rage
   (B) hope
   (C) truth
   (D) rapture
   (E) fear

6. CURSORY:

   (A) brief
   (B) easy
   (C) convoluted
   (D) shy
   (E) complicated

7. EXASPERATE:

   (A) subdue
   (B) irritate
   (C) trace
   (D) behave
   (E) despise

8. ABSOLUTION:

   (A) dinner
   (B) honesty
   (C) scent
   (D) pile
   (E) forgiveness

Answers to Lesson Seven

Word List Practice

1. psychiatrist
2. mortician
3. mediator
4. lobbyist
5. notary
6. cursory

Analogies Practice

1. psychiatrist
2. lobbyist
3. notary
4. mediator
5. proletariat

Roots Practice

1. to make, to do
2. to make
3. make easy
4. things are made
5. made greatly
6. made by man

Synonyms Practice

1. C
2. A
3. E
4. B
5. D
6. A
7. B
8. E

Lesson Eight

Words to Learn

Below are the twenty words used in Lesson Eight; refer back to this list as needed as you move through the lesson.

Nostalgia:	longing
Precocious:	advanced
Elegy:	funeral song
Recuperate:	recover
Enhance:	increase
Posterity:	descendants
Excavate:	dig
Precaution:	carefulness
Futile:	useless
Undaunted:	unafraid
Litigation:	legal proceeding
Prelude:	introduction
Instigate:	provoke (start a fight)
Curriculum:	studies
Fluctuate:	waver
Demoralize:	depress
Posthumous:	after death
Deteriorate:	worsen
Posterior:	rear
Curvature:	arc

Word List Practice

Use the words from the preceding list to complete the following activities.

1. If a book was published posthumously, would the author be able to read the finished edition? Why or why not?

2. Would a superhero more likely be described as demoralized or undaunted?

3. If something doesn't get better, it either stays the same or it _____.

4. It takes a long time to _____ after an illness like whooping cough.

_____

Analogies Practice

One of the common relationships used in the analogy part of the SSAT is the "used for" relationship. In this relationship, one word is used for the other word, such as "voice is to sing."

To complete the questions below, use the following word bank:

   Excavate
   Litigation
   Elegy
   Curriculum

Use the "occupation" relationship and the list of words above to complete the following questions.

1. Car is to transportation as jazz procession is to _____.
2. Recipe is to meal as lesson plans are to _____.
3. Pen is to writing as legal maneuver is to _____.
4. Broom is to sweep as shovel is to _____.

Roots Practice

For questions 1-2, write the definitions for the words on the lines provided. Based on their meanings, define the common root.

   Posterior _____
   Posterity _____
   Posthumous _____

1. The root *post* means:

   Prelude _____
   Precocious _____
   Precaution _____

2. The root *pre* means:

3. How does the meaning of the root *pre* factor into the meaning of *precocious*? If someone is *precocious*, they are "advanced before" what?

4. There is another word meaning "after death" with the root words *post* and *mort*. Can you guess what it is?

5. If the root word *inter* means "between," and a prelude is an introduction, when does an *interlude* happen?

6. If *posterior* means at the end (or rear), what very similar word means at the beginning? (Hint: *ante* means before)

_____

Synonyms Practice

To spend more time with the words in this lesson, complete the crossword puzzle below.

Lesson Eight

Across

2. longing
3. depress
5. worsen
8. after death
10. carefulness
11. introduction
13. recover
15. provoke
17. unafraid
18. increase
19. useless

Down

1. legal proceeding
4. advanced
6. waver
7. descendants
9. studies
12. rear
14. dig
16. arc
20. funeral song

Answers to Lesson Eight

Word List Practice

1. no, because the author would be dead
2. undaunted
3. deteriorates
4. recuperate

Analogies Practice

1. elegy
2. curriculum
3. litigation
4. excavate

Roots Practice

1. after, behind
2. before
3. what is normal for his or her age
4. postmortem
5. in the middle
6. anterior

Synonyms Practice

1. litigation
2. nostalgia
3. demoralize
4. precocious
5. deteriorate
6. fluctuate
7. posterity
8. posthumous
9. curriculum
10. precaution
11. prelude
12. posterior
13. recuperate
14. excavate
15. instigate
16. curvature
17. undaunted
18. enhance
19. futile
20. elegy

Lesson Nine

Words to Learn

Below are the twenty words used in Lesson Nine; refer back to this list as needed as you move through the lesson.

Potent:	powerful
Collaborate:	cooperate
Retribution:	punishment
Burnish:	polish
Convergence:	union
Stalwart:	robust (strong and dependable)
Coincide:	correspond (happen at the same time)
Gusto:	enjoyment
Spontaneous:	impulsive
Zealous:	fervent (passionate)
Deflect:	divert (turn away)
Fortuitous:	lucky
Succinct:	brief
Genuflect:	kneel
Deliberate:	intentional
Premeditated:	planned
Voluble:	talkative
Inflection:	tone (of voice)
Hybrid:	mixed
Resolute:	determined

Word List Practice

Use the words from the list on the previous page to complete the following activities.

When we are electing the next president, we hope that he or she is what three things?

1.

2.

3.

_____

4. If we have to watch her give a speech, however, we hope that she is not _____.

5. What is mixed about a *hybrid* car?

6. Is winning the lottery *fortuitous* or *deliberate*?

Analogies Practice

This lesson will give you more practice with the antonym relationship. Remember, antonyms are words with opposite meanings.

To complete the questions below, use the following word bank:

Potent
Deliberate
Spontaneous
Voluble

Use the antonym relationship and the list of words above to complete the following questions.

1. Up is to down as fortuitous is to _____.

2. In is to out as succinct is to _____.

3. Hard is to soft as powerless is to _____.

4. Wet is to dry as premeditated is to _____.

Roots Practice

For questions 1-2, write the definitions for the words on the lines provided. Based on their meanings, define the common root.

Deflect _____
Genuflect _____
Inflection _____

1. The root *flect* means:

Convergence _____
Coincide _____
Collaborate _____

2. The root *co/con* means:

3. What bends when it comes to *inflection*?

_____

83

4. What bends when someone *genuflects*?

5. If an *incident* is an event or occurrence, what happens in a *coincidence*?

6. Using the meaning of the root *di* (apart) and the word *convergence*, what is a word meaning "to go in different directions from a common point?"

Synonyms Practice

1. BURNISH:
   - (A) reduce
   - (B) roll
   - (C) light
   - (D) polish
   - (E) strike

2. ZEALOUS:
   - (A) hyper
   - (B) peaceful
   - (C) ragged
   - (D) slow
   - (E) fervent

3. STALWART:
   - (A) weak
   - (B) shy
   - (C) unavailable
   - (D) robust
   - (E) tired

4. GUSTO:
   - (A) hope
   - (B) fear
   - (C) enjoyment
   - (D) certitude
   - (E) flight

5. RETRIBUTION:
   - (A) punishment
   - (B) glee
   - (C) enjoyment
   - (D) happiness
   - (E) planning

6. HYBRID:
   - (A) sore
   - (B) mixed
   - (C) clean
   - (D) spinning
   - (E) clear

Answers to Lesson Nine

Word List Practice

1. potent
2. stalwart
3. resolute
4. voluble
5. power sources for the engine: gasoline and electric
6. fortuitous

Analogies Practice

1. deliberate
2. voluble
3. potent
4. spontaneous

Roots Practice

1. to bend
2. with, together
3. a voice, or the tone of a voice
4. knees
5. two events come together
6. diverge

Synonyms Practice

1. D
2. E
3. D
4. C
5. A
6. B

Lesson Ten

Words to Learn

Below are the twenty words used in Lesson Ten; refer back to this list as needed as you move through the lesson.

Sustenance:	nourishment
Lackluster:	dull
Trajectory:	path
Insurgent:	rebel
Genesis:	origin
Antagonistic:	hostile
Illustrious:	celebrated
Unkempt:	messy
Trite:	overused
Insurrection:	revolt
Contemplate:	ponder (think about)
Vogue:	popularity
Lustrous:	shining
Resurrect:	bring back
Excruciating:	agonizing
Subsistence:	survival
Provenance:	birthplace
Duplicity:	deceptiveness
Ruminate:	reflect
Averse:	opposing

Word List Practice

Use the words from the preceding list to complete the following activities.

List three words that you would like to have associated with you:

1.

2.

3.

List three words that you would NOT like to have associated with you:

4.

5.

6.

7. If a definition of *subsist* is "keep going," do you think *subsistence* living includes luxuries? Why or why not?

Analogies Practice

This lesson will give you more practice with the synonym relationship. Remember, synonyms are words with the same meaning.

To complete the questions below, use the following word bank:

Genesis
Antagonistic
Ruminate
Unkempt

Use the synonym relationship and the list of words above to complete the following questions.

1. Plush is to comfortable as averse is to _____.

2. Seek is to search as contemplate is to _____.

3. Illustrious is to celebrated as messy is to _____.

4. Provenance is to birthplace as creation is to _____.

Roots Practice

For questions 1-2, write the definitions for the words on the lines provided. Based on their meanings, define the common root.

        Insurgent _____
        Resurrect _____
        Insurrection _____

1.   The root *surg/surr* means:

        Lackluster _____
        Lustrous _____
        Illustrious _____

2.   The root *lust* means:

3.   Do you think supermodels prefer their hair to be *lackluster* or *lustrous*?

4.   Based on the meaning of *resurrect*, what do you think *resurrection* means?

5.   Based on the meaning of one of the roots above, what do you think it means when the tide *surges*?

Synonyms Practice

Use the crossword puzzle below to spend more time with the words in this lesson.

Lesson Ten

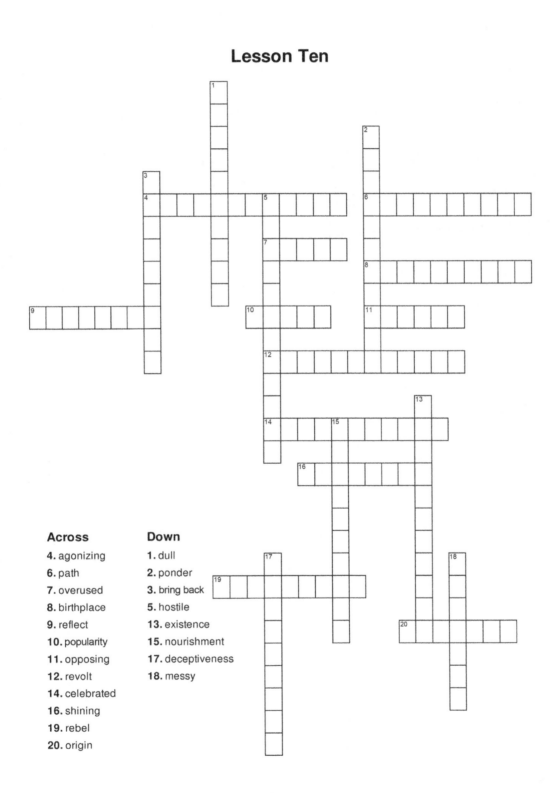

Across

4. agonizing
6. path
7. overused
8. birthplace
9. reflect
10. popularity
11. opposing
12. revolt
14. celebrated
16. shining
19. rebel
20. origin

Down

1. dull
2. ponder
3. bring back
5. hostile
13. existence
15. nourishment
17. deceptiveness
18. messy

Answers to Lesson Ten

Word List Practice

1. vogue
2. illustrious
3. lustrous
4. lackluster
5. unkempt
6. antagonistic
7. No, because you are living with just enough to keep going or just enough for existence.

Analogies Practice

1. antagonistic
2. ruminate
3. unkempt
4. genesis

Roots Practice

1. rise
2. shine
3. lustrous
4. the act of being brought back to life
5. the tides rise

Synonyms Crossword

1. lackluster
2. contemplate
3. resurrect
4. excruciating
5. antagonistic
6. trajectory
7. trite
8. provenance
9. ruminate
10. vogue
11. averse
12. insurrection
13. subsistence
14. illustrious
15. sustenance
16. lustrous
17. duplicity
18. unkempt
19. insurgent
20. genesis

SSAT Reading Section

In the SSAT reading section, you are given passages and then asked questions about these passages. In general, there are about eight passages in this section, but there can be slightly more or slightly less. There are typically four to six questions per passage, but again this is only a general guideline. For the entire section, there will be a total of forty questions. You will have forty minutes to complete the section. There will be only one reading section on your test.

- About 8 passages (can be more or less, though)
- Roughly 4-6 questions for each passage
- 40 total questions
- 40 minutes to complete section
- Only one reading section

You may be thinking, "I know how to read, I am good on this section." However, most people applying to independent school know how to read. In order to get the median 50th percentile score on the Middle Level reading section, you need to get a little more than half the questions correct (and not answer the others). This means that half the students taking this test are getting less than that.

- To get the median score for the Middle Level, you need to get a little more than half of the questions correct (and not answer the others)

The issue is that not every student can get a perfect score on the reading section, so the test writers have to create a test where some students who know how to read are going to miss several questions.

So how do the test writers get you to answer so many questions incorrectly? First of all, the questions can be very detail-oriented. Think of this not as a reading test, but as looking for a needle in a haystack – with very little time to find it. Secondly, they include answer choices that take the words from the passage and switch them around so that all the same words are there, but the combination suddenly means something else. Lastly, they use your own brain against you! How do they do this? As we read, we automatically fill in details to create a bigger picture. On this test, however, these details are often the wrong answer choices.

- Very detail-oriented questions
- Test writers rearrange words from the passage to mean something else in an answer choice
- We fill in details as we read, but they aren't always correct

By making a plan and sticking to it, you can overcome these obstacles and beat the average score – by a lot!

In this section, first we will cover the general plan of attack and then we will get into the details that make the difference.

Reading Section Plan of Attack

Students can significantly improve their reading scores by following an easy plan:

Step 1: Plan your time
Know how many passages there are, how many passages you need to answer before you are halfway through, and at what time you should be halfway through the passages.

Step 2: Prioritize passages
Play to your strengths. Don't just answer the passages in the order that they appear.

Step 3: Go to the questions first
Mark questions as either specific or general. You want to know what to look for as you read.

Step 4: Read the passage
If you run across the answer to a specific question as you are reading, go ahead and mark it so you can come back to it, but do not worry if you miss an answer.

Step 5: Answer specific questions
Go back to the passage and find the evidence to answers for specific questions.

Step 6: Answer general questions
Answer any questions that ask about the passage as a whole.

Step 7: Repeat steps 3-6 with next passage
You've got it under control. Just keep cranking through the section until you are done.

Keep in mind that this section is not a test of how well you read. It is a test of how well you test. You need to manage your time and think about the process rather than the actual reading.

Step #1 – Plan your time

Before you do anything, take thirty seconds to plan out how much time you have to complete half of the passages. To do this, count up the total number of passages and then divide this number by 2.

- If you have six passages, you should be done with about three passages when you are 20 minutes into the reading section

- If you have seven passages, you should have completed about three and a half of the passages when you are 20 minutes into the reading section

- If you have eight passages, you should have completed about four passages when you are 20 minutes into the reading section.

Now look at the starting time and make a quick chart of starting time, halfway point, and ending time. For example, let's say that you have a section with 7 passages and you start at 9:23, then your chart should look like this:

Start – 9:23
Halfway point – 9:43 – $3\frac{1}{2}$ passages
End – 10:03

Note that the number of passages is not evenly divisible by two. This means that we have to guesstimate whether we are done with half of a passage. In this example, if you have only completed three passages at the halfway point, you need to speed it up. If you have started and made progress on the fourth passage at the halfway point, then you are right on track. If you have completed four passages at this halfway point, that is good because you have saved your hardest passages for last. If you have done five passages at the halfway point, however, you may be rushing.

These times will give you rough milestones as you move through the test. Not every section will take you exactly the same amount of time, so don't stress if a long passage with six questions takes you a little longer. The point of planning out your time is that you will know if you are taking way too long on each passage – or if you are unnecessarily rushing.

- Make a chart with your halfway point and finish time before you begin the section
- This chart is a rough guideline – not an absolute schedule

Let's say you start a reading section at 9:32 and there are 8 passages. Fill in the chart below (be sure to fill in both time and number of passages completed for the halfway point):

Start –

Halfway point –

Finish –

Now let's say you start a reading section at 8:56 and there are 7 passages. Make your own chart below:

(Answers to this drill are found on page 125.)

Step #2 – Prioritize passages

Take a quick look at your passages. In general, do your non-fiction first, then your fiction, then poetry last (if there is any poetry). If there are any passages that stick out as being really long, save those for last as well. As long as you stay on track with the timing of other passages, you can use your extra time at the end to finish these passages.

- Save really long passages for last
- Save poetry passage for the end

The following are some of the types of passages that you may see:

- *Arts* – These passages may give you a brief biography of an artist or talk about the development of a certain type of art. These tend to be pretty straightforward, so look for them to answer early in the section.
  - Answer arts passages toward the beginning of the section

- *Science* – These passages describe some scientific phenomenon or advancement in the medical field. No need to worry about deep implying or inferring questions here – we won't be asked what the stethoscope was feeling! These are good passages to answer early on.
  - Answer science passages toward the beginning of the section

- *Native culture* – These passages describe some aspect or ritual of a native culture, whether it be Native American, Australian aboriginal, or some other group. Because they are also non-fiction, they tend to be more straightforward, so prioritize these passages.
  - Answer native cultures passages toward the beginning of the section

- *History* – These non-fiction passages tell about a particular era in history. Like our other non-fiction passages, these are good to answer early.
  - Answer history passages toward the beginning

- *Primary document* – These passages provide part of a document that was written during a different period in history. Generally, they come from American history, so you may see part of a speech by Abraham Lincoln, or a newspaper account from the First World War. These are a little less straightforward. Technically, no knowledge of the time period is necessary. However, if you know about the background of what the passage addresses, the odds of answering the inferring and implying questions correctly go up. With these passages, look for the ones that you know something about but save the others for later.
  - If you are familiar with the topic, answer primary document passages earlier in the section; if you are not familiar with the topic, save primary document passages for near the end

- *Essay* – These passages consist of an author writing eloquently about a particular topic or idea. The problem with essays is that they tend to use a lot of metaphor or analogy. Makes them more fun to read, but less fun to try to translate into multiple-choice questions. Save these for toward the end.
  - Save essays for near the end

- *Fiction or folktale* – A lot of the fiction passages that you see will be folktales. These are generally stories from other cultures that have a moral or lesson as the punchline. Fiction questions tend to be very picky and the correct answer may be found in just a word or two. Fiction passages don't have the same strict organization as other passages, so trying to find the answer can be like looking for a needle in a haystack – while someone times you. Save these for the end.

- Save fiction or folktale passages for near the end
- Questions tend to be pickier and organization makes it harder to find the right answer easily

- *Poetry* – If you get a poetry passage, it should be the absolute last passage that you answer. Poetry doesn't exactly lend itself to one-size-fits-all interpretation, but this is a multiple choice test. Don't be surprised if you find yourself disagreeing with the test writers about the correct answers on these passages. The kicker is that their vote counts and yours does not.
  - If you get a poetry passage, answer it last
  - Hard to turn a poem into good multiple-choice questions

Do you see the trend here? Straightforward non-fiction passages make it easy to pick out the right multiple choice answer. Fiction is a little trickier. And poetry as a multiple choice endeavor? Never a good idea.

- Non-fiction = good

- Fiction = less good

- Poetry = iffy at best

In general, you also want to answer passages that interest you most first. You don't want to wear yourself out by dragging your way through a dreadfully boring passage and then be mentally exhausted for a passage that you do like. For example, if you have more than one non-fiction passage, then you would first answer the one(s) that you find more interesting.

Drill #2

You start the reading section. After a quick scan of each passage, you have to prioritize the order of answering the passages. Quickly number the passages below in the order that you would answer them.

Number passages 1-7 with 1 being the first passage you would answer and 7 being the last passage you would answer.

Passage topics:

Native American folktale about how people got fire: #_____

Poem: #_____

Passage about the invention of the unicycle: #_____

News article from World War I: #_____

Traditional tale from China: #_____

Passage about why we have Leap Day: #_____

Passage from a novel #_____

(Answers to this drill are found on page 125.)

Step #3 - When you start a passage, go to questions first

It is important that you identify specific (S) and general (G) questions before you begin to read. You may come across the answer to a specific question as you read, so you also want to underline what the question is asking about for specific questions.

- Mark questions "S" or "G"
- For specific questions, underline the key word that it is asking about

So how do you know if it is specific or general? Here are some examples of the form that specific questions often take:

- In the first paragraph, the word _____ means
- In line 5, _____ means
- In line 7, _____ most likely refers to
- All of the following are mentioned EXCEPT
- All of the following questions are answered EXCEPT

If there is a line reference or the question has a lot of details in it, then it is probably a specific question.

If there is a line reference, go ahead and put a mark next to that line in the passage. That way you will know where to look for an answer. If the question asks about a specific detail, underline what it asks about so that you know what to look for when you read.

- If there is a line reference, mark that line reference in the passage
- If the question asks about a specific detail, underline that detail in the question so that you know what to look for when you read

For example, let's say our question was:

6. How many years did it take Johnny Appleseed to plant his trees?

   We would underline the word "years" since that is the detail we are looking for. Presumably, the whole passage would be about him planting trees so that would not be a helpful detail to look for.

-

Some questions may look general, but on the SSAT they are asking for a specific example.

Here is how these questions may look:

- The author would most likely agree
- Which of the following questions is answered by the passage?
- According to the passage/author
- It can be inferred from the passage
- This passage infers/implies which of the following

The reason that these questions are specific is that on the SSAT the answers to these questions will be found in a single sentence or two. In real life, that may not be true, but on this test, it is. We can't underline anything for these questions, however, since the details we are looking for are in the answer choices.

- In real life, these questions might not be specific, but on the SSAT they are
- Nothing to underline since it is the answer choices that give details and not the questions

General questions ask about the passage as a whole. They might look like:

- This passage primarily deals with
- This passage is mainly about
- What is the best title of this passage?
- The author's tone is

If you see the words *main* or *primary* you have a general question on your hands and should mark it with a "G."

Please keep in mind that you do not have to be correct every time when you mark "S" or "G." Do not obsess over whether a question is specific or general. The point of this strategy is to save you time and it just isn't that big of a deal if you mark one question incorrectly.

- Mark "S" or "G" quickly – not a big deal if you get it wrong

Drills 3-6 will give practice identifying specific and general questions. Mark each question as "S" or "G." If the question is specific, underline the key word or phrase to look for in the passage.

Time yourself on each drill so that you can see your improvement – and how easy it is to do this quickly! And remember, absolute accuracy is not a must. If we obsess over correctly labeling the questions "S" or "G," then we won't save ourselves any time.

For the following drills:

- Mark "S" or "G"
- Underline what the question is looking for if it is specific

Drill #3

1. This passage is primarily about

2. As used in line 7, "graciously" most nearly means

3. It can be inferred from the passage that all of the following statements about types of grasses are correct EXCEPT

4. According to the passage, how long did it take to travel across the country on the first transcontinental railway?

5. The author's style is best described as

Time:

Drill #4

1. The door to the barn was probably made from

2. The sounds referred to in the passage were

3. According to the author, the musicians stopped playing because

4. An *emu* is probably a type of

5. The mood of this passage can best be described as

Time:

(Answers to these drills are found on page 125.)

Drill #5

1. The sound that came from the floorboards can best be described as

2. It can be inferred that from the passage that earlier settlers did not have windows in their homes because

3. What made the citizens call a town meeting?

4. As it is used in line 15, the word "substantial" most nearly means

5. Which of the following questions is answered by information in the passage?

Time:

Drill #6

1. Which of the following best state the main idea of the passage?

2. In line 4, John Adams' use of the word "furious" is ironic for which of the following reasons?

3. How does Adams' speech reflect the idea that government is "for the people, by the people?"

4. The purpose of Adams' speech was to

5. Why does Adams use the word "mocking" in line 13?

Time:

(Answers to these drills are found on page 125.)

Step #4 – Read the passage

Now, you can go ahead and read the passage. If you happen to run across the answer to one of your specific questions, mark where it is so you can come back.

You have to be a little Zen about looking for the answers while you read. You can spend five minutes obsessing over finding the answer for one particular question, but if you just move on, you are likely to come across the answer later.

- It's a little like love, sometimes you just have to let it go and trust that it will come back to you

Step #5 – Answer specific questions

After you finish reading, answer any specific questions. For these questions, think of it as a treasure hunt. The right answer is there, you just have to find it. Generally, you should be able to underline the exact answer paraphrased in the passage. If you can't do that, you just haven't found it yet. Keep looking. You should also think about whether or not the question fits into a particular category (we will work on those in just a minute).

When you are looking for the answer to a specific question, skim! Don't read every word, you have already done that. Look quickly for the words that you underlined in the question. Also, remember our old friend ruling out.

- Skim when looking for the answers for specific questions
- Use ruling out
- For specific questions, you should underline the correct answer restated in the passage
- Look for questions that fit into a particular category of questions

Here are five categories of specific questions that you may see on the SSAT:

- Meaning
- Questions that look general but are really specific
- Inferred / implied
- EXCEPT
- Tone or attitude about a specific topic

There are many more specific questions that do not fall into a particular category. Just keep in mind that you want to underline the evidence for the correct answer in the passage for any specific questions.

Meaning questions

These questions ask you to identify the meaning of a word or statement. There are several different ways that the test writers might phrase this kind of question.

How they might look:

- In the first paragraph, the word _____ means
- Which word is closest in meaning to _____?
- Which word could be substituted for _____ without changing the meaning?

These questions aren't hard if you use our approach! Here is what you do:

- First locate the reference in the passage
- Then cross out the reference in the passage
- Plug in answer choices and see what makes the most sense

The trick for meaning questions is not to be afraid of words that you don't know.

Rule out what you know doesn't work, and if you have to guess, don't shy away from a word just because you aren't sure what it means. Remember how test writers have to make sure that not everyone is getting a perfect score? Well, students HATE to guess words that they are unsure of the meaning of. So the correct answer on these types of questions is often a word that you do not know.

- Don't shy away from a word that you do not know

Following is a sample passage. Use this passage to answer all of the drills for the specific question types. This book is designed so that you can tear out the passage instead of flipping back and forth. Be sure to do this so that you can develop good habits such as:

- Underline correct answers in the passage for specific questions
- Use ruling out – physically cross out answer choices that do not work

Use the passage on the following page to answer the questions.

Passage for Specific Questions Drills:

Once on a dark winter's day, when the yellow fog hung so thick and heavy in the streets of London that the lamps were lighted and the shop windows blazed with gas as they do at night, an odd-looking little girl sat in a cab with her father and was driven rather slowly through the big thoroughfares.

She sat with her feet tucked under her, and leaned against her father, who held her in his arm, as she stared out of the window at the passing people with a queer old-fashioned thoughtfulness in her big eyes.

She was such a little girl that one did not expect to see such a look on her small face. It would have been an old look for a child of twelve, and Sarah Crewe was only seven. The fact was, however, that she was always dreaming and thinking odd things and could not herself remember any time when she had not been thinking things about grown-up people and the world they belonged to. She felt as if she had lived a long, long time.

This page intentionally left blank so that passage can be removed from book to use for drills.

7.   When the author mentions "thoroughfares" in the first paragraph she is referring to

(A)   the driver
(B)   London
(C)   the cab that Sarah is riding in
(D)   roads
(E)   passengers

8.   As used in the first sentence of the passage, the word "blazed" most nearly means

(A)   darkened
(B)   shone
(C)   froze
(D)   limited
(E)   focused

(Answers to this drill are found on page 126.)

Questions that Look General but are Specific

On the SSAT, there will be questions that if you saw them outside of this test, you would think they were asking about the passage in general. Because we are experts on the SSAT, however, we know that these questions are really looking for a detail.

The answer can generally be found in a single sentence.

These questions might look like:

- The author would most likely agree
- Which of the following questions is answered by the passage?
- According to the passage/author
- The setting of the story is

Our approach to these questions is just like any other specific question. The trick to these questions is not in how to answer them, but rather in recognizing them in the first place. You may be asking why a question about setting would be specific. The reason is that the answer is often given in just a sentence or small phrase.

- You should be able to underline the correct answer

- Skim, skim, skim until you find the answer – it is often only one word

- Use ruling out – a lot

Tricks for questions that look general but are specific:

- The test writers often take a sentence from the passage and twist it around to mean something different – just make sure you can underline the answer in the passage

- You might think they are looking for a general theme, but they are usually looking for just one or two words

The following drill refers back to the passage about Sarah Crewe.

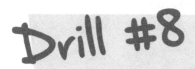

1. Which of the following statements would the author most likely agree with?

   (A) Sarah was twelve years old.
   (B) It was not safe to go on a drive on that particular day.
   (C) Sarah was smaller than other children her age.
   (D) Sarah seemed much older than she actually was.
   (E) Sarah's father is unusual looking.

2. Which of the following questions is answered by the passage?

   (A) In what city does this story take place?
   (B) In what year does this story take place?
   (C) Where were Sarah and her father going?
   (D) Did Sarah have any siblings?
   (E) Where did Sarah live?

(Answers to this drill are found on page 126.)

Inferred / Implied Questions

These questions make you think that you should be reading deeply into the passage. This is not the case, however.

Perhaps the passage says:

"The boy hung his head and held back the tears as he brushed the sand from his feet."

The question then asks:

1. Which of the following was implied by the passage?
    - (A) The boy was sad and upset that his friends did not include him.
    - (B) completely unrelated answer
    - (C) The boy had just returned from the beach.
    - (D) completely unrelated answer
    - (E) completely unrelated answer

You have ruled out three answer choices and are down to choices A and C. In school, you are expected to read into passages and look for emotions when there is an implied question, so it is tempting to select choice A. However, this is the SSAT and there is no evidence that he was sad BECAUSE his friends did not include him. However, he is brushing sand off of this feet, so we can assume that he was in a sandy place such as the beach. The context of the rest of the passage would matter, but the general idea is that we are not looking for deep emotions, but rather more literal answers.

- When debating between two answer choices, look for the more literal answer choice

These questions can look like:

- It can be inferred from the passage
- This passage infers/implies which of the following

To approach these questions:

- Don't do too much thinking of your own. While the words *infer* and *imply* suggest that you should be making your own leaps of thought and conclusions, they are really just looking for something paraphrased from the passage.
- These are still specific questions, so we are looking to underline an answer

Tricks for implying or inferring questions:

- The answer can often be found in just a few words and is not a main idea.

Complete the following drill. The question refers back to the passage about Sarah Crewe.

1. Which of the following can be inferred from the passage?

    (A) Sarah was an unhappy child.
    (B) The driver of the cab was driving cautiously.
    (C) Sarah did not like her father.
    (D) London was a very large city.
    (E) Sarah did not live with her mother.

(Answer to this drill is found on page 126.)

EXCEPT / NOT questions

How they might look:

- All of the following are mentioned EXCEPT
- All of the following questions are answered EXCEPT
- Which of the following is NOT true?

How to approach:

- Circle the word EXCEPT or NOT – even though they put them in all caps, it is really easy to forget once you start looking for an answer
- For these questions, you should be able to underline four of the answers in the passage – it is the answer that you cannot underline that is the correct one
- After you underline an answer in the passage, cross out that answer choice so that you don't choose it by mistake!

Tricks for EXCEPT questions:

- Students tend to forget the EXCEPT or NOT

The following drill refers back to the Sarah Crewe passage.

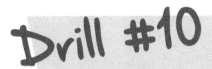

1. All of the following are mentioned in the passage EXCEPT

   (A) winter weather in London
   (B) Sarah's personality
   (C) Sarah's father's personality
   (D) how shop lights were powered in London at the time of this story
   (E) Sarah's physical appearance

(Answer to this drill is found on page 126.)

Tone or attitude about a specific topic questions

There are two types of tone and attitude questions. One type asks you about the author's tone or attitude in general, and the other type asks what the author feels about a particular subject. It is that second type that we will focus on here.

These questions may look like:

- The author's tone regarding _____ is
- The author's attitude about _____ is

Here is our approach for these tone and attitude questions that ask about only a small part of the passage:

- Locate the part of the passage that discusses this topic
- Stick to this area while you rule out answer choices

Tricks to look out for with tone or attitude questions:

- Rule out answers that are too extreme, in a positive or negative way
- Don't be afraid of words you don't know

Please complete the drill below. The question refers back to the passage about Sarah Crewe.

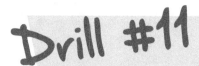

1. Which of the following describes the author's tone about winter weather in London?

(A) dreary
(B) hopeful
(C) defensive
(D) enthusiastic
(E) inquisitive

(Answer to this drill is found on page 126.)

Step #6 – Answer general questions

After answering the specific questions, you have probably reread the passage multiple times. The trick for the general questions is not to get bogged down by the details, however. How do we do this? By rereading the last sentence of the entire passage before we answer general questions. This will clarify the main idea.

- Reread last sentence of passage before answering general questions

General questions are those that are about the passage as a whole, and not just a specific part of the passage.

There are 4 main types:

1. Main idea
2. Tone or attitude
3. Organization
4. Style

Main idea questions

Main idea questions are looking for you to identify what the passage is about. You can identify them because they often use the words main or primarily.

- Often have the words *main* or *primarily* in them

Here is what they may look like:

- This passage primarily deals with
- The main purpose of this passage is to
- Which of the following best expresses the author's main point?

- What is the best title of this passage?

How to approach main idea questions:

- Reread the last sentence of the entire passage and look for the answer that comes closest to this sentence

Trick to look out for with main idea questions:

- Answers that give details from the passage but are not the main idea

Usually, the wrong answers are mentioned in the passage, but they are incorrect because they are not the main idea.

Following on page 113 is a passage to be used for all the general question practice drills. The book is designed so that you can tear out the page instead of flipping pages while trying to answer questions.

Please complete the following drill using the Hantavirus passage on the following page.

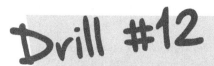

1. What is the main idea of this passage?

    (A) the symptoms of the hantavirus
    (B) the history of the hantavirus
    (C) the history of Yosemite Park
    (D) a recent outbreak of the hantavirus at Yosemite
    (E) how the hantavirus is spread

2. Which of the following would be the best title for this passage?

    (A) Terror at Yosemite Park
    (B) An outbreak of a virus at Yosemite
    (C) A brief history of the hantavirus
    (D) Summertime blues
    (E) The dangers of hiking in national parks

(Answers to this drill are found on page 126.)

Tone or attitude questions

Previously, we worked on tone and attitude questions that were about a particular topic. These tone and attitude questions refer to the entire passage.

They might look like this:

- The author's tone is
- The author's attitude is

If the question does not refer to a specific part of the passage, you can assume that it applies to the passage as a whole.

How to approach:

- Reread the last sentence of the passage
- Use ruling out

Tricks to look out for with tone or attitude questions:

- Rule out answers that are too extreme, in a positive or negative way
- Don't be afraid of words you don't know
- Think about the type of passage that you are reading (fiction or non-fiction)

————

Passage for General Questions Drills

Many recent visitors to Yosemite National Park have been diagnosed with Hantavirus Pulmonary Syndrome. The disease is caused by infected mice, and in particular, deer mice. Exposure to the mouse feces or urine could result in human infection.

California Department of Public Health and Yosemite National Park Public Health Service officers conduct routine inspections and monitor rodent activity and mouse populations. Park officials also actively perform rodent proofing inspections of all facilities and buildings throughout the park.

The CDPH recommended the park increase rodent control measures to reduce the risk of exposing visitors to the hantavirus. Extra inspections, more thorough cleaning of the cabins, and increased overall sanitation measures have been implemented to discourage mouse infestations.

Symptoms of the disease usually appear between one and six weeks after exposure and are similar to those of influenza, including fever, headaches, and muscle aches. The infection progresses rapidly into severe breathing problems and sometimes death. Because of these severe consequences, the park rangers at Yosemite have taken the current outbreak of Hantavirus very seriously and are working to let visitors know who might have been affected.

This page intentionally left blank so that passage can be removed from book to use for drills.

- Non-fiction passages tend to have correct answers that are like the words *objective, informative, interested*, etc.

- Fiction passages tend to have more emotional answers such as *nervous, excited, determined*, etc.

The following drill refers back to the passage about hantavirus at Yosemite.

1. The author's tone can best be described as

    (A) disappointed
    (B) ambivalent
    (C) jealous
    (D) outraged
    (E) informative

(Answer to this drill is found on page 126.)

Organization questions

Some questions require you to think about the organization of the passage a whole.

They might look something like this:

- Which of the following will the author discuss next?

- What will (name of a character) do next?

To approach these questions:

- Next to each paragraph, label in a word or two what it is talking about

- Use these labels to look for a natural flow in what would come next

Tricks to look out for on organization questions:

- Answers that repeat the main idea of another paragraph – authors are not likely to repeat themselves

- Answers that relate to the main idea, but are pretty far removed or are a much broader topic than the passage

The following drill refers back to the passage about hantavirus at Yosemite.

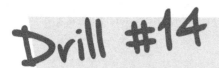

1. Which of the following is the author most likely to discuss next?

    (A) where the hantavirus was first discovered
    (B) the history of outbreaks at other parks
    (C) what park rangers at Yosemite have learned from this outbreak
    (D) how viruses change over time
    (E) the future of vaccines

(Answer to this drill is found on page 126.)

Style questions

These questions ask you to identify where you might find a passage.

They might look like:

- What is the style of the passage?
- This passage can best be described as
- The answer choices will give different types of writing such as a newspaper article, propaganda, a manual, etc.

How to approach:

- First, ask yourself if it is fiction or non-fiction. If it is fiction, rule out any non-fiction forms. If it is non-fiction, then rule out any fiction forms.
- If it is more scholarly non-fiction (i.e. dry and boring), then the correct answer is likely to be something like a textbook or encyclopedia entry.
- If it is non-fiction but still telling a story, it might be an account of an event, a news article or item, or found in a newspaper.
- If it is trying to persuade the reader, then it could be propaganda (selling an idea) or an advertisement (selling a product).
- Fiction passages tend to be found either in a novel or in some sort of anthology.

Trick for style questions:

- Any form of writing that is too technical won't show up on this test (medical journals, manuals, etc.)

The following drill refers back to the passage about hantavirus.

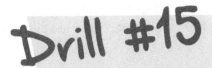

1. Where would this passage most likely be found?

   (A) a personal diary
   (B) a newspaper
   (C) a diagnosis manual
   (D) correspondence between two physicians
   (E) a novel

(Answer to this drill is found on page 126.)

Step #7 – Move on to your next passage and repeat!

When you complete a passage, check your time against the chart your created before starting the section and then move on to the next passage.

- Keep track of time
- Just keep on truckin'

Secrets to Choosing the Types of Answers that Test Writers Prefer

Ruling out is particularly important on the reading section. Often, you will read through the answer choices and right away you can rule out two or three answer choices.

The art of answering reading questions correctly comes down to three things:

- Look for answer choices that are harder to argue with
- Watch out for answer choices that take words from the passage and move them around so that the meaning is different
- Be careful not to let your brain fill in details that are not there

Secret #1: Look for answer choices that are harder to argue with

The people who write the SSAT have to make sure that there is no dispute over which is the correct answer to a question.

How do they do this? When they write a question, they come up with five answer choices. Then they go back and make sure that four of those answer choices have something in them that makes them wrong. Those are the details that we want to look for!

Basically, when you are debating between two answer choices, ask yourself which one is easiest to make a case against. Rule that one out.

- Four answer choices for every question have something that makes them wrong
- Wrong answer choices are easier to argue with
- Rule out the answer choices that are easier to argue with

So what is it that makes an answer choice easy to argue with?

1. Extreme words
2. Words that leave no room for negotiation (always, never, all, etc.)

What are extreme words?

Think of words existing on a spectrum. Words in the middle are pretty neutral, but words on either end are extreme.

Here is an example:

Let's say you were looking for a word to describe your experience with the latest phone app. Here is one possible range of the words that you might use:

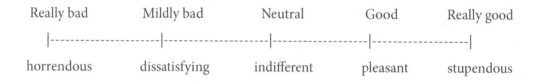

Really bad Mildly bad Neutral Good Really good

horrendous dissatisfying indifferent pleasant stupendous

Horrendous and *stupendous* are very extreme words, so they would not likely be the right answer choice on the SSAT. They are too easy to argue with. The words *dissatisfying*, *indifferent*, and *pleasant*, however, are more in the middle. It is harder to argue with them, so they are more likely to be correct on the SSAT.

- When you are trying to decide whether a word is extreme, think of where it would fall on a spectrum compared to other words with a similar meaning

To complete the following drill, rule out answer choices that are too extreme and choose from what is left. Yes, there is no passage! The point here is to use your knowledge of the type of answer choices that are preferred in order to answer the question.

Answer the following drill using just what you know about what types of answers tend to be right on the SSAT.

Drill #16

1. The author's attitude toward juvenile imprisonment can be described best as one of

   (A) hostile attack
   (B) enthusiastic support
   (C) sarcastic criticism
   (D) jubilant support
   (E) cautious optimism

2. Which of the following phrases would the author use to describe George Washington?

   (A) Triumphant warrior
   (B) Vile wretch
   (C) Committed patriot
   (D) Untalented ruler
   (E) Tyrant

(Answers to this drill are found on page 126.)

Which words leave no room for negotiation?

Words such as *always*, *never*, and *all* are too easy to argue with. Let's say that I tell you that the bus is always late. That would be a really easy statement to argue with. If the bus was on time even once, then I would be wrong because I used the word *always*. Let's say that I tell you that Abraham Lincoln never thought that the union would actually break apart. How could I possibly know that? A correct answer would say something like "there is no evidence that Abraham Lincoln thought that the union might break apart" rather than "Abraham Lincoln never thought the union would break apart."

- Words such as *all*, *none*, *entirely*, *always*, and *never* are too easy to argue with

———

For the following drill, pretend that you are down to two answer choices. You have ruled out the other three as definitely incorrect and now you have to choose the answer choice that is hardest to argue with. Circle the one that you would choose on the actual test.

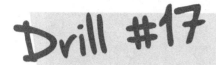

Choice 1: Asteroids never hit the Earth.
Choice 2: Scientists have not observed an asteroid colliding with the earth.

Choice 1: The facts of the story all point to the same conclusion.
Choice 2: The story is described in a way that suggests one conclusion.

Choice 1: No sailors were found on the decks of the ship.
Choice 2: None of the sailors survived the storm.

Choice 1: The basketball players were disappointed by the loss.
Choice 2: All of the basketball players left the game upset because of the loss.

(Answers to this drill are found on page 126.)

Secret #2: Watch out for answer choices that take words from the passage and move them around so that the meaning is different

On the SSAT, answer choices often have words from the passage. More often than not, however, these words are twisted around so that the meaning is different. Usually the right answer choice has synonyms for words in the passage. That doesn't mean you should rule out all choices that repeat words from the passage, it just means that you should be careful when words are repeated from the passage.

- Be cautious when choosing an answer that repeats words from the passage

———

Here is an example:

Let's say that the passage states:

John was upset when Sam got into the car with Trish.

The question may look something like:

1. Which of the following is implied by the author?
   (A) John was upset with Trish when Sam got into the car
   (B) John was upset with Trish when he got into the car
   (C) Sam and Trish were upset when John got into the car
   (D) John and Sam were cousins
   (E) John was not happy because Sam rode with Trish

Answer choices A, B, and C all use words from the passage, but do not have the same meaning as what the passage says. Choice D is just unrelated – which happens on the SSAT! Choice E restates the passage without using exact words from the passage.

In the drill on the next page, there is a sentence from a passage. There is then a list of answer choices. You have to decide whether the answer choice has the same meaning as the passage, or whether the words have been twisted around to mean something else.

———

Drill #18

Passage 1: After being persuaded by the pleading of Father Thomas O'Reilly, when Sherman ordered the city of Atlanta burned, he spared the city's hospitals and churches.

Answer states:	Same meaning	Twisted meaning
1. When Sherman burned the city of Atlanta, only Father Thomas O'Reilly's church was spared.		
2. Atlanta's hospitals and churches were not ordered to be burned by Sherman.		
3. When Atlanta was burned, due to the influence of Father Thomas O'Reilly the city's churches and hospitals remained standing.		
4. Sherman ordered that Atlanta's hospitals and churches not be spared, despite the pleadings of Father Thomas O'Reilly.		

Passage 2: When the morning sun rose high above the horizon, a small boy could be spotted as he carried a bucket along the ridge of a hill in the distance.

Answer states:	Same meaning	Twisted meaning
1. A small boy was spotted along the horizon, looking almost like a bucket on the hill.		
2. Along the ridge, a child was carrying a pail in the morning.		
3. The small boy spotted the sun rising over a ridge as he carried a bucket.		
4. Far away, it was possible to see a boy carrying a bucket as he walked along the top of a hill in the morning sun.		

(Answers to this drill are found on page 126.)

Secret #3: Be careful not to let your brain fill in details that are not there

As we read, we automatically fill in details. However, the writers of the test know this and use this against you! Remember, the average student is missing a whole lot of reading comprehension questions, despite the fact that he or she probably knows how to read well.

For example, let's say that the passage says:

> "Samuel came from a family of enormous height – it was said that
> even his mother was six feet four inches tall."

Look at the following question and decide what answer choice would be a trap (we don't have enough information to pick out the right answer, we are just trying to identify the trick answer choice.)

2.   Which of the following about Samuel can be inferred from the passage?
   (A)   He is well educated
   (B)   He is very tall
   (C)   His favorite pastime is basketball
   (D)   He left school at an early age
   (E)   He was the first astronaut to be a pet owner

As we read, our mind probably filled in that Samuel is tall since the passage says that his family was tall. However, the passage does NOT say that Samuel is tall. Odds are good that we won't remember this, however, since our mind has already filled in the blank. The test writers know this and throw in choice B as a trick. This is exactly how they get proficient readers to miss so many questions!

So how do we overcome this trick? By underlining the evidence in the passage for each answer choice for specific questions. Do not go on what you remember – if you can't underline it, it isn't the right answer choice.

- Underlining the evidence for the correct answer choice will keep you from choosing an answer where your brain has drawn its own conclusions

Also watch out for assigning emotions to other people. Let's say a story tells us that a little boy lost his dog. You might assume that he would be sad and choose an answer choice that indicates that. But maybe he always hated that dog! Unless there is evidence of a particular emotion, don't assume that the character would think or feel what you would think or feel.

- Don't assume what a character would feel, there has to be concrete evidence of that emotion

For the following drill, read the passage and then answer the question that follows. Remember to look out for our tricks!

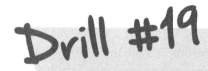

On a dark night, when there was no moon in the sky, a peddler pulled into an inn. He had come from very far away with wares to sell. When the peddler told the innkeeper why he was travelling, the innkeeper was distrustful. He had heard of peddlers and the tricks they liked to play. He said to the peddler, "I will give you a room tonight, but in the morning I want you to show me one of your tricks for which you are so famous." The peddler wearily agreed. He stowed his nag for the night and barely made it to his room upstairs before falling asleep. In the morning, the peddler was feeling much better. As the innkeeper walked through the breakfast room, he saw the peddler talking with the innkeeper's wife and showing her a quilt that matched one that the inn already had. The wife was quite excited as she was in need of another quilt. She counted out the coins for the quilt and the peddler was soon on his way once more. As he drove away, the innkeeper yelled after him, "Hey! I thought you were going to show me one of your famous tricks!" The peddler replied, "I just did. I just sold your wife the quilt off of your own bed."

1.   From the passage, which of the following can be inferred?

(A)   the innkeeper was furious at the peddler
(B)   the peddler was tired after his long journey
(C)   the innkeeper's wife was in charge off all the money in the inn
(D)   the quilt on the innkeeper's bed was worn out
(E)   there were no other guests at the inn that night

(Answer to this drill is found on page 126.)

Now you know what you need to in order to excel on the reading section!

Answers to Drills

Drill #1

Start – 9:32
Halfway point – 9:52, 4 passages
Finish – 10:12

Start – 8:56
Halfway point – 9:16, 3.5 passages
Finish – 9:36

Drill #2

There is not an absolute right order to answer these passages. The passage about the invention of the unicycle, the news article from WWI, and the passage about why we have Leap Day are all non-fiction, so they should have been in your top 3. Your order will vary depending upon what you find interesting! The Native American folktale, the traditional tale from China, and the novel passage should have been #4-6. Again, their exact order will depend on what looked good to you. The poem should be answered last. Always.

Drill #3

1. G
2. S
3. S
4. S
5. G

Drill #4

1. S
2. S
3. S
4. S
5. G

Drill #5

1. S
2. S
3. S
4. S
5. S

You might be asking yourself, would there really be a passage with all specific questions? There could be!

Drill #6

1. G
2. S
3. S or G – it depends on what the whole passage is about. Remember, we have to stay flexible when we do this.
4. G
5. S

Drill #7

1. D
2. B

Drill #8

1. D
2. A

Drill #9

1. B

Drill #10

1. C

Drill #11

1. A

Drill #12

1. D
2. B

Drill #13

1. E

Drill #14

1. C

Drill #15

1. B

Drill #16

1. E
2. C

Drill #17

1. Choice 2
2. Choice 2
3. Choice 1
4. Choice 1

Drill #18

Passage 1:
1. twisted meaning
2. same meaning
3. same meaning
4. twisted meaning

Passage 2:
1. twisted meaning
2. same meaning
3. twisted meaning
4. same meaning

Drill #19

1. B

———

Additional Reading Practice

The following are some passages and questions for you to practice your skills. You will see that after each passage and set of questions, there are additional questions about the process. Be sure to answer these. It is important that you don't just whip through the passages, but rather that you think about what you are doing as you go.

- Be sure to answer process questions after the questions that go with the passage

Each passage has a time recommended. You will notice that the times vary. This is because not every passage should take the same amount of time. On the real test, you will always be given the same number of minutes to complete each reading section, but the number of passages will vary so the minutes per passage will also be different. Don't think of the times given as a strict cut-off. Just know that if you take a lot longer than recommended, you need to work on speeding up the process. Alternately, if you are answering the passages a lot more quickly than recommended, you need to slow it down. Note that the process questions should NOT be included in the time given.

- Recommended times vary by passage
- Recommended times are not strict cut-offs but rather a guideline
- Process questions should NOT be done within the recommended time

Here is a general process for completing each passage:

1. Circle recommended time for each passage.
2. Start timer.
3. Mark questions "S" or "G".
4. Read, answering specific questions as you go if you can.
5. Answer any specific questions that you have not already answered.
6. Answer general questions.
7. STOP TIMER.
8. Answer process questions.
9. Check your answers – and think about WHY you missed any questions.

———

Passage 1
Recommended Time: 6 minutes

When America engaged in the Civil War, men on both sides left their domestic posts and set off to meet their fates upon the battlefield. Very likely, there were many tearful farewells as husbands parted from wives and sons from mothers. Yet, in the wake of these departed warriors, most women did not sit idly by or wallow in their sorrow. Rather, they took hold of the swords passed on to them and led the charge of their households.

Line 5

Both within and beyond their homes, many women employed their talents to contribute to the war efforts. Their passionate spirits were set ablaze with the desire for victory. Like the gallant soldiers sacrificing their lives for their beliefs, women were also motivated by their views in support of or opposition to abolition, secession, and the goal of a united America.

10

Some, like Clara Barton, became "angels of the battlefield," nursing the wounded and providing them comfort. Some, like Rose O'Neal Greenhow, worked as spies, secretly collecting and sharing intelligence. And others, like Jennie Hodgers, disguised their feminine attributes, adopted alter egos, and enlisted as soldiers. Whatever their role, these contributors displayed bravery, courage, and often, a blatant disregard for the expectations of female behavior that most people held at the time.

15

Passage Questions

1. According to the passage, during the American Civil War women

   (A) learned to sword fight
   (B) sat idly and waited for their husbands to return
   (C) sometimes acted as spies and soldiers
   (D) were united in support of abolition
   (E) did not have an opinion on the war

2. It can be inferred that the women mentioned in the passage were greatly concerned with

   (A) what other people thought of them
   (B) defining the role of the American president
   (C) rebuilding the United States
   (D) creating nursing societies
   (E) supporting the work of male soldiers

3. This passage was probably written in order to

   (A) correct a misunderstanding about soldiers during the Civil War
   (B) explain the contribution of a particular group during the Civil War
   (C) describe the contributions of Clara Barton
   (D) prove that the Civil War would not have ended without the contribution of women
   (E) provide evidence that spies played an important role in the Civil War

4. All of the following are mentioned in the passage EXCEPT

    (A) how nurses were viewed during the Civil War
    (B) how women felt when their male relatives went off to battle
    (C) the contribution of Jennie Hodgers
    (D) causes of the Civil War
    (E) how females were expected to behave during the time of the American Civil War

5. The author's attitude toward women who lived during the American Civil War is one of

    (A) admiration
    (B) skepticism
    (C) nostalgia
    (D) amazement
    (E) indifference

6. The passage implies that an "alter ego" (line 14) is

    (A) a nurse
    (B) a soldier
    (C) a disguise
    (D) a battle
    (E) a period in American history

Process Questions

Answer these questions AFTER you have stopped the timer.

1. How long did it take you to complete the passage and questions? Do you need to work more quickly next time or slow down?

2. Did you remember to mark questions as S or G before answering them? Which questions were specific? Which questions were general?

Passage 2
Recommended Time: 5 minutes

Have you ever wondered what happens to a plastic bottle after you deposit it in a recycling bin? Each empty vessel placed in a recycling container takes a multi-step journey of reincarnation.

Line 5   This journey begins when a recycling company collects the bottle and transports it to the local recycling plant. Since there are many types of plastic that must be processed separately, recycling facilities have workers or special equipment to sort the bottles. Then, after the bottles are sorted, food particles or other contaminants are removed. The plastic is cut into small pieces and melted down. Once this process is complete, the newly formed material is sold to other companies.

10   What happens next is more open-ended. Depending on the type of plastic and the company that buys it, there are many possibilities for what the plastic might become. Did you ever imagine while drinking from a plastic bottle that it could one day be used to make a piece of furniture, a road, or a T-shirt? Even uniforms worn by some athletes during the 2010 World Cup and 2012 Olympics were made partly from recycled plastic. Consider that

15   the next time you finish a bottle and have to decide whether to trash it or recycle it. Why doom a bottle to endless years in a crowded landfill when it has the potential for a much more meaningful existence?

Passage Questions

1. The passage implies that an important step in the recycling process is

   (A) buying the right type of plastic container
   (B) sorting different types of plastics
   (C) promoting recycled products
   (D) passing laws that encourage recycling
   (E) distributing recycling bins

2. This primary purpose of this passage is to

   (A) convince readers of the importance of a certain action
   (B) explain the different types of plastic
   (C) provide instructions for someone wanting to operate a recycling facility
   (D) describe how uniforms were made for the 2012 Olympics
   (E) create a sense of suspense about what happens to recycled bottles

3. From the passage it can be inferred that

   (A) recycling rates are falling
   (B) more people are recycling
   (C) containers must be cleaned before they can be recycled
   (D) recycling trucks should be outfitted with automatic sorters
   (E) the same company collects used containers and produces recycled products

4. The passage mentions that all of the following products can be made from recycled plastic bottles EXCEPT

   (A) roads
   (B) uniforms
   (C) furniture
   (D) t-shirts
   (E) plastic bottles

5. The passages states that the type of product that is made from recycled plastic depends upon

   (A) the company that picks up the plastic containers from the recycling bin
   (B) how many containers are being recycled
   (C) the distance that the recycled plastic must be shipped
   (D) the type of plastic
   (E) incentives offered by the local government

Process Questions

Answer these questions AFTER you have stopped the timer.

1. How long did it take you to complete the passage and questions? Do you need to work more quickly next time or slow down?

2. Did you remember to mark questions as S or G before answering them? Which questions were specific? Which questions were general?

3. Did you remember to use ruling out to answer #4? How did you know to use ruling out for this question?

4. Questions #1, #3, and #5 are all pretty straightforward specific questions. Did you underline the answer to these questions in the passage?

Answers to Passage 2

Passage Questions

1. B is the correct answer. The best way to answer this question is using process of elimination. There is simply not evidence for choices A, C, D, and E, so we can rule those out. This is a specific question and we can underline evidence for choice B, so that is the correct answer.

2. A is the correct answer choice. This is definitely a persuasive passage. The last line even asks the reader, "Why doom a bottle to endless years in a crowded landfill when it has the potential for a much more meaningful existence?" Don't be thrown by the fact that answer choice A does not mention the word "recycling". The words "a certain action" refer to recycling.

3. C is the correct answer. Remember that on the SSAT, we have to be able to underline evidence for the correct answer choice. The passage states that "after the bottles are sorted, food particles or other contaminants are removed", which is evidence that answer choice C is the right answer.

4. E is the correct answer. Although the passage talks about plastic bottles being recycled, it does not mention that new plastic bottles can be made from recycled plastic bottles. There is evidence for answer choices A-D, but since this an EXCEPT question we can rule out those answer choices.

5. D is the correct answer. In the third paragraph, the passage states "depending on the type of plastic and the company that buys it, there are many possibilities for what the plastic might become". This is evidence that we can underline for choice D. The other answer choices might affect the type of product that is made, but they are not mentioned in the passage, so they are not the correct answers.

Process Questions

1. Answers will vary for this question.
2. Questions #1, #3, #4, and #5 are specific questions. Question #2 is general.
3. Any time we have an "EXCEPT" question, we have to use ruling out in order to find the answer choice that is NOT mentioned.
4. It is very important to underline the exact answer restated in the passage. These questions all have answer choices that could make sense but are wrong because they are not mentioned in the passage.

Passage 3
Recommended Time: 4 minutes

Over the course of several years, all the residents of Everwood Drive had transformed from mere acquaintances to the closest of friends, with the exception, that is, of Ms. Harrington. While everyone else greeted each other with a polite smile and friendly wave, Ms. Harrington's countenance had only two states: grimace and scowl. The two masks
Line 5 looked quite similar; sharp lines cut into the forehead, furrowed brow, and downturned lips, all highlighted by a look of scorn projecting from the dark spheres set deep in their sockets. The sole difference between the two expressions was that while the grimace suggested a strong dislike, the scowl reflected an absolute hatred for whatever was within its line of sight.

In fact, the only thing that Ms. Harrington didn't seem to have an intense disdain
10 for was her flowers. The passing of months could be marked by the changing blooms that punctuated her lawn: tulips in April; rhododendrons in May; lilies in June; hydrangea in July. Despite the dark shadow that the gardener cast over the street, her charges were a bright presence that imbued cheer and a joy for life. The other neighbors repeatedly marveled at the irony of it all. How could the one solitary weed within their garden of a community also be
15 the most gifted green thumb any of them had ever seen?

Passage Questions

1. The primary purpose of this passage is to

   (A) inform the reader about different types of plants
   (B) build to an exciting climax
   (C) describe a character
   (D) describe the residents of Everwood Drive
   (E) instruct readers on how to make a garden thrive

2. The passage implies that

   (A) the only time Ms. Harrington spoke with her neighbors was when they asked about her flowers
   (B) Ms. Harrington smiled when talking about her flowers
   (C) Ms. Harrington's house was not well cared for
   (D) Ms. Harrington grew different flowers in different months
   (E) Ms. Harrington lived alone

3. Ms. Harrington's countenance can best be described as

   (A) friendly
   (B) threatening
   (C) ambivalent
   (D) disinterested
   (E) calm

4. According to the passage, what leaves the residents of Everwood Drive puzzled?

    (A) how Ms. Harrington could be so mean and yet grow cheerful flowers
    (B) why Ms. Harrington is so unfriendly
    (C) how Ms. Harrington grows such a lovely lawn
    (D) why their yards look so bleak
    (E) how Ms. Harrington knows what to grow during each month

Process Questions

Answer these questions AFTER you have stopped the timer.

1. How long did it take you to complete the passage and questions? Do you need to work more quickly next time or slow down?

2. Did you remember to mark questions as S or G before answering them? Which questions were specific? Which questions were general?

3. On question #1, why is answer choice D so appealing?

4. On question #2, why is answer choice E so appealing?

Answers to Passage 3

Passage Questions

1. C is the correct answer choice. This passage is primarily a description of Ms. Harrington. Other answer choices are mentioned, but are details and not the main idea.

2. D is the correct answer. The passage states, "The passing of months could be marked by the changing blooms that punctuated her lawn". This is our evidence for choice D.

3. B is the correct answer choice. The word countenance is another way to say facial expression. Since she alternates between a grimace and a scowl, threatening is the best description of her expression. It isn't a perfect fit, but on this test remember that we are looking for the "best" answer choice and since choice D is better than the other choices, it is the best answer choice.

4. A is the correct answer choice. The very last sentence of the passage tells us "How could the one solitary weed within their garden of a community also be the most gifted green thumb any of them had ever seen?" Answer choice A restates this question, so it is the correct answer.

Process Questions

1. Answers will vary for this question.

2. Questions #2, #3, and #4 are all specific questions. Question #1 is general.

3. Answer choice D is mentioned in the very first sentence of the passage. It is tempting to think that the first sentence introduces the main idea, but on this test it is actually the LAST sentence that we want to look at for general questions. Answer choices that repeat the idea from the first sentence are generally a trap.

4. As a good reader, you could easily infer that Ms. Harrington lived alone. She was cranky, had no friends, and had a lot of time on her hands for gardening. However, because there is no evidence that we could underline in the passage that she lived alone, answer choice E is not correct. This is an example of why it is so important to underline answers to specific questions because wrong answers are often logical conclusions from the passage and unless we go back and look for evidence, we don't realize that our brain has filled in that detail.

Passage 4
Recommended Time: 5 minutes

I had for my winter evening walk—
No one at all with whom to talk,
But I had the cottages in a row
Up to their shining eyes in snow.

Line 5   And I thought I had the folk within:
I had the sound of a violin;
I had a glimpse through curtain laces
Of youthful forms and youthful faces.

I had such company outward bound.
10   I went till there were no cottages found.
I turned and repented, but coming back
I saw no window but that was black.

Over the snow my creaking feet
Disturbed the slumbering village street
15   Like profanation, by your leave,
At ten o'clock of a winter eve.

Passage Questions

1. Which word best describes the speaker of this poem?

   (A) lonesome
   (B) optimistic
   (C) tired
   (D) friendly
   (E) thankful

2. Why does the speaker of the poem "repent" in the middle of the poem?

   (A) He has not lived a good life.
   (B) He was mean to people who passed by.
   (C) He walked by the houses and chose not to spend time with the people inside the cottages.
   (D) He disturbed the parties in the cottages.
   (E) He had not exercised enough.

3. The poem suggests that the "shining eyes" (line 4) are most likely

   (A) musical instruments
   (B) neighbors
   (C) a snow fort
   (D) cottage windows
   (E) a winter night

4. Which statement best summarizes the main lesson of this poem?

   (A) Always bundle up when you go for a walk on a winter night.
   (B) Music is important for happiness.
   (C) Walking can be lonely.
   (D) Enjoy yourself when you are young.
   (E) Do not pass up a chance to spend time with other people because you may not be given that chance again.

5. What do the black windows at the end of the poem represent?

   (A) nighttime
   (B) loneliness
   (C) death
   (D) triumph
   (E) winter

Process Questions

Answer these questions AFTER you have stopped the timer.

1. How long did it take you to complete the passage and questions? Do you need to work more quickly next time or slow down?

2. Did you remember to mark questions as "S" or "G" before answering them? Which questions were specific? Which questions were general?

3. What do you notice about the questions for a poem passage?

4. Are poems a strength for you or are they better to answer last?

Answers to Passage 4

Passage Questions

1. A is the correct answer choice. The poem describes a person walking who is looking in on other people but is not a part of the socializing. The poem also states that the speaker had "No one at all with whom to talk". This is evidence that the speaker was lonesome.

2. C is the correct answer. With poem questions, we want to stick to the words of the poem as closely as possible. To repent is to try to make up for something, so we need to look at the poem to see what the speaker might be trying to make up for. He has walked past houses without stopping in the first part of the poem and answer choice C best restates this idea.

3. D is the correct answer. Lines 3-4 state "But I had the cottages in a row/ Up to their shining eyes in snow". The speaker then goes on to describe how he can see the people who are in the cottages. This implies that the lights are on in the cottages, causing the windows to look like shining eyes.

4. E is the correct answer choice. This is a general question, so we want to be sure that we pick an answer choice that summarizes the main idea and not a detail from the passage.

5. B is the correct answer choice. At the beginning of the poem, the "shining eyes" or windows allow the speaker to feel like he is present in what is going on in the cottages. When he walks back though the village, there are no lights on, so he does not feel that he has a connection to the people in the cottages.

Process Questions

1. Answers will vary for this question.
2. Questions #2, #3, and #5 are all specific questions. Questions #1 and #4 are general questions.
3. Poems have questions that require a better understanding of metaphorical (or not literal) language.
4. Answers will vary for this question. If you were very comfortable with reading into the poem then by all means answer poem passages earlier in the section. For most students, however, trying to translate a poem into multiple-choice answers is difficult and poem passages should be answered last.

Passage 5
Recommended Time: 3 minutes

> To the casual observer, that luminous ball of fire above us may appear to move across the heavens. It may even deceive witnesses into believing that it takes a daily journey along a path from east to west.
>
> *Line 5* However, such perceived motion is merely an illusion. That magnificent star is static; frozen in its designated position at the heart of our solar system. The object which is actually moving is the massive globe upon which we stand. At breakneck speeds it spins us round its axis, each and every day. And year after year, it propels us in a ceaseless orbit around that central star.

Passage Questions

1. The star referred to in the passage is most likely

    (A) the moon
    (B) the sun
    (C) the North star
    (D) Earth
    (E) Venus

2. The passage implies that some people who view the sun may believe

    (A) the distance from the Earth to the sun changes
    (B) the Earth is not round
    (C) the solar system spins
    (D) the sun moves from east to west
    (E) we do not actually know whether it is the sun or the Earth that moves

3. What object is actually moving in the passage?

    (A) the sun
    (B) the moon
    (C) the Earth
    (D) the witnesses
    (E) no objects are actually moving

4. According to the passage, which of the following best describes the motion of the Earth?

    (A) it spins slowly
    (B) it is static
    (C) it is frozen in position
    (D) it rotates very quickly
    (E) it moves from east to west

Process Questions

Answer these questions AFTER you have stopped the timer.

1. How long did it take you to complete the passage and questions? Do you need to work more quickly next time or slow down?

2. Did you remember to mark questions as S or G before answering them? Which questions were specific? Which questions were general?

3. In question #4, why are answer choices B, C, and E traps?

Answers to Passage 5

Passage Questions

1. B is the correct answer choice. At the beginning of the passage, it refers to a "luminous ball of fire above us". Later, the passage refers to the same object as "that magnificent star". The star is the luminous ball of fire above us, or the sun.
2. D is the correct answer choice. In the first paragraph, the passage states that the sun may "deceive witnesses into believing that it takes a daily journey along a path from east to west". While it is not correct that the sun is moving, the passage does provide evidence that some people believe that.
3. C is the correct answer choice. The passage tells us that the "magnificent star", i.e. the sun, is static, or not moving. The object that actually is moving is the "the massive globe upon which we stand". Don't be confused by choice D. The witnesses standing on the Earth would be moving, but they are not an "object".
4. D is the correct answer choice. The passage states that the "globe upon which we stand…. at breakneck speeds it spins us round its axis". This is the evidence you should have underlined to support answer choice D.

Process Questions

1. Answers will vary.
2. All of the questions for this passage were specific. Could this happen on the real SSAT? Absolutely.
3. Answer choices B, C, and E all contain words that show up somewhere in the passage, they just aren't describing the motion of the Earth.

Passage 6
Recommended Time: 4 minutes

Edward sat next to his mother, analyzing the grass beneath his feet. The blades glistened with tiny dew drops, smaller than the occasional tears that slid down his mother's cheek. Every few minutes, he glanced up at the box in front of them. Behind the box stood a large portrait of his grandfather, and as long as Edward kept this picture from his view, he

Line 5 could pretend that it was a stranger in the casket.

He flipped through the memories of his grandfather arranged in his mind like files in a drawer, and one-by-one, he pulled out each memory and recalled its contents. He saw pastel colors painting the sky as the sun rose over the shore where they fished together. His nostrils filled with the smell of burnt firewood from the fires they built while camping. He

10 heard his grandfather's voice echo through his ears like rolling thunder. Often the stories told by that resounding voice were ones of far-off places full of fantastic creatures. Yet the tales Edward held dearest were the ones about a young soldier who developed his sense of moral fortitude amidst the horrors of war.

So absorbed was Edward in his memories that he didn't even notice that the service

15 had ended or that an elderly mourner stood stooped over in front of him.

"I'm sure you are going to miss your grandfather a great deal." Edward startled to attention.

"Did you know my grandfather well?" he asked.

"Very well, indeed. I wouldn't even be standing here if it weren't for him saving my

20 hide back in Normandy. Fifty years of my life are owed to him."

"Wow, sir. I didn't know my grandfather saved anyone. He told me stories but never that one."

"I'm not surprised, young man. I'm not surprised at all..."

Passage Questions

1. Which of the following best describes the relationship between Edward and his grandfather?

   (A) Edward resented his grandfather's success.
   (B) Edward did not know his grandfather well.
   (C) Edward and his mother lived with Edward's grandfather.
   (D) Edward was bored by his grandfather's stories.
   (E) Edward and his grandfather had a close relationship.

2. The passage suggests which of the following about Edward's grandfather?

   (A) He died too young.
   (B) He had very white hair.
   (C) His voice was deep.
   (D) He often retold the same stories.
   (E) He was gloomy by nature.

3. Why was the elderly mourner not surprised that Edward had not heard the story of his grandfather saving the elderly mourner's life?

    (A) Edward's grandfather had a strong character and would not boast.
    (B) Edward did not listen closely to his grandfather's stories.
    (C) Edward's grandfather was not actually responsible for saving the man's life.
    (D) Edward's grandfather did not like to share stories from war.
    (E) Edward did not often remember the stories that his grandfather told.

4. It can be inferred from the passage that the funeral was held

    (A) at a funeral home
    (B) outside
    (C) in a church
    (D) at Edward's house
    (E) at Edward's grandfather's house

Process Questions

Answer these questions AFTER you have stopped the timer.

1. How long did it take you to complete the passage and questions? Do you need to work more quickly next time or slow down?

2. Did you remember to mark questions as "S" or "G" before answering them? Which questions were specific? Which questions were general?

3. In question #2, what words in the question let us know that this question is specific and looking for a little detail?

Answers to Passage 6

Passage Questions

1. E is the correct answer. The passage tells us that Edward is quite upset by his grandfather's passing and gives examples of all the activities that the two did together. This is evidence that Edward and his grandfather had a close relationship.

2. C is the correct answer choice. The passage mentions "the stories told by that resounding voice". This question is looking for a detail and not the main idea, so we are expecting to find the answer in just a sentence or two.

3. A is the correct answer choice. This question is best answered by ruling out. Answer choice A uses the word "boast", which is kind of a strong word for the SSAT. Answer choices B-E are clearly wrong, however.

4. B is the correct answer choice. The passage states that Edward was "analyzing the grass beneath his feet". Since grass is found outside, answer choice B is correct.

Process Questions

1. Answers will vary.

2. Questions #2, #3, and #4 are specific. Question #1 is general. You may not have marked question #1 as general to begin with because you may not have realized that the whole passage was about the relationship between Edward and his grandfather. Don't worry if you marked question #1 as specific. The point of this strategy is to save time and we don't want to obsess over getting the specific or general categorizations right every time. We need to stay flexible and adjust as we go.

3. The words "the passage suggests" indicates that we looking for some picky detail. The question could also be phrased as "the passage implies which of the following" or "which of the following could be inferred from the passage". Since these questions do not give a key word to skim for, it would be tempting to think that they are general questions. Because we are experts on the SSAT, however, we know that these questions are specific and we should be able to underline the correct answer in the passage.

Passage 7
Recommended Time: 5 minutes

> In 1909, The New York Times declared that Robert Peary had discovered the North Pole. He was hailed as a hero after finally making it to the North Pole on his eighth attempt in 23 years. There was only one problem with this story, however. A mere week earlier, the New York Herald had declared that Frederick Cook had discovered the North
>
> *Line 5* Pole a full year earlier.
>
> One problem with determining who first discovered the North Pole lies with the geography of the North Pole itself. Unlike the South Pole, which is located on a fixed landmass, the North Pole is set atop floating sea ice.
>
> Generally, modern archaeologists can put together the observations of many
>
> 10 explorers from the same era and current land features to determine exactly where an explorer travelled. In the case of the North Pole, however, the sea ice could have drifted so that land features that were once over the North Pole could now be located a hundred miles from the North Pole.
>
> Another complicating factor was that Frederick Cook wandered through the
>
> 15 wilderness for several months before being able to return to civilization again. Therefore, he was unable to report his discovery in a timely manner.

Passage Questions

1. This passage is primarily about

   (A) the geography of the North Pole
   (B) Robert Peary's greatest achievement
   (C) conflicting reports about a discovery
   (D) the friendship between Robert Peary and Frederick Cook
   (E) how Frederick Cook got lost

2. According to the passage, the South Pole

   (A) is on solid ground
   (B) is covered with floating sea ice
   (C) was discovered by Robert Peary
   (D) was discovered by Frederick Cook
   (E) is a diverse ecosystem

3. The passage implies that Frederick Cook

   (A) was a friend of Robert Peary's
   (B) was the real discoverer of the North Pole
   (C) got lost in the South Pole
   (D) did not immediately tell other people that he had discovered the North Pole
   (E) was not a very good navigator

4. It can be inferred from the passage that modern archaeologists

    (A) think that Robert Peary first discovered the North Pole
    (B) do not find reports from other explorers of the North Pole to be helpful
    (C) consider Frederick Cook to be the real discoverer of the North Pole
    (D) credit native tribes as the first people to set foot on the North Pole
    (E) resist taking sides in the debate

5. This passage would most likely be found in

    (A) a novel
    (B) a scientific journal
    (C) an almanac
    (D) an autobiography
    (E) a history magazine

Process Questions

Answer these questions AFTER you have stopped the timer.

1. How long did it take you to complete the passage and questions? Do you need to work more quickly next time or slow down?

2. Did you remember to mark questions as S or G before answering them? Which questions were specific? Which questions were general?

3. In question #3, why is answer choice D a better answer choice than answer choice E?

4. In question #1, what makes answer choice B wrong?

Answers to Passage 7

Passage Questions

1. C is the correct answer. Other answer choices provide details, but not what the passage is "primarily" about.
2. A is the correct answer. This question is easy to miss because most of the passage is about the North Pole so it is easy to answer the question as if it asked about the North Pole. The only thing that the passage says about the South Pole, however, is that it is "located on a fixed landmass".
3. D is the correct answer choice. The very last sentence of the passage tells us "he was unable to report his discovery in a timely manner". Answer choice D restates this. Answer choice C is tempting because it seems as though Frederick Cook did get lost. He would have gotten lost around the North Pole, however, and choice C says he got lost in the South Pole.
4. B is the correct answer choice. The passage describes how sea ice could have drifted since Peary and Cook explored the North Pole so historical accounts would not be as helpful.
5. E is the correct answer choice. The best way to answer this question is to use process of elimination. It is a non-fiction passage, so we can rule out choice A. It is not a technical piece, however, so choice B can be ruled out. An almanac has maps in it but not historical descriptions therefore choice C can be eliminated. An autobiography is written in first person so we can rule out choice D. We are left with choice E.

Process Questions

1. Answers will vary.
2. Questions #2, #3, and #4 are specific questions. Questions #1 and #5 are general.
3. It would be easy to infer that Frederick Cook was not a good navigator since he wandered in the wilderness for months. However, the passage does not give us evidence that he was lost because he was not a good navigator. On this test, the answer with the most evidence wins. Answer choice D is restated in the passage. The main lesson here is that even though the question uses the word "inferred", the better answer choice is the one that is restated in the passage.
4. The word "greatest" makes answer choice B wrong. Can you see how that word makes the answer choice easy to argue with? If the test writers had written "a great accomplishment of Robert Peary", then it would be much harder to argue with. But by saying that it was his "greatest" accomplishment, that is much more subjective to personal opinion and therefore a deal breaker on the SSAT.

Passage 8
Recommended Time: 4 minutes

> Men who write journals are usually men of certain marked traits—they are idealists, they love solitude rather than society, they are self-conscious, and they love to write. At least this seems to be true of the men of the past century who left journals of permanent literary worth—Amiel, Emerson, and Thoreau. Amiel's journal has more the character of a diary
>
> Line 5 than has Emerson's or Thoreau's, though it is also a record of thoughts as well as of days. Emerson left more unprinted matter than he chose to publish during his lifetime.
>
> The journals of Emerson and Thoreau are largely made up of left-overs from their published works, and hence as literary material, when compared with their other volumes, are of secondary importance. You could not make another "Walden" out of Thoreau's journals,
>
> 10 nor build up another chapter on "Self-Reliance," or on "Character," or on the "Over-Soul," from Emerson's, though there are fragments here and there in both that are on a level with their best work.

Passage Questions

1. In line 2, the author states that men who write journals "love solitude rather than society". What does this imply about men who keep journals?

    (A) They enjoy writing.
    (B) They would prefer to be alone rather than in a group.
    (C) They have high ideals.
    (D) They are all exactly alike.
    (E) Their journals are very literary in nature.

2. What does the author mean when he writes that "Amiel's journal has more the character of a diary" (line 4)?

    (A) Amiel's journal shares just his personal thoughts.
    (B) Amiel's journal is more self-conscious.
    (C) Amiel's journal records more daily happenings.
    (D) Much of Amiel's journal is published in other places.
    (E) Amiel's journal has not been found in modern times.

3. Which of the following best describes the author's tone in this passage?

    (A) dismissive
    (B) amused
    (C) indifferent
    (D) excited
    (E) informative

4. Why does the author say that the journals of Emerson and Thoreau are of "secondary importance" (line 9)?

   (A) The author does not like to read those journals.
   (B) Amiel's journal has more description of daily life.
   (C) Much of the material in Emerson and Thoreau's journals was what remained from their
       published works.
   (D) The journals are not their best works.
   (E) They lack character.

Process Questions

Answer these questions AFTER you have stopped the timer.

1. How long did it take you to complete the passage and questions? Do you need to work more
   quickly next time or slow down?

2. Did you remember to mark questions as S or G before answering them? Which questions were
   specific? Which questions were general?

3. In question #1, why are answer choices A and C both traps?

4. In question #2, why are answer choices B and D traps?

Answers to Passage 8

Passage Questions

1. B is the correct answer choice. Solitude refers to being alone and society refers to being in a group. Answer choice B best restates the phrase that is referenced in the question.

2. C is the correct answer choice. We can use process of elimination for this question. We can easily rule out answer choices B, D, and E as being unrelated. Now we have to debate between choices A and C. The passage tells us that Amiel's journal is a record of daily happenings in addition to thoughts, and choice A says it "shares just his personal thoughts." We can rule out choice A. Answer choice C is the correct answer.

3. E is the correct answer choice. The passage is very dry and lacks emotion. We can rule out choices A, B, and D because they are too emotional. We can also rule out indifferent (choice C) because people do not choose to write about a subject that they are indifferent about. Informative is a great description of this passage, so choice E is the correct answer.

4. C is the correct answer. The author states that the "journals of Emerson and Thoreau are largely made up of left-overs from their published works". This implies that the journals are not as important because the best material from them is already published. Answer choice C best restates this idea.

Process Questions

1. Answers will vary.

2. Questions #1, #2, and #4 are all specific questions. Question #3 is general.

3. Answer choices A and C are both restated in the same sentence as the phrase that the question references, so they are very tempting. However, the question does not ask about the whole sentence, it asks only about the meaning of a small part of the sentence.

4. Answer choices B and D repeat ideas that are found elsewhere in the passage. You could underline evidence for these answer choices, but the problem is that they do not answer the question that is asked.

Quantitative Sections – Basic Strategies

On the quantitative sections, there are problems from arithmetic, algebra, and geometry. The math is really not that hard. The SSAT is more about figuring out what concepts they are testing rather than remembering complicated equations.

- The SSAT is more about figuring out what they are testing than hard math

You will NOT be allowed to use a calculator on the SSAT. Yes, you read that correctly. By using strategies, however, we can get to the right answers, often without using complicated calculations.

- No calculator allowed

The goal is for you to get a general understanding of the key strategies for the math section. Following the basic strategies are content lessons where you will get to apply your new skills.

Drumroll, please! The strategies are:

- Estimate – this is a multiple choice test!
- If there are variables in the answer choices, try plugging in your own numbers
- If they ask for the value of a variable, plug in answer choices

Strategy #1: Estimate

You can spend a lot of time finding the exact right answer on this test, or you can spend time figuring out what answers couldn't possibly work and then choose from what is left.

For example, let's say the question is:

1. Which addition problem is closest to 49+31+28?

    (A) 50+30+20
    (B) 50+40+30
    (C) 50+30+30
    (D) 40+30+30
    (E) 40+30+20

If you were to complete the first addition problem and then find each of the sums in the answer choices, that would take a long time without a calculator. However, if we look at our answer choices, we can see that they are not asking us to do the actual addition! They just want to see if we know how to round off in order to estimate. Answer choice C is correct.

You can use estimating on many of the problems, but be sure to estimate when the question uses the words "closest to" or "approximately." If you are not sure of how to round off in order to estimate, read the next section carefully.

Rules for rounding

Is the number 78 closer to the number 70 or 80? If you said 80, you have a good idea of how rounding works. You have rounded 78 to the nearest 10, which is 80.

Now, what if you are to round a decimal number, like 3.43 to the nearest whole number? Would it be closer to 3 or to 4? The answer is that it is closer to 3. The special name for the "4" of the number 3.43 is the "rounding digit." Notice that when you round down, you drop the rounding digit and all the digits to its right.

Now that you see how rounding works, here are the rules:

- Round down if the rounding digit is 0, 1, 2, 3, or 4. This means to drop the rounding digit and all digits to its right.

For example, rounding 41.278543 to the nearest whole number means that the rounding digit is 2. Since 2 is less than 5, you will round down, meaning that you will drop the rounding digit 2 and all the numbers to its right. So 41.278543 will round to just plain 41.

- Round up if the rounding digit is 5, 6, 7, 8, or 9. This means to make the number to the left of the rounding digit one unit higher, and then drop the rounding digit and all the digits to its right.

For example, when we round the number 46.81 to the nearest whole number, the rounding digit is 8. It is 5 or greater, so we will round up. This means that the number 46.81 will be rounded up to 47.

Here are some other examples, with the rounding digit underlined:

- Rounding to a whole number – The number 3.<u>5</u> is rounded up to 4.
- Rounding to the nearest tenth – The number 2.7<u>3</u>22, rounded to the nearest tenth, will be 2.7. Look at the rounding digit, which is 3, and you see that you will round down. So drop the rounding digit and all the digits to its right, and you are left with 2.7.

Drill #1 has questions that show how rounding is tested on the SSAT.

1. The sum 78+52+29 is approximately

    (A) 70+50+20
    (B) 70+60+20
    (C) 70+50+30
    (D) 80+50+30
    (E) 80+60+30

2. Which difference is closest to 5.97−3?

    (A) 5−3
    (B) 6−3
    (C) 60−3
    (D) 600−3
    (E) 500−3

(Answers to this drill are found on page 166.)

Strategy #2: Plug in Your Own Numbers if There are Variables in the Answer Choices

What do I mean by variables in the answer choices? If you look at the answer choices and some or all of them have letters in addition to numbers, then you have variables in your answer choices.

- Look for letters in the answer choices

Here is how this strategy works:

1. Make up your own numbers for the variables

    Just make sure they work within the problem. If it says that x is less than 1, do not make x equal to 2! If it says $x + y = 1$, then don't make x equal to 2 and y equal to 3. Also, make sure that you write down what you are plugging in for your variables. EVERY TIME. You think you will remember that x was 4, but then you go to try out answer choices and it gets all confused. Just write it down the first time. Also, try to avoid using −1, 1, and 0 because they have funky properties and you might get more than one answer that works. The exception to this rule is when the question asks you what must be true. In that case, you want to use the funky numbers to try to rule out answer choices.

2. Solve the problem using your numbers

    Write down the number that you get and circle it. This is the number you are trying to get with your answer choices when you plug in your value for the variable.

3. Plug the numbers that you assigned to the variables in step 1 into the answer choices and see which answer choice matches the number that you circled.

Here is an example:

2. Suzy has q more pencils than Jim. If Jim has 23 pencils, then how many pencils does Suzy have?

(A) $\dfrac{q}{23}$

(B) $q - 23$

(C) $q + 23$

(D) $23 - q$

(E) $\dfrac{23}{q}$

Step 1: Plug in our own number.

Let's make q equal to 4. Suzy now has 4 more pencils than Jim.

Step 2: Solve using our own numbers.

If Jim has 23 pencils, and Suzy has four more than Jim, then Suzy must have 27 pencils. This is our target. Circle it. 27 is the number that we want to get when we plug in 4 for q in our answer choices.

Step 3: Plug into answer choices.

We are looking for the answer choice that is equal to 27.

(A) $\dfrac{q}{23} = \dfrac{4}{23}$

(B) $q - 23 = 4 - 23 = -19$

(C) $q + 23 = 4 + 23 = 27$

(D) $23 - q = 23 - 4 = 19$

(E) $\dfrac{23}{q} = \dfrac{23}{4}$

Choice C gives us 27, which is what we were looking for. C is the correct answer.

If the question asks you which answer choice is greatest or least, then you won't come up with a target number to circle. Rather, you will just plug your values into the answer choices and see which one is greatest or least, depending on what the question asked for.

- If the question asks which answer choice is greatest or least, you won't come up with a target, you will just plug into answer choices

———

Here is an example:

3. Two times which number is greatest?

   (A) $X + 2$
   (B) $X - 2$
   (C) X
   (D) $X + 1$
   (E) $X - 1$

Step 1: Choose our own numbers.

Let's make X equal to 2. This is a nice, easy number to work with.

Step 2: Solve using our own numbers.

For this kind of problem, we skip step 2. There is no target since we are looking to compare answer choices.

Step 3: Plug into answer choices and then multiply by 2 (since the question asks "two times which number") and see what gives us the GREATEST number:

   (A) $X + 2 = 2 + 2 = 4 \times 2 = 8$
   (B) $X - 2 = 2 - 2 = 0 \times 2 = 0$
   (C) $X = 2 \times 2 = 4$
   (D) $X + 1 = 2 + 1 = 3 \times 2 = 6$
   (E) $X - 1 = 2 - 1 = 1 \times 2 = 2$

By plugging in our own numbers, we can clearly see that choice A gives us the GREATEST number, so we pick choice A.

Another type of problem with variables in the answer choices will ask what "must be true." For questions like this, plug in your own numbers and rule out any answer choices that don't work for your numbers. If there is more than one answer choice that works, then pick different numbers. Since it is a "must be true" problem, the correct answer choice has to work with ALL numbers. If you need to, keep picking new numbers until you have only one answer choice that has not been ruled out.

- With "must be true" problems, if you have ruled out all that you can but there is more than one answer choice left, pick new numbers and keep ruling out until there is only one choice left

Here is an example:

4. If b is 3 more than w, then w must be

    (A) 3
    (B) less than 3
    (C) more than 3
    (D) 3 more than b
    (E) 3 less than b

To solve, let's make b equal to 4. That would make w equal to 1. This allows us to rule out answer choices A, C, and D. However, choices B and E are still in the running. So let's choose another number for b. Let's make b equal to 10. This would make w equal to 7. That is greater than 3, so we can rule out choice B. That leaves us with choice E, which is the correct answer.

To solve the problems in Drill #2, try plugging in your own numbers!

Drill #2

1. If Q is an even number, which values must also be even

   I. $Q + 1$
   II. $Q + 2$
   III. $2Q$
   IV. $3Q$

   (A) I only
   (B) I and II
   (C) II and III
   (D) II, III, and IV
   (E) I, II, III, and IV

2. Sheila had w baseball cards. She gave five cards to Tommy but then she received three cards from Jill. In terms of w, how many cards did Sheila now have?

   (A) $w - 15$
   (B) $w - 8$
   (C) $w - 2$
   (D) $w + 2$
   (E) $w + 5$

3. Charlotte paid for an ice cream cone with a $5 bill. She received d dollars in change. How many dollars did she pay for the ice cream cone?

   (A) $5 + d$
   (B) $5 - d$
   (C) $d - 5$
   (D) $d + 5$
   (E) $5d$

Drill #2 (continued)

The next three problems are pretty challenging. If you are in 5th (or even 6th) grade, remember that your percentile score is what matters and that score will only compare you to other students your age. So if these problems seem really tough, don't worry about it!

Challenge problems:

4. To ride in a certain taxicab costs X dollars for the first two miles and Y dollars for each additional mile traveled. How much does it cost, in dollars, to ride for 7 miles?

   (A) $X + (5 \times Y)$
   (B) $X + (7 \times Y)$
   (C) $2 \times X + (5 \times Y)$
   (D) $2 \times X + (7 \times Y)$
   (E) $7 \times (X + Y)$

5. K is a number less than 1. If K is multiplied by a positive whole number, then the answer must be which of the following?

   (A) 0
   (B) less than K
   (C) greater than K
   (D) greater than the number K was multiplied by
   (E) less than the number K was multiplied by

6. If the width of a rectangle is 4 times the length, l, which of the following gives the perimeter of the rectangle in terms of l?

   (A) $3l$
   (B) $5l$
   (C) $10l$
   (D) $2(4 + l)$
   (E) $4(4 + l)$

(Answers to this drill are found on page 166.)

Strategy #3: If a Question Asks for the Value of a Variable, Plug in Answer Choices

On the SSAT, it is often easier to plug in answer choices and see what works. In particular, you may find this strategy most helpful on word problems. After all, this is a multiple choice test so one of those answers has to work!

- Can often use this strategy on word problems
- This is a multiple choice test!

For this strategy, keep in mind that a variable is not always a letter. The problem might define x as the number of cars, or it might just ask you what the number of cars is. Either way, it is still asking for the value of a variable and you can use this strategy.

- A variable may not always be a letter, it can be any unknown quantity

Whenever a question asks for the value of a variable, whether it is a letter or something like the number of bunnies, one of those answer choices has to work. Since this is a multiple-choice test, you just have to figure out which one. Ruling out is one of our most important strategies, and this scenario is just another example of how valuable a tool ruling out can be.

- Remember the mantra: Ruling out is good

Here are the steps for using this strategy:

Step 1: Put your answer choices in order from least to greatest if they are not already in that order (they usually are already in order, but the writers sometimes mix things up)

Step 2: Plug the middle answer choice into the problem to see if it works. The exception to this rule is if the question asks what is the smallest number or greatest number. If they ask for the smallest number, start with the smallest number, and if they ask for the greatest number, then start with the largest number.

- Usually we start in middle
- If they ask for the smallest number, start with the smallest number
- If they ask for the greatest number, start with the largest number

Step 3: If the middle choice does not work, go bigger or smaller depending on what you got for the middle answer choice.

Here is an example:

5.   If three times a number is 18, what is the number?

    (A) 3
    (B) 6
    (C) 12
    (D) 15
    (E) 18

In this case, the answer choices are already in order (they usually are), so we can skip step 1 and go right to step 2.

Step 2: Plug in middle answer choice.

We make our number equal to answer choice C, which is 12. It says that three times a number is 18, but three times 12 is 36. That means we can rule out answer choice C.

Step 3: Go bigger or smaller if the middle answer choice did not work.

Answer choice C gave us a number that was too big, so we will try choice B next. If we plug in 6, three times 6 would give us 18. That tells us that choice B is correct.

For the following drill, try plugging in answer choices to see what works. Even if you know how to solve another way, you need to practice this strategy because there will be a time when you need it to bail you out.

Drill #3

1. Sam is thinking of a number halfway between 15 and 21. What number is he thinking of?

   (A) 16
   (B) 17
   (C) 18
   (D) 19
   (E) 20

2. If four times a number is 32, what is the number?

   (A) 4
   (B) 8
   (C) 12
   (D) 16
   (E) 128

3. Carol has a jar with pennies, nickels, dimes and quarters in it. She needs to take 57 cents from the jar. What is the least number of coins she can take from the jar and have exactly 57 cents?

   (A) 2
   (B) 3
   (C) 4
   (D) 5
   (E) 7

(Answers to this drill are found on page 166.)

Those are the basic strategies that you need to know for the math section. As you go through the content sections, you will learn content and the strategies that work for specific problem types.

Answers to Math Strategies Drills

Drill #1

1. D
2. B

Drill #2

1. D
2. C
3. B
4. A
5. E
6. C

Drill #3

1. C
2. B
3. D

Math Content Sections

We have covered the basic strategies for the math section. Now, we are going to take a look at some of the problem types that you will see on this test.

On the SSAT, sometimes the math to solve a problem is not that hard. However, the tough part of the problem might be recognizing what direction to go and what concept is being tested.

Doing well on the math section is often a matter of decision making. You need to decide what type of problem you are working on as well as what the most efficient way to solve will be.

Each lesson will:

- Teach you the facts that you need to know
- Show you how those facts are tested
- Give you plenty of practice

That is the book's side of the bargain, but you also have to keep up your end of the deal.

As you work through the content always ask yourself:

- What makes this problem unique?
- How will I recognize this problem in the future?

You are on your way to crushing the SSAT math section!

Math Fundamentals

Now let's put the fun in fundamentals.

On the SSAT, they are testing your ability to recognize and apply concepts. You probably already have the knowledge that you need, but might have to learn to recognize how it is tested on the SSAT. That is what this section is all about.

This section will cover:

- Different kinds of numbers
- Ordering numbers
- Estimating
- Operations
- Divisibility
- Place value

Different Kinds of Numbers

On the SSAT, you will need to know what some different kinds of numbers are. They include:

- Integer
- Whole Number
- Positive
- Negative
- Even
- Odd
- Consecutive
- Prime
- Composite

Integers and whole numbers are very similar. Simply put, they are numbers that do not have decimals or fractions. For example, 0, 1, 2, and 3 are all integers as well as whole numbers. The difference is that integers include negative numbers. On this test, however, they don't really require you to know the difference between integers and whole numbers. You just need to know that if they ask for an integer or a whole number, the correct answer cannot have a fraction or decimal.

- If they ask for an integer or whole number, no decimals or fractions

Positive numbers are those that are greater than zero. Negative numbers are those that are less than zero. The only tricky thing about positive and negative numbers is that zero is neither positive nor negative. The SSAT is not likely to ask you if zero is positive or negative, but they might tell you that a variable is positive, in which case you have to know that it can't be equal to zero.

- Zero is neither positive nor negative

Even numbers are those numbers that can be divided by 2 without a remainder. That means that you can divide even numbers into groups of two with nothing left over. Odd numbers are those that cannot be divided by 2 without a remainder. By this definition, zero is an even number because it can be divided by two with nothing left over. Even numbers are 0, 2, 4, 6, and so on. Odd numbers are 1, 3, 5, and so on.

- Zero is an even number

Consecutive numbers are simply integers that are next to each other when you count. For example, 1 and 2 are consecutive numbers. There are also consecutive even numbers and consecutive odd numbers. These are just the numbers that would be next to each other if you counted by twos. For example, 2 and 4 are consecutive even numbers and 1 and 3 are consecutive odd numbers. The SSAT is not going to ask you if numbers are consecutive, but they will ask you to apply this information. If you see the words "consecutive even numbers" or "consecutive odd numbers," circle them because it is really easy to use just plain consecutive numbers and forget about the even or odd part.

- Consecutive just means in a row
- Look out for consecutive even and consecutive odd numbers because it is easy to forget the even or odd part

A prime number has only two factors: 1 and itself. A composite number is the product of at least two numbers other than itself and 1. The number is 1 is tricky- because it is not the product of two different numbers, it can be neither prime nor composite. The only even number that is prime is 2 since all other even numbers have two as a factor.

- A prime number has two factors: itself and 1
- A composite number has at least two factors other than itself and 1
- The number 1 is neither prime nor composite
- The number 2 is the only even prime number

―――――

Below are some examples of questions that ask you to apply this information about different kinds of numbers.

1. If H is an odd number, which of the following must also be an odd number?

    (A) $\dfrac{H}{3}$

    (B) $H + 3$

    (C) $H \times 2$

    (D) $H \times 3$

    (E) $H - 1$

    In order to answer this question, let's plug in our own numbers. Since it is a must be true question, we will use 1 since exceptions often pop up when we plug in the number 1. If we plug in 1 for H in answer choice A, then we get $\dfrac{1}{3}$ as our answer. Since this is not an odd number, we can eliminate choice A. If we plug in 1 for H in answer choice B, we get 4 as an answer, which is also not an odd number. If we keep going, when we get to choice D, if we plug in 1 for H, we get 3 as an answer, which is an odd number. This question was testing the fact that an odd number multiplied by an odd number results in an odd number. We don't need to know that, however, if we plug in our own numbers to see what works. Answer choice D is correct.

2. Which set of numbers contains only composite numbers?

    (A) 2, 4, 6, 8, 10
    (B) 2, 4, 5, 10, 12
    (C) 4, 6, 8, 9, 11
    (D) 4, 5, 6, 7, 8
    (E) 4, 6, 8, 9, 200

    Composite numbers are numbers that are not prime. Another way to state this is that composite numbers have factors other than themselves and 1. Answer choices A and B can be eliminated because 2 is a prime number (it is the only even prime number). Answer choice C can be eliminated because 11 is a prime number and answer choice D can be ruled out because 7 is a prime number. The numbers in answer choice E can all be divided by either 2 or 3 with no remainder, so answer choice E is correct.

3. Which is a prime number?

    (A) 52
    (B) 53
    (C) 55
    (D) 56
    (E) 63

    In order to answer this question, we can first rule out answer choices A and D because the only even prime number is 2 and 52 and 56 are even numbers. The number 55 (choice C) can easily be eliminated as well because it has 5 and 11 as factors. We now have to decide if 53 or 63 is prime. Since both digits in 63 can be

―――――

divided by 3 without a remainder, we can know that 3 is a factor of 63 and eliminate choice E. We are left with choice B, which is correct since 53 is a prime number.

Ordering Numbers

Some questions on the SSAT may require you to identify whether numbers are greater than or less than each other. You may be asked to use inequality signs.

Here is a cheat sheet for some of what you may see:

If the question states:	Then it can be written as:
X is between 3 and 5	$3 < X < 5$
X is greater than 6	$X > 6$
X is less than 10	$X < 10$

The thing that you need to keep in mind about *between*, *greater than*, and *less than* is that they don't include the numbers themselves. For example, if X is between 3 and 5, then it cannot be either 3 or 5.

Here are some examples of how these concepts are tested:

4. M is a whole number that is between 5 and 8. M is also between 6 and 13. Which of the following is M?

    (A) 5
    (B) 6
    (C) 7
    (D) 7.5
    (E) 8

    We can begin by eliminating choice D because 7.5 is not a whole number. If we look at the first statement, M could be 6 or 7 because those are the two whole numbers between 5 and 8. However, the second statement says that the number is between 6 and 13. Since this doesn't include the number 6, we are left with the number 7, and choice C is correct.

5. If $-1 < R < 4$, which of the following could be the value of R?

    (A) –2
    (B) –1
    (C) 0
    (D) 4
    (E) 5

    The question tells us that R must be greater than –1, so answer choices A and B can be eliminated – for choice B, –1 is equal to –1, not greater than –1. The value of R must also be less than 4, so choices D and E can be ruled out. The number 0 is both less than 4 and greater than –1, so answer choice C is correct.

6. The value of H is less than the value of J but greater than the value of G. The value of F is greater than the value of J. Which answer choice correctly shows these relationships?

   (A) $F < G < H < J$
   (B) $F > G > H > J$
   (C) $F < J < H < G$
   (D) $J < H < G < F$
   (E) $G < H < J < F$

   The question states that the value of H is less than the value of J. Answer choices B, C, and D can be eliminated because they show H as being greater in value than J. We are only left with choices A and E. The question also states that F is greater than J, and answer choice E shows this relationship correctly. Answer choice E is the correct answer.

Estimating

Some of the easiest questions on this test just require you to estimate. The question may tell you to estimate, or it could ask you which answer is "closest to" or "approximately" equal to a value. If you see this language, you can round off and then use the fact that this is a multiple-choice test to choose the correct answer.

If you see the words "estimate," "closest to," or "approximately," you can estimate to get close enough to the correct multiple-choice answer.

Here are a couple of problems for you to try:

7. Estimate: $\dfrac{42,032}{1,998}$

   (A) 21
   (B) 210
   (C) 410
   (D) 2,100
   (E) 21,000

   The first step in answering this question is to round each number. The numerator (top number) is close to 42,000, and the denominator (bottom number) is close to 2,000. Our problem becomes $\dfrac{42,000}{2,000}$. Now we can simplify. If we divide both the numerator and denominator by 1,000, we now have $\dfrac{42}{2}$, or 21. Answer choice A is correct. Did you choose answer choice E? Many students forget that when we simplify and divide both the top and bottom by the same number, those zeroes do not come back!

8. Which is closest to $\dfrac{97 \times 1,032}{19 \times 21}$?

    (A) 25
    (B) 250
    (C) 400
    (D) 2,500
    (E) 4,000

We see the words "closest to," so the first step is to round off so we can estimate. The problem becomes $\dfrac{100 \times 1,000}{20 \times 20}$. Now we can perform the operations on the top and bottom. If we multiply $100 \times 1,000$, we can simply count up the zeroes (there are five of them) and see that the result is 100,000. On the bottom, we can rewrite the problem as $2 \times 10 \times 2 \times 10$. Using the commutative property of multiplication, this is equal to $2 \times 2 \times 10 \times 10$, or 400. Our problem is now $\dfrac{100,000}{400}$. To simplify, we can divide both the numerator and denominator by 100. The result gives us $\dfrac{1,000}{4}$, or 250. Answer choice B is correct.

Operations

There are some questions that test your ability to calculate or perform basic operations.

The simplest of these questions have just two numbers and one operation. Sometimes the answer choices are close enough to each other that you need to perform the calculation. Other times, you just need to estimate to figure out which multiple-choice answer comes closest.

- First see if you can estimate and use ruling out to choose the correct multiple-choice answer
- If the answer choices are very close in value, it is hard to estimate

Some of these questions are also testing your ability to use number sense to solve more efficiently. You can always use traditional methods to solve, but the questions are often written in such a way that they can be answered more quickly if you take a shortcut such as breaking apart a number, simplifying before solving, etc.

- Look for shortcuts to save work with calculations

Here are some examples for you to try:

9. What is the value of 302×206?

    (A) 7,852
    (B) 60,012
    (C) 62,212
    (D) 69,012
    (E) 72,120

One approach is to calculate 302×206 using long multiplication. However, we can also estimate to come close enough on this question. It is easy to figure out that 300×200 is equal to 60,000. This allows us to eliminate answer choice A. We know that the answer should be a little bit more than 60,000 since we rounded down to find 60,000. Answer choice B is a trap, though. If we multiplied just the last digits, we would add 12 to the value. The problem is that multiplication is not like addition; you can't just combine the same place values since we multiply each digit by all the place values. Answer choice B can be eliminated. Since answer choices D and E are a lot more than 60,000 they can also be ruled out. Answer choice C is correct. If you were to do the calculation, you would find that answer choice C is indeed the correct answer choice.

10. What is the value of 700 divided by 25?

    (A) 25

    (B) 28

    (C) 30

    (D) 280

    (E) 675

You can use long division to answer this question. However, it is possible to use properties of multiplication and division to solve more efficiently. We can turn 700 into 7×100. Now our problem becomes:

$$\frac{7 \times 100}{25}$$

We can then rearrange this expression.

$$\frac{7 \times 100}{25} = 7 \times \frac{100}{25} = 7 \times 4 = 28$$

The correct answer is 28, or answer choice B. If you haven't learned how to take these shortcuts in school, then don't worry about trying to learn them now. You can still do well on this test. The shortcuts just give you a little more time to puzzle through some of the harder questions.

11. Which is the value of $2{,}987 \times 51$?

    (A) 46,898

    (B) 51,308

    (C) 152,337

    (D) 152,437

    (E) 153,337

For this question, we can estimate that $3{,}000 \times 50$ is 150,000. However, we have three answer choices that are very close to each other in that range. The best approach is to do the calculation since the answer choices are not far enough apart to estimate. The correct answer is choice C.

Some questions on the SSAT will also be simple word problems that are testing whether you can identify the correct operation to use and then perform a basic calculation.

The wording often gives a hint as to what operation should be performed.

Here is a guide to some of the language you may see:

If the question states:	Then you should:
…of…	Multiply
…how many more…	Find the difference (subtract)
…how many times…	Divide
…sum…	Add
…difference…	Subtract
…divisible by…	Divide and look for a number that does not leave a remainder
…into how many…	Divide

Here are some examples of how this information is tested:

12. On Wednesday, Sheila had sold 324 boxes of cookies. Her goal was to sell 410 boxes by Sunday. How many more boxes of cookies must she sell between Wednesday and Sunday?

   (A) 34
   (B) 76
   (C) 86
   (D) 410
   (E) 734

The question uses the words "how many more," so we know we need to subtract, or find the difference. When we subtract 324 from 410, the result is 86, so choice C is correct.

Here is an example of a multi-step question that tests your ability to apply equation language:

13. Ben brought 3 dozen donut holes to share with his classmates. If he wants to evenly divide them among the nine students in his class, and there will be none left over, then how many donut holes does each student get?

   (A) 1
   (B) 2
   (C) 3
   (D) 4
   (E) 5

There are a total of 36 donut holes – a dozen means 12, so 3 dozen is 3 × 12, which is equal to 36. There are 9 kids in the class, so we divide 36 by 9 to find that each student gets 4 donut holes. Choice D is correct.

Here is a similar question that uses slightly harder numbers to work with:

14. In the year 2000, City X had 2.3 million residents. By 2010, the population had grown by 630,000 residents. How many residents did City X have in 2010?

    (A) 2.93 million
    (B) 2.9063 million
    (C) 2.763 million
    (D) 2.363 million
    (E) 2.3063 million

    The first step is to identify the operation. Since the population grew, we need to use addition to find the total population. Now we need to convert the number 630,000 into millions. We do this by moving the decimal point six places to the left and we get that 630,000 is equal to 0.63 million. If we add 2.3 million and 0.63 million, remembering to line up the decimal points, the total population is 2.93 million and answer choice A is correct.

Sometimes the test will have a question where the division problem does not come out evenly. Then we have to decide whether to round up or to round down.

Here is an example:

15. Julie has 75 cents. She wants to buy lollipops that are 14 cents each. How many lollipops can she buy?

    (A) 4
    (B) 5
    (C) 6
    (D) 7
    (E) 8

    To solve this problem, we have to see how many 14's we can get from 75. If we divide 75 by 14, we get 5 with a remainder of 5. Since Julie can only buy a lollipop when she has the full 14 cents, she can only buy 5 lollipops. Choice B is correct.

Here is another one to try:

16. Grace needs to buy 23 t-shirts for her class. The t-shirts come in packages of 10. How many packages must she buy?

    (A) 1
    (B) 2
    (C) 3
    (D) 4
    (E) 5

The trick to this problem is that Grace has to buy more t-shirts than she needs. If we divide 23 by 10, then we get 2 with a remainder of 3. However, Grace needs a t-shirt for everybody, so the remainder tells us to round up with this type of problem. The correct answer is C.

Other questions may ask for what is left over (or the remainder) without ever using the word *remainder*.

Here is an example:

17. A bottle contains 24 ounces of juice. If five glasses are each filled with 4.5 ounces of the juice, how many ounces of juice are left in the bottle?

    (A) 1.5 ounces
    (B) 2.5 ounces
    (C) 3 ounces
    (D) 5 ounces
    (E) 22.5 ounces

The first operation we must perform is multiplication. There are 4.5 ounces in each of 5 glasses, so we multiply 4.5 by 5 and find that 22.5 ounces of juice have been poured out. Don't forget that the question asks how much is left, however. If we subtract 22.5 from 24, we get that there are 1.5 ounces left. Answer choice A is correct.

There are also questions on the SSAT that do not test your ability to perform operations as much as to recognize what an operation (or the steps in an operation) means. For these questions, you need to think about how the operation works and not spend time performing calculations. The best way to identify these questions is to look at the answer choices and see if they are numbers or expressions. If the answer choices are not just numbers, they are generally testing a concept and not a calculation.

- Some questions are not asking you to calculate, they are asking you to use the concepts of operations
- Before jumping into a calculation, always look at the answer choices first

Here is an example:

18. If $35 + 35 + 35 + 35 + 35 = 5 \times \lozenge$, then what number goes in the $\lozenge$?

    (A) 5
    (B) 30
    (C) 35
    (D) 55
    (E) 175

This question is testing your ability to recognize what multiplication really means and does not require you to perform the calculation. The left side of the equation is an addition problem, and the right side is asking you to turn it into a multiplication problem. When we add 35 to itself 5 times, that is the same thing as multiplying 35 by 5, so the multiplication problem is 5×35. The correct answer is C.

Another problem type asks you to apply what you know about carrying numbers when you add.

Remember that when you add 2 numbers together, you have to carry a 1 to the next place if the sum of any column is greater than 10. Look at this example.

$$3724$$
$$\underline{+1198}$$
$$4922$$

In the first column to the right, we add 4 and 8 and get 12. We write down the 2 then carry the 1 to the next column over. We add $2 + 9 + 1$ (this is the one that we carried over), and get 12 again. So we write down the 2 and carry the 1 to the next column to the left. We add $7+1+1$ (this is the one that we carried over) and get 9. Since 9 is not a two-digit number, we don't have to carry over anything to the last column on the left.

Now try this problem.

19. What are the possible values for Δ in the problem below?

$$3724$$
$$\underline{+11\Delta8}$$
$$49\blacklozenge2$$

(A) 0, 1, or 2
(B) 2, 3, or 4
(C) 5, 6, or 7
(D) 6, 7, or 8
(E) 7, 8, or 9

Let's look at each column. In the first column to the right, we added the $4 + 8$ and got 12, so we wrote down the two and carried the one to the next column. Now we will add $2 + 1 + \Delta$ to get $\blacklozenge$. We can't figure this out, not yet. But go to the next column on the left and notice that since $7 + 1$ doesn't add up to 9, we must have carried a 1 from the previously added column. So now we know that $2 + 1 + \Delta$ has to be greater than or equal to 10. This happens only if Δ is 7, 8, or 9. Any of these values would work. Answer choice E is correct.

Now try this problem:

20. The value of Δ could be which of the following digits?

$$738$$
$$\underline{+11\Delta6}$$
$$19\blacklozenge4$$

(A) 0
(B) 1
(C) 3
(D) 5
(E) 6

The easiest way to solve this problem is to go through the process of adding. If we add the first column on the right, we get a total of 14 and carry the 1 to the next place. That gives us a total of 4 plus the triangle in the next column. If we look at the next column to the left, we can see that a 1 must have been carried from the previous column. Since the column with the missing digit adds to 4 without the missing digit, we can see that the missing digit must be at least 6 in order for us to have to carry a 1. Answer choice E is correct.

Similar problems exist for multiplication and division. Let's review these basic operations.

When you have a division problem, such as $6\overline{)43}$ the work is:

$$
\begin{array}{r}
7 \\
6\overline{)43} \\
\underline{42} \\
1
\end{array}
$$

Remember that you can say that the quotient (7) times the divisor (6) plus the remainder (1) is equal to the original number that was being divided.

- Quotient × divisor + remainder = number that was divided

Now try this problem:

21. Chloe divides a number by 6 and gets 4 with a remainder of 3 as her answer. What was the original number?

    (A) 20
    (B) 21
    (C) 24
    (D) 27
    (E) 28

    In order to solve this problem, we first have to multiply the divisor (6) times the quotient (4). This gives us 24. Then we add the remainder (3) to find that the original number was 27. Answer choice D is correct.

Here is another one:

22. For the division problem $8\overline{)\square}$, if the answer is between 6 and 7, then a possible value for $\square$ is

    (A) 24
    (B) 32
    (C) 36
    (D) 48
    (E) 54

If the answer to $8\overline{)\square}$ were 6, then the problem would look like this:

$$\begin{array}{r} 6 \\ 8\overline{)\square} \end{array}$$

In this case, the value for $\square$ would be 48 if we multiply the quotient (answer) by the divisor. If the answer to $8\overline{)\square}$ were 7, then the problem would look like this:

$$\begin{array}{r} 7 \\ 8\overline{)\square} \end{array}$$

and the value of $\square$ would be 56. The problem states that the answer is between 6 and 7, and so the value of $\square$ is between 48 and 56. Thus, the correct answer choice is E.

Another type of problem that tests your understanding of operations uses multiplication. Consider this problem:

$$\begin{array}{r} 12 \\ \times 43 \\ \hline 36 \\ 48 \\ \hline 516 \end{array}$$

Another way to write this problem would be $(12 \times 3) + (12 \times 40)$. This is where the values of 36 and 48 come from in the work shown just above the answer. But look again at the 48. It is NOT really 48. It is really 480, because it is the answer to (12×40) which is 480. There should really be a 0 after the 48, but we use a quick version to shorten the problem, and so we don't write the 0. In school, you probably learned to put in your own zero to mark the place value. On the SSAT, this is what they are really testing with this problem type.

Use this information to answer the following question.

23. What is the value of the digit 7 in the line with the arrow?

$$\begin{array}{r} 137 \\ \times 24 \\ \hline 548 \\ \underline{274} \Leftarrow \end{array}$$

(A) 7
(B) 70
(C) 700
(D) 7,000
(E) 70,000

If you remember the hint from the discussion above, you know that 274 is really 2,740. Thus, the value of the 7 is really 700. The correct answer is C.

Now try this one:

24. What is the value of the 5 in the line with the arrow?

$$
\begin{array}{r}
137 \\
\times 24 \\
\hline
548 \Longleftarrow \\
274 \quad \\
\hline
\end{array}
$$

(A) 5
(B) 50
(C) 500
(D) 5,000
(E) 50,000

In this case, the number 548 is in the first line of the multiplication problem, so it isn't too tricky. There is no missing digit, so the answer is C.

Divisibility

Some questions may ask you if a number is divisible by another number. This simply means that it can be divided by that number with no remainder, or nothing left over.

It can be helpful to know some basic divisibility rules. You don't absolutely have to know these as long as you can do the problems out by hand, but it can save you a lot of time if you know the rules.

Here are some of the easier rules. There are rules for numbers divisible by 7 and 8, but they are really hard to remember and therefore not so helpful!

If ...	Then it is divisible by ...
the number is even	2
you add up all the digits of the number and the result is divisible by 3 (ex: 231 = 2 + 3 + 1 = 6 and 6 is divisible by 3)	3
the last two digits of your number are divisible by 4 (ex: 549,624 and 24 is divisible by 4)	4
the number ends in 0 or 5	5
the number is divisible by both 2 and 3	6
you add up all the digits and the result is divisible by 9 (ex: 3726 = 3 + 7 + 2 + 6 = 18 and 18 is divisible by 9)	9
the number ends in 0	10

Here is a basic example of how divisibility could be tested:

25. Which of the following answer choices is divisible by 6?

    (A) 824
    (B) 826
    (C) 828
    (D) 866
    (E) 904

If a number is divisible by 6, it must be divisible by both 2 and 3. All of the answer choices are even, so they are all divisible by 2. Now, to see if the numbers are divisible by 3 we have to add up the digits and see if that number is divisible by 3.

    (A) 8 + 2 + 4 = 14 – not divisible by 3
    (B) 8 + 2 + 6 = 16 – not divisible by 3
    (C) 8 + 2 + 8 = 18 – IS divisible by 3
    (D) 8 + 6 + 6 = 20 – not divisible by 3

_____

(E) 9 + 0 + 4 = 13 – not divisible by 3

Since only answer choice C is divisible by both 2 and 3, it is the only answer choice that is divisible by 6. Answer choice C is correct.

Some other questions don't use the word *divisible* at all! But they are still testing divisibility.

Here is an example:

26. If $\frac{t}{4}$ is a whole number, which of the following could be *t*?

(A) 748
(B) 758
(C) 774
(D) 802
(E) 814

In order for $\frac{t}{4}$ to be a whole number, *t* would have to be evenly divisible by 4. To figure out if a number is evenly divisible by 4, we look just at the last two digits. If we look at answer choice A, the last two digits are 48. 48 is divisible by 4, so choice A is correct.

Other problems set up a situation where items must be distributed evenly. In these problems, look for the answer choice that is divisible by the number of people that the item will be distributed among.

Here is an example:

27. Tommy brought a cake to school for his birthday. There are 12 kids in his class. If he wants every student to get an equal number of pieces of cake with none left over, into how many pieces could he cut his cake?

(A) 6
(B) 18
(C) 20
(D) 36
(E) 40

This question uses the words "into how many," so we know that we have to divide. It also tells us that he wants each student to have the same number of pieces of cake, so we are looking for a number that is divisible by 12, since there are 12 students. The only answer choice that is evenly divisible by 12 is choice D, so it is correct.

_____

Here is a similar question:

28. A group of students each contributed $9 to go on a fieldtrip. Which of the following could be the amount collected?

(A) $319

(B) $324

(C) $339

(D) $345

(E) $356

The important part of this question is that $9 was collected from each person. That means that the total amount collected must be a multiple of 9, or that the total must be divisible by 9. Remember that in order to be divisible by 9, the digits must add up to a number divisible by 9.

Let's try each answer choice

(A) 3 + 1 + 9 = 13 – not divisible by 9

(B) 3 + 2 + 4 = 9 – IS divisible by 9

(C) 3 + 3 + 9 = 15 – not divisible by 9

(D) 3 + 4 + 5 = 12 – not divisible by 9

(E) 3 + 5 + 6 = 14 – not divisible by 9

Answer choice B is correct.

Finally, we have a doozy of a problem. It uses the word *average*, but it isn't really an average problem. Since an average is equal to sum ÷ # of items, if the average is to be a whole number, then the sum must be evenly divisible by the number of items. We can also rearrange the average equation so that it is sum ÷ average = # of items.

Also, you should know that if a number is divisible by another number, then it is also divisible by the factors of the other number. This is actually what our rule for being divisible by six is based on. Two and three are the prime factors of six, so if a number is divisible by both two and three, then the number will be divisible by six. This is particularly helpful when you are dealing with bigger numbers than we have rules for. For example, let's say a question asks whether something is divisible by 15. Three times five is 15, so if the number was divisible by BOTH three and five, it would be divisible by fifteen.

The following problem is very challenging.

29. Maria wanted to know what the average class size was at her school. She took the total enrollment at her school and divided it by the number of classes. She found that the average class size was exactly 18 students. Which of the following could NOT have been the total number of students at her school?

(A) 1,080

(B) 1,140

(C) 1,134

(D) 1,152

(E) 1,170

In order to solve this problem, we need to find the answer choice that is NOT evenly divisible by 18. Since sum ÷ average = # of classes, the sum must be divisible by 18, otherwise we would wind up with a fractional class, which is not possible. If we divide 18 into factors, we can see that nine times two gives us 18. That means that if an answer choice is divisible by both two and nine, then it is divisible by 18. All of the answer choices are even, so we can't rule any out for not being divisible by 2. We need to look for the answer choice that is NOT divisible by nine, since it is a NOT question. If we add up the digits of answer choice B, we get six, which is not divisible by nine, and therefore 1,140 is not divisible by nine.

Choice B is correct.

Place Value

Another basic concept that is tested is place value.

Consider the number 354. This number is really made up of 3 separate numbers. The "4" is 4 ones. The "5" is 5 tens, and the "3" is 3 hundreds. These 3 numbers are added up as 4 + 50 + 300 to get 354. Here is a chart to help you remember place values.

We will use the number 457,208.196 as an example.

4	5	7	2	0	8	.	1	9	6	3	4
Hundred thousands	Ten thousands	Thousands	Hundreds	Tens	Ones	Decimal point	Tenths	Hundredths	Thousandths	Ten-thousandths	Hundred-thousandths

Look at the digit 2, which is in the hundreds place. It represents a value of 200, because it represents 2 hundreds. Similarly, the digit 5 represents 5 ten thousands, so its value is 50,000.

For another example, think of the number 829. The number 829 is the result of adding three numbers together: 8 hundreds (800) plus 2 tens (20) plus 9 ones (9).

Another way to think of the number 829 is: $(8 \times 100) + (2 \times 10) + (9 \times 1)$.

Let's do a sample problem:

462.3<u>4</u>1

30. In the above number, what is the value of the underlined digit?

(A) 4 hundredths
(B) 4 tenths
(C) 4 ones
(D) 4 tens
(E) 4 hundreds

In this question, the underlined digit is in the hundredths place. That means that the value of the 4 is 4 hundredths, so answer choice A is correct. The trick with this type of question is to pay close attention to whether the answer choice has a "–th" at the end of it.

Here is another place value problem that may look a little different from how you have seen place value tested before.

31. In the number 537.981, which digit has the GREATEST value?

(A) 3
(B) 5
(C) 7
(D) 8
(E) 9

This question is a little tricky. Be careful not to just choose the greatest number. 9 may be the largest digit, but in the context of the whole number, the 9 is only worth 0.9. The digit 5 is worth 500 in the number given, so that digit has the greatest value. Choice B is correct.

Here is another question that uses place value:

8☐,649

32. In the number given above, the thousands digit has been replaced with a box. If the number above is less than 86,649, then what is the largest digit that could replace the box?

(A) 1
(B) 2
(C) 6
(D) 5
(E) 7

If the total number is less than 86,649, then we know that the missing thousands digit must be less than 6. Answer choice D is correct.

Here are a couple of questions that look like calculations but are really testing place value:

33. $634 \div 7 =$

(A) $\dfrac{4}{7} + \dfrac{30}{7} + \dfrac{600}{7}$

(B) $\dfrac{4}{7} + \dfrac{3}{7} + \dfrac{6}{7}$

(C) $\dfrac{4}{7} \div \dfrac{30}{7} \div \dfrac{600}{7}$

(D) $\dfrac{4}{7} \div \dfrac{3}{7} \div \dfrac{6}{7}$

(E) $\dfrac{4}{7} \times \dfrac{30}{7} \times \dfrac{600}{7}$

This question is not asking you to perform the calculation, but rather to break down the calculation by place value. We could rewrite $634 \div 7$ as:

$$\dfrac{634}{7}$$

If we break down 634 into expanded form, we can write the problem as:

$$\dfrac{(600 + 30 + 4)}{7}$$

which could also be written as

$$\dfrac{4}{7} + \dfrac{30}{7} + \dfrac{600}{7}$$

Answer choice A is correct.

34. $495 \times 6 =$

(A) $(400 \times 6) \times (90 \times 6) \times (5 \times 6)$
(B) $(400 \times 6) + (90 \times 6) + (5 \times 6)$
(C) $400 \times 90 \times 5 \times 6$
(D) $(400 \times 90 \times 5) \times 6$
(E) $(400 + 90 + 5) + 6$

We will break down 495 by place value and it becomes $400+90+5$. Now we can use the distributive property to turn $(400 + 90 + 5) \times 6$ into $(400 \times 6) + (90 \times 6) + (5 \times 6)$. Answer choice B is correct.

The next problem uses place value, but it is pretty challenging!

35. Which fraction is equal to the decimal $\square.4$?

(A) $\dfrac{10\times(\square+4)}{10}$

(B) $\dfrac{(10\times\square)+4}{10}$

(C) $\dfrac{\square+3}{10}$

(D) $\dfrac{\square+3}{100}$

(E) $\dfrac{(10\times\square)+4}{100}$

The easiest way to solve this problem is to fill in our own number for $\square$. Let's make $\square$ equal to 2. That means that $\square.4$ would be equal to 2.4. Now we can plug in 2 for $\square$ in the answer choices and see which answer choice gives us 2.4.

(A) $\dfrac{10\times(\square+4)}{10} = \dfrac{10\times(2+4)}{10} = \dfrac{60}{10} = 6$

(B) $\dfrac{(10\times\square)+4}{10} = \dfrac{(10\times2)+4}{10} = \dfrac{24}{10} = 2.4$

(C) $\dfrac{\square+3}{10} = \dfrac{2+3}{10} = \dfrac{5}{10} = 0.5$

(D) $\dfrac{\square+3}{100} = \dfrac{2+3}{100} = \dfrac{5}{100} = 0.05$

(E) $\dfrac{(10\times\square)+4}{100} = \dfrac{(10\times2)+4}{100} = \dfrac{24}{100} = 0.24$

From this, we can see that only choice B gives us 2.4 when we plug in 2 for the $\square$ symbol. Answer choice B is correct.

Frequency

Another concept that is tested on the SSAT is frequency. Frequency simply refers to how often something shows up in a set. These questions are pretty straightforward so if you see one on the actual test, rejoice.

Here are a couple of questions for you to try:

36. {2, 3, 7, 9, 12, 16, 17, 18, 20, 22, 27, 29, 30, 31, 33, 34, 35, 38, 40, 42, 44}

    In the set of numbers above, what is the frequency of even numbers?

    (A) 9
    (B) 10
    (C) 11
    (D) 12
    (E) 14

    To answer this question, we simply need to count up the number of even numbers in the set. Since 2, 12, 16, 18, 20, 22, 30, 34, 38, 40, 42, and 44 are the even numbers in the set and there are 12 of these numbers, answer choice D is correct.

37. Greg makes a list of various animals (shown below). How many letters are in the least frequent length of animal name?

toucan	tiger	ferret	elephant	chicken	gerbil
cat	horse	dog	zebra	lion	blue jay
hamster	rat	cardinal	mule	cow	hawk

    (A) 3
    (B) 4
    (C) 6
    (D) 7
    (E) 8

    Let's go ahead and make a chart showing the length of each animal name (on the real test, you would just write on the chart given).

toucan – 6	tiger – 5	ferret – 6	elephant – 8	chicken – 7	gerbil – 6
cat – 3	horse – 5	dog – 3	zebra – 5	lion – 4	blue jay – 7
hamster – 7	rat – 3	cardinal – 8	mule – 4	cow – 3	hawk – 4

There are only two eight letter words, which is the least frequent, so choice E is correct.

Probability

A concept related to frequency is probability. Probability simply gives the frequency of a desired outcome over the total number of possible outcomes.

$$\text{probability} = \frac{\text{frequency of desired outcome}}{\text{total number of outcomes}}$$

For example, if there are 10 markers and 3 of them are red, if a marker is randomly selected, the probability that it will be red is $\frac{3}{10}$.

Here is an example for you to try:

38. A jar has 5 red marbles, 10 blue marbles, 3 green marbles, and 7 yellow marbles. If a marble is randomly selected, what is the probability that it will be yellow?

(A) $\frac{7}{25}$

(B) $\frac{7}{18}$

(C) $\frac{7}{15}$

(D) $\frac{7}{10}$

(E) $\frac{10}{25}$

If we add together the number of marbles of each color, there is a total of 25 marbles. Since 7 of these marbles are yellow, there are 7 yellow marbles out of a total of 25 marbles, and the probability of choosing a yellow marble is $\frac{7}{25}$. Answer choice A is correct.

It is also important to know how to find the probability of multiple events occurring. To do this, we just multiply the probabilities of each individual event occurring.

For example, let's say we are flipping a coin twice and want to know the probability of it landing on heads twice. Since the probability of it landing on heads the first time is $\frac{1}{2}$ and the probability of it landing on heads the second time is $\frac{1}{2}$, the probability of the coin landing on heads both times is $\frac{1}{2} \times \frac{1}{2} = \frac{1}{4}$.

- To find the probability of multiple events occurring, multiply the probabilities of each individual event occurring

Here is a question for you to try:

39. In a certain game, a player must roll two cubes, each with sides labeled 1-6. What is the probability that a player will have one cube land with a 4 facing up and one cube land with an odd number facing up?

(A) $\dfrac{1}{12}$

(B) $\dfrac{1}{6}$

(C) $\dfrac{1}{4}$

(D) $\dfrac{1}{3}$

(E) $\dfrac{2}{3}$

The probability of landing with a 4 facing up is $\dfrac{1}{6}$, since there are 6 faces to a cube and only one is labeled 4. The probability of landing with an odd number face up is $\dfrac{1}{2}$, since there are 6 faces and 3 of them (or half of them) are labeled with an odd number. If we multiply these two probabilities together, $\dfrac{1}{6} \times \dfrac{1}{2} = \dfrac{1}{12}$ so the probability of both events occurring is $\dfrac{1}{12}$. Answer choice A is correct.

Now you have the fundamentals that you need to do well on the math section of the SSAT. Be sure to complete the math fundamentals practice set to reinforce your learning. Remember, the most important part of the practice set is figuring out WHY you missed the questions that you answer incorrectly.

Math Fundamentals Practice Set

1. Kim plans to buy balloons for a party. She wants one balloon for the back of each chair and there are a total of 27 chairs at the party. If the balloons come in packages of six, how many packages of balloons must she buy?

   (A) 4
   (B) 5
   (C) 6
   (D) 8
   (E) 9

2. In the number 253.$\underline{8}$74, what is the value of the underlined digit?

   (A) 8 hundredths
   (B) 8 tenths
   (C) 8 oneths
   (D) 8 ones
   (E) 8 tens

3. John can't remember the number of home runs that Daniel hit last season. Daniel writes down $16 < x < 20$ and $x > 18$. If x is the number of home runs that Daniel hit, what is the value of x?

   (A) 16
   (B) 17
   (C) 18
   (D) 19
   (E) 20

4. Estimate: $(4{,}996 \times 301) \div (29 \times 51)$

   (A) 100
   (B) 1,000
   (C) 1,500
   (D) 5,000
   (E) 50,000

5. Let k be an even number. What is the next consecutive even number?

   (A) $k - 2$
   (B) $k + 1$
   (C) $k + 2$
   (D) $2k + 1$
   (E) $2k + 2$

6. What is the value of the digit 6 in the line with the arrow pointing to it?

$$\begin{array}{r} 276 \\ \times 12 \\ \hline 552 \\ 276 \quad \Leftarrow \\ \end{array}$$

(A) .6
(B) 6
(C) 60
(D) 600
(E) 6,000

7. At Lora's grandmother's 90th birthday party, there are 5 identical cakes. A total of 60 people are at the party, and each person should receive exactly one piece of cake. If each cake is to be cut into identical pieces, into how many pieces should each cake be cut?

(A) 6
(B) 7
(C) 8
(D) 9
(E) 12

8. What is the digit represented by □ in the following addition problem?

$$\begin{array}{r} 6\,2\,3 \\ +9\,\square\,\triangle \\ \hline 1\,5\,7\,1 \\ \end{array}$$

(A) 0
(B) 1
(C) 2
(D) 3
(E) 4

9. If $\dfrac{x}{3}$ is a whole number, which of the following could be x?

(A) 234
(B) 236
(C) 359
(D) 451
(E) 502

10. Which is the value of 740 divided by 20?

   (A) 30
   (B) 37
   (C) 74
   (D) 148
   (E) 370

11. Which of the following numbers is divisible by 9?

   (A) 234
   (B) 256
   (C) 302
   (D) 436
   (E) 469

12. If $26 + 26 + 26 + 26 = 4 \times \Diamond$, then what number should replace $\Diamond$?

   (A) 3
   (B) 4
   (C) 26
   (D) 52
   (E) 104

13. If $(14 + 35) \times 6 = (9 \times 10) + (K \times 100) + (4 \times 1)$, then what is the value of K?

   (A) 2
   (B) 3
   (C) 4
   (D) 7
   (E) 9

14. A teacher had 126 pencils that he divided evenly among the students in his class. Which could have been the number of students in his class?

   (A) 15
   (B) 16
   (C) 17
   (D) 18
   (E) 22

15. Which is the value of 412×124?

   (A) 2,884
   (B) 14,008
   (C) 51,078
   (D) 51,084
   (E) 51,088

16. A company had sales of $1.23 million dollars in 2014. In 2016, its total sales were $1.49 million. What was its increase in sales from 2014 to 2016?

    (A) $26,000,000
    (B) $2,600,000
    (C) $260,000
    (D) $26,000
    (E) $2,600

17. If $K < M$, $M < L$, and $J < L$, which of the following shows the correct order from least to greatest?

    (A) $K < L < J < M$
    (B) $K < M < J < L$
    (C) $K < M < L < J$
    (D) $J < M < L < K$
    (E) cannot be determined from information given

18. When a number is divided by 7, the answer is 4 with a remainder of 3. What is the number?

    (A) 24
    (B) 25
    (C) 28
    (D) 31
    (E) 34

19. If P is a prime number, which of the following must be a composite number?

    (A) $P + 1$
    (B) $P + 2$
    (C) $P \div P$
    (D) $(P + 1) \div P$
    (E) $P \times 3$

20. In a bouquet of flowers, there are 5 red flowers, 6 green flowers, 10 yellow flowers, 12 pink flowers, and 12 purple flowers. If a flower is selected at random, which color flower has a 1 in 9 chance of being chosen?

    (A) Red
    (B) Green
    (C) Yellow
    (D) Pink
    (E) Purple

21. Sheila created a chart showing the number of days of rain per month in her town, as shown below.

Month	Days of rain
January	12
February	10
March	14
April	16
May	9
June	14
July	11
August	10
September	9
October	5
November	11
December	9

How many days of rain were there in the most frequent number of rainy days?

(A) 5

(B) 9

(C) 10

(D) 11

(E) 12

22. In a box, there is a red marker, a green marker, a blue marker, and a black marker. There is also a red crayon, a blue crayon, and a green crayon. In addition, there is a black pen and a blue pen. If a marker, a crayon, and a pen are randomly chosen, what is the chance that they will all be blue?

(A) $\dfrac{1}{24}$

(B) $\dfrac{1}{12}$

(C) $\dfrac{1}{9}$

(D) $\dfrac{1}{3}$

(E) $\dfrac{3}{4}$

Challenge problems – Do not worry if you cannot solve these problems. Remember that schools are looking at your percentile score!

23. If $e \div \Delta = W$ plus a remainder of 1, then what is an expression for e?

(A) $e \times W - 1$

(B) $\Delta \times W + 1$

(C) $e \times \Delta + 1$

(D) $\Delta + W \times 1$

(E) $W \times \Delta - 1$

24. Which fraction is equal to the decimal $\square.3$?

(A) $\dfrac{10 \times (\square + 3)}{10}$

(B) $\dfrac{(10 \times \square) + 3}{10}$

(C) $\dfrac{\square + 3}{10}$

(D) $\dfrac{\square + 3}{100}$

(E) $\dfrac{(10 \times \square) + 3}{100}$

25. Karl wanted to know the average class size at his school. He took the total number of students at his school and then divided by the number of classes. He found that the average class size was exactly 15 students. Which of the following could have been the total number of students at his school?

(A) 650

(B) 725

(C) 805

(D) 845

(E) 855

Answers to Math Fundamentals Practice Set

1. B
2. B
3. D
4. B
5. C
6. C
7. E
8. E
9. A
10. B
11. A
12. C
13. A
14. D
15. E
16. C
17. E
18. D
19. E
20. A
21. B
22. A

Challenge problems

23. B
24. B
25. E

Advanced Math Fundamentals

This section covers some of the harder math fundamentals. If you are in fifth grade, some of this information will be new to you. Keep in mind that you will only be compared to other students your age, so you do not need to master all of this material. If you are in 7th grade, however, then it is more important to learn this material.

In this section, we will cover:

- Factors and multiples
- Exponents
- Order of operations
- Operations with negative numbers
- Absolute value

Factors and Multiples

Factors are numbers that another number can be divided by without a remainder. For example, the factors of 4 are 4, 2, and 1. The factors of 8 are 8, 4, 2, and 1. Note that the number itself and 1 are always factors. On the SSAT, you may see a question that asks you to identify the greatest common factor. The greatest common factor is the largest factor that two or more numbers both have. For example, the greatest common factor of 8 and 4 is 4 since that is the largest number that is a factor of both numbers. The greatest common factor is not always one of the numbers, however. For example, let's say we need to find the greatest common factor of 6 and 8. The factors of 6 are 6, 3, 2, and 1. The greatest common factor of 6 and 8 would therefore be 2 because that is the largest number that is a factor of both numbers.

- A factor is a number that another number can be divided by with no remainder
- The greatest common factor is the largest number that is a factor of two or more other numbers

You may see a question that simply asks you how many factors a number has. One approach to this is to create a factor tree. In a factor tree, each branch splits into numbers that can be multiplied to create that number. This splitting continues until you are down to only prime numbers. The factors are then any of these prime numbers as well as the products of any of these prime numbers.

- Factor trees show numbers split into factors until you reach prime numbers
- The possible factors are these prime numbers, the product of any combination of these prime numbers (including the number itself), and 1

For example, let's look at the factors of 60:

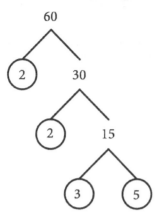

The factors are:

1
60
2
3
5
2 × 2 = 4
2 × 2 × 3 = 12
2 × 3 = 6
2 × 3 × 5 = 30
3 × 5 = 15

Here is a question for you to try:

1. How many positive integer factors does 80 have?

    (A) 2
    (B) 4
    (C) 5
    (D) 8
    (E) 10

If we draw out a factor tree, it would look like this:

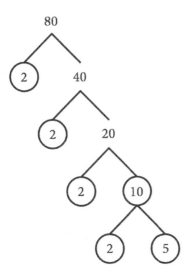

The factors are:

1
80
2
5
$2 \times 2 = 4$
$2 \times 2 \times 2 = 8$
$2 \times 2 \times 2 \times 2 = 16$
$2 \times 5 = 10$
$2 \times 2 \times 5 = 20$
$2 \times 2 \times 2 \times 5 = 40$

Therefore, the factors of 80 are 1, 2, 4, 5, 8, 10, 16, 20, 40, and 80. Since there are 10 of these factors, answer choice E is correct.

Some other questions will ask you to find the greatest common factor. Here are some for you to try:

2. What is the greatest common factor of 12 and 16?

   (A) 1
   (B) 2
   (C) 4
   (D) 6
   (E) 12

In order to answer this question, we need to list the factors of each number:

12: 1, 2, 3, 4, 6, 12

16: 1, 2, 4, 8, 16

From these two lists, we can see that the largest number that shows up as a factor of both 12 and 16 is 4. Therefore, 4 is the greatest common factor, and answer choice C is correct.

3. If the greatest common factor of a number M and 54 is 18, which of the following could be the value of M?

   (A) 24
   (B) 36
   (C) 64
   (D) 108
   (E) 162

We can use the process of elimination for this question. We can eliminate choices A and C because 18 is not a factor of 24 or 64. If we look at choice B, the factors of 36 are 1, 2, 3, 4, 6, 9, 12, 18, and 36. The factors of 54 are 1, 2, 3, 4, 6, 9, 18, 27, 54. The largest number that shows up on both lists of factors is 18, so 18 is the greatest common factor of both 36 and 54 so M could be 36. Answer choices C and E can be eliminated because 54 is a factor of both 108 and 162 (as well as of itself), so 54 would be the greatest common factor, not 18. Answer choice B is correct.

A multiple of a number is a number that is a product of that number and another number. For example, the multiples of 4 are 4, 8, 12, 16, and so on. The least common multiple is the smallest number that is a multiple of two or more other numbers. To find this, we can start a partial list of the multiples but stop when we get to a multiple that they have in common. For example, let's say we are looking for the least common multiple of 4 and 6.

   Multiples of 4: 4, 8, 12….
   Multiples of 6: 6, 12….

The first number that was a multiple of both 4 and 6 was 12. Therefore, 12 is the least common multiple.

Since this test is multiple-choice, however, our options are limited. Start with the smallest number in the answer choices and see if it is a multiple of both. If it isn't, go on to the next biggest number, and continue this process until you find a number that is a multiple of both numbers given in the question.

-   Since this is a multiple-choice test, you only have to find the smallest multiple-choice answer that is a multiple of both numbers given if the question asks for the least common multiple

Here are a couple of questions for you to try:

4. What is the least common multiple of 24 and 36?

    (A) 2
    (B) 6
    (C) 12
    (D) 72
    (E) 144

To answer this question, we can first eliminate choices A, B, and C because these answer choices give factors instead of multiples. If we look at choices D and E, both 72 and 144 are multiples of 24 and 36. However, the question asks for the least common multiple, and 72 is less than 144, so answer choice D is correct.

5. What is the least common multiple of 16 and 32?

    (A) 8
    (B) 16
    (C) 32
    (D) 48
    (E) 64

To answer this question, we can first rule out choices A and B because they are factors and not multiples of 32. When we evaluate choice C, we have to remember that a number is a multiple of itself. Therefore, 32 is a multiple of both 32 (32×1) and 16 (16×2). Answer choice C is the correct answer.

Here is a question that tests your ability to list multiples but not identify the least common multiple:

6. How many positive integers less than 80 are multiples of both 6 and 9?

    (A) 4
    (B) 6
    (C) 8
    (D) 10
    (E) 12

For this question, we could list out all of the multiples. However, that would be a lot of work. Another approach is to list out the multiples of the largest number (there are fewer of these than of the smaller number) and see which of those is also a multiple of the smaller number. The multiples of 9 that are positive integers less than 80 are: 9, 18, 27, 36, 45, 54, 63, 72. Of these numbers, only 18, 36, 54, and 72 are also multiples of 6. Therefore, there are 4 positive integers that are less than 80 that are multiples of both 6 and 9. Answer choice A is correct.

Exponents

Squaring a number means multiplying it by itself. For example, if we square 6, we write it as $6^2 = 6 \times 6 = 36$.

Taking a square root of a number is going backwards from squaring. To find the square root of 36, we ask ourselves, "What number times itself is equal to 36?" The answer is 6.

We use a special symbol for a square root. To take the square root of 36, we write it in symbols as $\sqrt{36} = 6$. Here is another square root: $\sqrt{64} = 8$.

On the SSAT it is helpful just to know a few perfect squares:

Number	Square of number
1	$1^2 = 1$
2	$2^2 = 4$
3	$3^2 = 9$
4	$4^2 = 16$
5	$5^2 = 25$
6	$6^2 = 36$
7	$7^2 = 49$
8	$8^2 = 64$
9	$9^2 = 81$
10	$10^2 = 100$

Here is how this concept is tested on the SSAT:

7. If a number multiplied by itself is 400, what is the number?

(A) 2
(B) 10
(C) 20
(D) 40
(E) 100

The question is a restatement of the definition of squaring a number. It really is asking what number squared is equal to 400. The easiest way to solve this is to try each answer choice.

(A) 2: $2^2 = 2 \times 2 = 4$ No
(B) 10: $10^2 = 10 \times 10 = 100$ No
(C) 20: $20^2 = 20 \times 20 = 400$ Yes
(D) 40:
(E) 100:

The correct answer is C. We don't have to do the work for choices D and E since we found an answer that works.

_____

Here are a couple more problems to try:

8. If $\#x\# = x^2$, then what is $\#4\#$ equal to?

    (A) 4
    (B) 8
    (C) 16
    (D) 20
    (E) 24

    The trick to solving this problem is to not get thrown off by the # symbols. You aren't supposed to know what they mean – they are made up. The question is telling us what we should do with them. If x is surrounded by # symbols, then we are supposed to square x. Since 4 is surrounded by # symbols, we have to square 4 in order to find the answer. We know that 4 squared is 16, so answer choice C is correct.

9. The expression $\sqrt{49} \times (2x + 5)$ is equal to

    (A) $5 + 14x$
    (B) $35 + 2x$
    (C) $35 + 14x$
    (D) $40 + 16x$
    (E) 49

    To solve this problem, we first have to take the square root of 49. Since $7 \times 7 = 49$, the square root of 49 is 7. We now have $7(2x + 5)$, so we have to use the distributive property. We are left with $14x + 35$. If we look at our answer choices, however, $14x + 35$ is not one of them. We are using addition, though, so we can use the commutative property to rearrange the equation and get $35 + 14x$. Answer choice C is correct.

When we square a number, we can also say that the exponent is 2. We can have an exponent other than 2 as well. The exponent tells us how many times we multiply a number by itself. For example, $2^3 = 2 \times 2 \times 2 = 8$, and $3^4 = 3 \times 3 \times 3 \times 3 = 81$.

Here are a couple of questions that test this concept:

10. What is the value of 2^4?

    (A) 2
    (B) 4
    (C) 8
    (D) 12
    (E) 16

    The exponent indicates that we should multiply four two's. This would look like $2 \times 2 \times 2 \times 2$. If we perform the calculations, the answer is 16. Answer choice E is correct.

11. If $x = 2$ and $y = 3$, what is the value of $3x^3y^2$?

   (A) 12

   (B) 36

   (C) 54

   (D) 72

   (E) 216

To answer this question, we have to substitute in 2 for x and 3 for y. Our problem becomes $3 \times 2^3 \times 3^2$. We first need to deal with the exponents (see following section on order of operations). Once we do that, our problem becomes $3 \times 8 \times 9$, which is equal to 216. Answer choice E is correct.

You will get more practice with exponents in the following order of operations section.

Order of Operations

You may have learned order of operations as PEMDAS in school. You may have also learned "Please Excuse My Dear Aunt Sally." These are both memory tricks used to remember the order of operations.

     PEMDAS stand for:

     P- Parentheses

     E- Exponents

     M/D- Multiplication or Division, from left to right

     A/S- Addition or Subtraction, from left to right

What this means is that we first perform any operations that are in parentheses, then we multiply out any numbers that have exponents, then we perform multiplication or division as it shows up in the problem from left to right, and finally we perform any addition or subtraction operations from left to right.

Here is an example:

     $4 + 6 \times 3^2 \div (5 - 2)$

     First we perform any operations in parentheses:

     $4 + 6 \times 3^2 \div 3$

     Now we perform any operations with exponents:

     $4 + 6 \times 9 \div 3$

     Now we perform multiplication or division from left to right:

     $4 + 54 \div 3$

     $4 + 18$

Finally, we perform addition or subtraction:

22

Here are a couple of problems that show how this could be tested on the SSAT:

12. The expression $9 - 2 \times 3 + 6$ is equivalent to

(A) 3
(B) 6
(C) 9
(D) 18
(E) 27

The key to this question is to recognize that we can't just perform operations from left to right (if you chose answer choice E, this is the mistake that you made). Since the order of operations tells us that we must perform multiplication or division before addition or subtraction, the math looks like this:

$9 - 2 \times 3 + 6$

$9 - 6 + 6$

$3 + 6$

9

Answer choice C is correct.

13. $9 + (16 - 8) \times 3 =$

(A) 17
(B) 33
(C) 42
(D) 51
(E) 63

Again, we have to remember to follow order of operations. First we must perform the operations in parentheses. If we do that, our expression becomes $9 + 8 \times 3$. Now we have to perform multiplication before addition and the expression becomes $9 + 24$, which is equal to 33 – if you performed addition before multiplication you would have gotten answer choice D, which is incorrect. Answer choice B is correct.

You often see problems with exponents that are testing order of operations as well.

Here are a few examples for you to try, just remember to use PEMDAS:

14. Simplify: $18 - 3^2 + 4 \times 2^3$

 (A) 41
 (B) 47
 (C) 104
 (D) 257
 (E) 1,832

The first step in PEMDAS is to perform operations in parentheses. This problem has no parentheses, though, so we move on to exponents. Our expression becomes $18 - 9 + 4 \times 8$. The next step is to perform multiplication or division. The expression becomes $18 - 9 + 32$. Now we perform addition and subtraction, remembering to go from left to right. This leaves us with 41, so answer choice A is correct.

15. The expression $10 - 2^3 + 4 \div 2 + 5^2$ is equivalent to

 (A) 3
 (B) 28
 (C) 29
 (D) 112
 (E) 283

In order to answer this question, we must apply PEMDAS. We don't have any parentheses, so we will start with exponents. This gives us $10 - 8 + 4 \div 2 + 25$. The next step is to perform the division operation, which results in $10 - 8 + 2 + 25$. Now we must perform addition and subtraction, from left to right. The result is 29. Answer choice C is correct.

16. Which is the value of the expression $2(4 + 1) \times (7 - 3)^2 \div 2^3$?

 (A) 10
 (B) 20
 (C) 40
 (D) 60
 (E) 80

The first step is to perform the operations in parentheses:

$2(4 + 1) \times (7 - 3)^2 \div 2^3 = 2(5) \times 4^2 \div 2^3$

Now we simplify the parts of the expression with exponents:

$2(5) \times 4^2 \div 2^3 = 2(5) \times 16 \div 8$

_____

Finally, we multiply/divide from left to right:

$10 \times 16 \div 8$

$160 \div 8$

20

Answer choice B is correct.

Operations with negative numbers

There are generally two types of problems that test the rules of negative numbers. The first is a short word problem that requires you to recognize a situation where using negative numbers would be appropriate and then solve using addition or subtraction. The second requires you to use the basic rules of multiplying with negative numbers.

You will recognize the word problems requiring you to use addition or subtraction with negative numbers because they include a value that is below the normal level.

The easiest way to solve these word problems is to sketch out a basic number line and think about whether we should go from the starting point to the left or right.

- Using a basic number line is one approach for solving problems with negative numbers.

For example, let's say we start with a temperature that is 13 degrees below zero and then the temperature rises by 25 degrees.

We could sketch out this situation as follows:

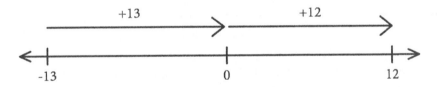

We started out at –13. The temperature increased, so we add degrees, or move to the right. To get from –13 to zero only required adding 13 degrees, so we need to add another 12 degrees in order to add a total of 25 degrees. The new temperature is 12 degrees above zero.

Here are a couple of problems for you to try:

17. At a school book fair, at 10 AM sales were 34 books below the goal for book sales. By 12 PM, another 56 books had been sold. At 12 PM, how did book sales compare to the goal?

    (A) 22 less than the goal had been sold
    (B) 12 books less than the goal had been sold
    (C) the number of books sold equaled the goal
    (D) 12 books more than the goal had been sold
    (E) 22 books more than the goal had been sold

_____

In this situation, at 10 AM, the number of books sold was 34 books less than the goal. We can represent this as –34 books sold. Now we can create a number line, moving 56 spots to the right since 56 more books were sold by 12 PM.

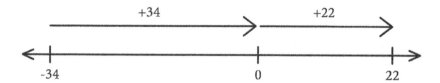

If we add 56 to –34, we wind up with positive 22, so answer choice E is correct.

18. In order to run a fieldtrip, a community center needed a minimum number of participants to register. Three days before the registration deadline, the community center needed another 7 participants to register. When the registration deadline passed, another 15 participants had registered. What was the final number of participants for the fieldtrip?

(A) 8 less than the minimum number required
(B) 7 less than the minimum number required
(C) 7 more than the minimum number required
(D) 8 more than the minimum number required
(E) 22 more than the minimum number required

Let's draw out the number line again. This time, we can represent needing 7 more registrants as –7 because they are 7 registrants below the goal.

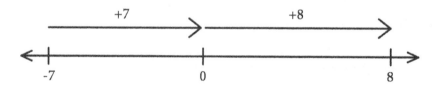

From the number line, we can see that adding a total of 15 participants to -7 leaves us with 8 participants more than the minimum. Answer choice D is correct.

Another type of negative number problem that you may see requires you to know the rules of multiplying negative numbers.

Here are the basic rules:

$$+ \times + = +$$

$$- \times - = +$$

$$+ \times - = -$$

If we multiply a positive number by a positive number, or a negative number by a negative number, the result will be positive. If we multiply a positive number by a negative number, the result will be negative.

Here are a couple of questions that test these rules:

19. $-3 \times -4 =$

    (A) -12

    (B) -7

    (C) -1

    (D) 7

    (E) 12

In this question, there is a negative number multiplied by a negative number. This means that the result will be positive. We multiply 3 and 4, and the result is 12. Since it should be positive 12, answer choice E is correct.

20. $(4 + 5)^2 \times -2$

    (A) -162

    (B) -82

    (C) -18

    (D) 82

    (E) 162

This question tests operations with negative numbers as well as PEMDAS. We first have to perform the operation in parentheses, which results in $9^2 \times -2$. Next we take care of exponents by squaring 9, and now our expression is 81×-2. Since $81 \times 2 = 162$, and we have a negative multiplied by a positive, we know that the end result is -162. Answer choice A is correct.

You may also see more involved PEMDAS questions where there isn't a negative sign to begin with but one of the operations in parentheses results in a negative number. The key to these questions is to remember that if we have a negative sign in parentheses and that number is raised to an exponent, we have to include the negative sign when we multiply.

For example:

$(-2)^2 = -2 \times -2 = 4$ (note that negative × negative = positive)

$(-2)^3 = -2 \times -2 \times -2 = -8$ (note that negative × negative × negative = positive × negative = negative)

- If a negative number is raised to an exponent that is an even number, the result will be positive
- If a negative number is raised to an exponent that is an odd number, the result will be negative

Here are a couple of questions for you to try:

21. Calculate: $(3 - 4)^5 - 2$

    (A) –3
    (B) –1
    (C) 0
    (D) 1
    (E) 3

Our first step is to perform the operation in parentheses. Since $3 - 4 = -1$, the expression becomes $(-1)^5 - 2$. Now we have to take care of the exponent. Since $(-1)^5 = -1 \times -1 \times -1 \times -1 \times -1 = -1$, the expression is now $-1 - 2$. Since $-1 - 2 = -3$, answer choice A is correct.

22. What is the product of $4 - 4^2$ and $3 - 5 \times 2$?

    (A) –84
    (B) –48
    (C) 28
    (D) 48
    (E) 84

The first step in answering this question is to simplify each expression using PEMDAS.

$4 - 4^2 = 4 - 16 = -12$

$3 - 5 \times 2 = 3 - 10 = -7$

Now we have to find the product of -12 and -7. Since the product is the result of multiplication, we calculate -12×-7. The result is 84 since a negative number multiplied by a negative number results in a positive number. Answer choice E is correct.

Absolute value

Another concept that you may or may not have learned is absolute value. When we take the absolute value of a number, we simply take the positive value of the number. We use two lines to represent absolute value, such as $|-4| = 4$ and $|4| = 4$. In the order of operations, we treat the absolute value brackets as parentheses.

- Absolute value brackets tell us to take the positive value of what is in the brackets, for example, $|-3| = 3$ and $|3| = 3$

- In the order of operations, absolute value brackets are treated in the "parentheses" step

Here are a couple of examples:

23. Calculate: $|5 - 7| \times 4 - 6$

    (A) -14

    (B) -12

    (C) 2

    (D) 6

    (E) 10

The first step in answering this question is perform the operation in the absolute value brackets: $|5 - 7| = |-2| = 2$. Now our expression is $2 \times 4 - 6$. At this point we need to perform any multiplication or division. Since the $\times$ represents multiplication in an expression, we need to multiply 2 and 4, and our expression becomes $8 - 6$, which is equal to 2. Answer choice C is correct.

24. What is the value of the expression $4 - |6 - 3|^2 + 12$?

    (A) 7

    (B) 13

    (C) 25

    (D) 27

    (E) 36

Following the order of operations, this is what the math looks like for solving this problem:

$4 - |6 - 3|^2 + 12$

$4 - 3^2 + 12$

$4 - 9 + 12$

$-5 + 12$

7

Answer choice A is correct.

Now that you have worked on some of these harder concepts, be sure to complete the practice set to reinforce what you have learned!

_____

Advanced Math Fundamentals Practice Set

1. How many positive integers are factors of 64?

   (A) 6
   (B) 7
   (C) 8
   (D) 10
   (E) 12

2. What is the value of $|3 - 5|^3$?

   (A) −8
   (B) −4
   (C) 2
   (D) 4
   (E) 8

3. What is the least common multiple of 4 and 15?

   (A) 1
   (B) 4
   (C) 30
   (D) 60
   (E) 120

4. Calculate: $-4 \times 6 \times -3$

   (A) −72
   (B) −24
   (C) −1
   (D) 24
   (E) 72

5. Which is equivalent to $8 - 2^2 \times 5 + 7$?

   (A) −20
   (B) −19
   (C) −5
   (D) 27
   (E) 54

6. How many positive integers less than 50 are multiples of both 2 and 3?

   (A) 8
   (B) 10
   (C) 16
   (D) 24
   (E) 25

7. What is the value of the expression $5 + (3 \times 2)^2 - 9 \div 3$?

   (A) 10
   (B) 11
   (C) 22
   (D) 38
   (E) 83

8. At 3 PM, the temperature was 9 degrees. By midnight, the temperature had fallen by 22 degrees. What was the temperature at midnight?

   (A) 31 degrees below zero
   (B) 13 degrees below zero
   (C) 4 degrees above zero
   (D) 13 degrees above zero
   (E) 31 degrees zero

9. What is the greatest common factor of 63 and 72?

   (A) 3
   (B) 6
   (C) 9
   (D) 12
   (E) 18

10. What is the value of $4 \times |8 - 5| + 16 \div 4$

   (A) –16
   (B) –7
   (C) 4
   (D) 7
   (E) 16

Answers to practice set

1. B
2. E
3. D
4. E
5. C
6. A
7. D
8. B
9. C
10. E

Patterns

On the SSAT, you will generally find a few questions that require you to recognize and use patterns.

Here are the problem types we will cover in this section:

- Identify the pattern
- Translate a pattern from words
- Find the rule and apply it
- Find a distant term

Identify the Pattern

The most basic type of question simply asks you to identify the pattern being used. These questions are not hard. Since the test is multiple-choice, you can just try out the answer choices and see which pattern predicts the elements in the pattern.

- If the question asks you to describe a pattern, just try out the answer choices and use process of elimination

Here are a couple of examples for you to try:

1. {3, 9, 27, 81, ...}

   To find the next term in this sequence, the previous term is

   (A) multiplied by itself
   (B) increased by 6
   (C) divided by 3
   (D) multiplied by 3
   (E) multiplied by 6

   To answer this question we can just try out the rules. Answer choice A is tempting because this rule works for the first two terms. However, 9 multiplied by itself is not 27, so we can eliminate choice A. Choice B works for finding the second term but not the third or fourth, so choice B can be ruled out. Choice C doesn't work for any of the terms, so it is easy to eliminate. Now let's try choice D. Since $3 \times 3 = 9$, $9 \times 3 = 27$, and $27 \times 3 = 81$, we know that choice D works for all numbers in the sequence, and it is correct.

2. Which rule is true for the sequence 4, 2, 1, $\frac{1}{2}$, $\frac{1}{4}$?

   (A) divide each term by 4 to find the next term
   (B) multiply each term by 4 to find the next term
   (C) subtract 2 from each term to find the next term
   (D) multiply each term by 2 to find the next term
   (E) multiply each term by $\frac{1}{2}$ to find the next term

If we use the same process as we did before, we can see that only choice E accurately predicts the next term for every term in the sequence. Choice E is correct.

Questions that are a little harder give you terms that are not consecutive (in a row) and ask you for the rule. The trick to these is to remember that the terms were not consecutive.

- If they give you terms not in a row, circle this information so that you don't forget when you start trying out the rules in the answer choices.

Here is one for you to try:

3. Shaun writes down a number pattern. The first number in his pattern is 20.5 and the third number is 64. Which could be the rule for Shaun's number pattern?

   (A) add 43.5
   (B) add 22
   (C) multiply by 2 and then subtract 6
   (D) multiply by 3 and then add 2.5
   (E) multiply by 4 then subtract 18

The key to this question is remembering that we are NOT given two terms in a row. We are given the first and third terms so there must be another term in between. One way to represent this is:

   20.5, _____, 64

That blank helps us remember to put a number between 20.5 and 64. Now we can try the rules. If we try answer choice A and add 43.5 to 20.5, we get 64 as an answer. This is incorrect because that would mean the second term was 64, but the question says that the third term is 64. Choice A can be ruled out. Now let's try choice B. If we add 22 to 20.5, the second term would be 42.5. If we add 22 to 42.5, then the next (or third) term would be 64.5. However, the third term is 64, so we can rule out choice B. Let's try choice C. If we multiply 20.5 by 2 and then subtract 6, our second term would be 35. If we multiply that by 2 and then subtract 6, the third term would be 64. Since this is our third term, answer choice C is correct. If you chose answer choices D or E, you forgot that 64 was the third term and not the second.

_____

Translate a Pattern from Words

A closely related problem type is one where a pattern is described in words and then you have to predict a term. To answer these questions, just slow down so you can follow each step carefully.

Here are a couple of questions for you to try:

4. Here is a pattern of numbers: 1, 1, 2, 3, 5, 8, …

    To get the third number, add the first and second numbers. To get the fourth number, add the second and third numbers. To get the fifth number, add the third and fourth numbers. If we continue this pattern, then what is the seventh number in the pattern?

    (A) 9
    (B) 12
    (C) 13
    (D) 16
    (E) 20

    This one isn't so bad, even though it looks kind of scary. You just have to follow the instructions that are given for creating the pattern. To get the seventh number, you simply add together the fifth and sixth number, or 5 + 8. Answer choice C is correct.

5. A number is 3 more than twice the previous number. The first number in the pattern is 1. What is the 3rd number in the pattern?

    (A) 3
    (B) 5
    (C) 7
    (D) 10
    (E) 13

    You start with the number 1. The directions say to take twice the number 1 and then add 3 to it. Twice the number 1 is 2, and then when you add 3 to it, you get 5. So 5 is the second number in the pattern. Now repeat the directions to find the next number, but start with the number 5. Take twice 5 and add 3. This gives 10 + 3, which is 13, so answer choice E is correct.

These questions can also ask for terms that are not consecutive, or in a row.

Here is an example for you to try:

6. The rule for Tomas's number pattern is to divide a number by 2 and then add 3. Which pair of numbers could be the second and fourth terms in Tomas's pattern?

    (A) 20 and 13
    (B) 15 and 33
    (C) 25 and 7.75
    (D) 30 and 12
    (E) 40 and 13

_____

We can use process of elimination on this one. If we start with answer choice A, when we divide 20 by two and add 3, the result is 13. However, this would make 20 and 13 consecutive terms, not leave one term in between them, so choice A can be ruled out. Now let's try choice B. If we divide 15 by 2 and add 3, the result is 10.5. Now we need to do that again since there should be a term in between the pair of numbers. 10.5 divided by 2 is 5.25 and if we add 3 to that the result is 8.25 and not 33. Answer choice B can be eliminated. If we go through the same process with 25 as the first number, the second number in the pattern would be 15.5, and the third number would be 10.75, and answer choice C is also wrong. If we start with 30 as the first number, the missing term would be 18, and the final number in the pair given would be 12. Since answer choice D gives 30 and 12 as a pair, it is the correct answer choice.

Find the Rule and Apply it

Sometimes the question will give you the numbers in a sequence and you need to identify a future term. The key to these questions is to first put into words the rule for predicting the next term. Often, you have to guess and check a bit to come up with the rule. It could be adding the same number each time, multiplying by the same number, and there could be more than one step to each rule as well.

- If the question doesn't give you a rule in words, you will need to figure out the rule on your own before trying to predict a future term

Some of these questions use fractions or decimals in the sequence. The rules for these questions tend to be more straightforward.

- The rules for patterns with fractions or decimals tend to be pretty straightforward with one step

Here are some questions for you to try that use patterns with fractions or decimals:

7. What is the next number in this set of fractions? $\frac{1}{5}, \frac{2}{6}, \frac{3}{7},$ _____

(A) $\frac{1}{8}$

(B) $\frac{2}{8}$

(C) $\frac{3}{4}$

(D) $\frac{4}{8}$

(E) $\frac{5}{6}$

Look at the numerators (top numbers). Their pattern is to increase by 1 each time. The next numerator will be 4. Now look at the denominators (bottom numbers). They also get bigger by 1 each time, so the next denominator will be 8. Thus, the answer is $\frac{4}{8}$, or answer choice D.

8. Given the pattern $\dfrac{1}{4}, \dfrac{2}{8}, \dfrac{3}{12}, \dfrac{4}{\odot}$, then what is the value for $\odot$?

   (A) 1
   (B) 8
   (C) 14
   (D) 16
   (E) 20

If we look closely at the pattern, we can see that with each fraction, the top number has one added to it. But the bottom number has four added to it each time. If we add 4 to 12, we get 16, so choice D is correct. Here is one for you to try with decimals:

9. What is the next term in the sequence 2.3, 3.95, 5.6, 7.25, _____?

   (A) 8.9
   (B) 9.95
   (C) 10.3
   (D) 11.35
   (E) 11.9

In order to answer this question, we need to find the pattern. We can start with looking for the difference between each term. Since 3.95 – 2.3 = 1.65, we know that to get from the first to second term we had to add 1.65. If we subtract 3.95 from 5.6, we can see that the difference between the second and third terms is also 1.65. Since 7.25 – 5.6 = 1.65, we know that our rule to get from one term to the next is to add 1.65. Since 7.25 + 1.65 = 8.9, answer choice A is correct.

Other questions use integers or whole numbers. Just remember to put the pattern into words first. Generally, the rules for questions with integers or whole numbers have two or more steps.

- The rules for patterns with integers are generally not one step

Here are a few examples for you to try:

10. Which number comes next in the series 2, 4, 8, 14, 22, ___ ?

   (A) 24
   (B) 26
   (C) 32
   (D) 34
   (E) 36

This pattern is tough to figure out at first. One strategy is to look for the difference between each term. If we look for that, we notice that to get from 2 to 4, we have to add 2. To get from 4 to 8, we have to add 4. To get from 8 to 14, we need to add 6. To get from 14 to 22, we add 8. To find the next term, we would therefore add 10 since the amount we add to each term increases by 2. Since 22 plus 10 is 32, answer choice C is correct.

———

11. Abraham wrote the first 8 numbers of a sequence: 3, 7, 13, 18, 22, 28, 33, 37. If this pattern continues, what will be the 10th number in this sequence?

    (A) 43
    (B) 44
    (C) 45
    (D) 47
    (E) 48

We can make a chart looking for the difference between each of the terms:

Order of term	Term	How to get to next term?
1	3	+4
2	7	+6
3	13	+5
4	18	+4
5	22	+6
6	28	+5
7	33	+4
8	37	?

If we look at the pattern for the terms given, we can see that we add 4, then 6, then 5, then repeat. Therefore, to find the 9th term, we would add 6 to the 8th term (37), and the 9th term is 43. To find the 10th term, we add 5 to the 9th term (43) and the 10th term is 48. Choice E is correct.

12. Marla wrote the first five terms of a sequence: 5, 8, 14, 26, 50. What is the sixth term of this sequence?

    (A) 98
    (B) 99
    (C) 100
    (D) 102
    (E) 104

We have to look for the pattern here. To get from 5 to 8, we have to add 3. However, to get from 8 to 14, we don't add 3 so we know that our rule is not "add 3." If we look at the differences between the terms, they are +3, +6, +12, +24. We can see that we double the difference each time. Therefore, we would add +48 to find the next (or 6th) term. Since 50 + 48 = 98, the 6th term is 98, and choice A is correct.

Find a Distant Term

Sometimes the question will establish a pattern and then ask what a distant term will be, such as the 50th term. These questions are designed so that it would take you forever to list out the items, but you can use reasoning to solve.

Let's say our pattern is red, blue, green, red, blue, green, and so on. The question asks for the 50th term. Our first step is to count up the elements in our pattern before it repeats. Since it is only red, blue, green, there are three elements in the pattern. Our next step is to divide the number of the term we are looking for by the number of elements in the pattern. The key is not how many times the number of elements goes into the term number, but rather what the remainder is. The number 50 can be divided by 3 sixteen times with a remainder of 2. This means that there are 16 complete sets of red, blue, and green through the 48th element in the pattern, the pattern starts again with red on the 49th element, and the 50th element is therefore blue. Notice that the remainder was 2 and the correct answer was the 2nd element in the pattern. If the remainder had been 1, the answer would have been the 1st element in the pattern. If there had been no remainder, the answer would have been the last element in the pattern, because there would be a complete pattern with nothing left over.

Here are the steps for finding a distant element in a pattern:

1. Count up the number of elements in the pattern before it repeats.

2. Divide the number of the desired term by the number of elements in the pattern.

3. Look at the remainder – if it is 1, then the answer is the 1st element in the pattern, if it is 2, it is the 2nd element in the pattern, and so on. If there is no remainder, it is the last element in the pattern.

Here are a couple of examples for you to try:

1. Pam is making kabobs, where you put meat and vegetables on a skewer. She always puts the meat and vegetables on the skewer in the same order: beef, onion, green pepper, and tomato. The skewer is very long, so Pam will repeat this pattern many times. What is the 18th item that Pam will put on the skewer?

   (A) Beef
   (B) Onion
   (C) Green Pepper
   (D) Tomato
   (E) Cannot be determined

   First we count up the elements in the pattern before it repeats. She puts on beef, onion, green pepper, and tomato, so there are 4 elements in the pattern. We divide 18 (the desired term) by 4. The answer is 4 with a remainder of 2. Therefore, the 18th item will be the 2nd element in the pattern, or onion. Choice B is correct.

2. Mark is sorting coins and putting them in a pattern of penny, nickel, dime, and repeating this over and over. What is the 37th coin that he would put in the pattern?

   (A) Penny
   (B) Nickel
   (C) Dime
   (D) Quarter
   (E) Cannot be determined

   In this case, there are 3 elements in the pattern: penny, nickel, and dime. We divide 37 (the desired term) by 3. The answer is 12 with a remainder of 1. Therefore, the first element of the pattern, penny, will be the 37th term. Answer choice A is correct.

Now you know how to ace pattern problems on the SSAT! Be sure to complete the patterns practice set.

Patterns Practice Set

1. A teacher is collecting photos of all the 6th graders' pets. She ends up with 20 dog photos, 20 cat photos, 20 hamster photos, and 20 snake photos. She puts them on a big display board, always putting a dog, then a cat, then a snake, then a hamster photo, and then she starts over with the same pattern. What is the 54th photo that she will put on the display board?

   (A) Dog
   (B) Cat
   (C) Snake
   (D) Hamster
   (E) Cannot be determined

2. A number is said to be a square number if that number of objects can be arranged in rows such that a square can be built from the number of objects. Here is a diagram for the first three square numbers:

   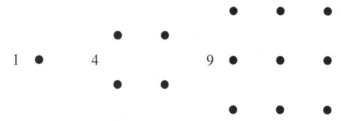

   What are the next 2 square numbers?

   (A) 10 and 12
   (B) 12 and 16
   (C) 16 and 20
   (D) 16 and 25
   (E) 25 and 36

3. Find the value of Δ in this pattern: $\dfrac{1}{5}, \dfrac{4}{5}, \dfrac{7}{5}, \dfrac{10}{5}, \dfrac{\Delta}{5}$

   (A) 11
   (B) 12
   (C) 13
   (D) 15
   (E) 17

4. Here is a pattern: $\dfrac{2}{5}, \dfrac{3}{6}, \dfrac{4}{7}, \dfrac{5}{8}, ..., \dfrac{13}{\blacklozenge}$

   If this pattern is continued, what is the value of $\blacklozenge$?

   (A) 16
   (B) 18
   (C) 20
   (D) 24
   (E) 30

5. Janice is stringing colored popcorn on a long string. She always puts white, then green, then red, in that order. Which piece of popcorn could not be green?

   (A) the 5th piece
   (B) the 14th piece
   (C) the 21st piece
   (D) the 29th piece
   (E) the 65th piece

6. (3, 11, 43, 171, …)

   To find the next term in the sequence above, the previous term is

   (A) multiplied by itself and increased by 2
   (B) multiplied by 3 and increased by 2
   (C) increased by 8
   (D) multiplied by 5 and decreased by 4
   (E) multiplied by 4 and decreased by 1

7. In a pattern, each number is 4 times 1 less than the previous number. The first number in this pattern is 2. What is the third number in this pattern?

   (A) 2
   (B) 4
   (C) 7
   (D) 12
   (E) 27

8. Which number comes next in the series 3, 6, 10, 13, 17, 20, 24, …?

   (A) 27
   (B) 28
   (C) 29
   (D) 30
   (E) 31

9. The rule for Glenda's number pattern is to multiply a number by 2 and subtract 3. Which could be the second and fourth terms in this sequence?

   (A) 2 and 3
   (B) 1 and –5
   (C) 1 and –1
   (D) 2 and –5
   (E) 3 and 5

10. What is the next term in the series 3, 4, 5, 7, 10, 15, 23, …?

   (A) 31
   (B) 33
   (C) 36
   (D) 38
   (E) 41

Answers to Patterns Practice Set

1. B
2. D
3. C
4. A
5. C
6. E
7. D
8. A
9. B
10. C

Fractions

Fractions on the SSAT really are not very hard. The questions tend to be pretty predictable problem types. Remember to pay attention to what makes each problem type unique as you work through this section.

In this section, we will cover:

- Pictures showing fractions
- Operations with fractions
- Word problems with fractions
- Comparing fractions

Pictures Showing Fractions

The first type of fraction problem that we will go over is how to tell what fraction of a picture is shaded.

The basic strategy for this problem type is that you need to divide your picture into pieces.

- Divide your pictures into pieces

This is easy if it is a figure that can be divided into equally sized pieces.

For example, if we have the following picture:

In this picture, we can see that there are four equally-sized pieces. Two of those four pieces are shaded, so $\frac{1}{2}$ of the figure is shaded.

Here is an example of how this could be tested on the SSAT:

1. In the hexagon pictured below, what fraction of the hexagon is shaded?

   (A) $\dfrac{1}{2}$

   (B) $\dfrac{1}{3}$

   (C) $\dfrac{1}{4}$

   (D) $\dfrac{1}{5}$

   (E) $\dfrac{1}{6}$

In order to solve this problem, draw in lines that divide the hexagon into equal pieces.

It should look like this:

Now we can clearly see that one part out of six is shaded, so the correct answer is choice E.

Here is another problem to try:

2. Kim drew these shapes on a piece of paper:

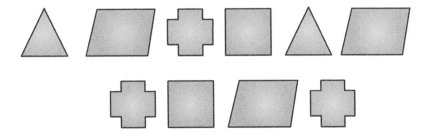

What fraction of the shapes are triangles?

(A) $\dfrac{1}{10}$

(B) $\dfrac{1}{5}$

(C) $\dfrac{3}{10}$

(D) $\dfrac{2}{5}$

(E) $\dfrac{4}{9}$

Our first step is to count up the total number of shapes. There are 10 shapes, so that becomes our denominator. Then we count up the number of triangles. There are 2 triangles, so this is our numerator. Our fraction now looks like this:

$$\dfrac{2}{10}$$

That is not an answer choice, however. We have to simplify the fraction in order to answer the question. We can see that both 2 and 10 can be divided by 2 with no remainder, so we will divide both the top and the bottom by 2.

$$\dfrac{2 \div 2}{10 \div 2} = \dfrac{1}{5}$$

Answer choice B is correct.

Sometimes you will have to divide a figure into unequal pieces to see what works. This question type always asks you to identify which figures have one-half shaded. It would be possible to write this question without using $\dfrac{1}{2}$ as the fraction that is shaded, but that would be a much harder problem type so the SSAT uses $\dfrac{1}{2}$.

Here is an example of a figure that has one-half shaded but isn't easily divisible into pieces that are all the same size.

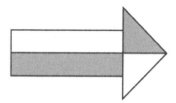

The key to these questions is to match up parts that are the same and then make sure that half of those parts are shaded.

Here is one for you to try:

3. Which of the following figures is NOT shaded in one-half of its region?

(A)

(B)

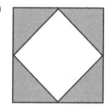

(C)

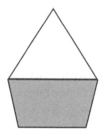

(D)

(E)

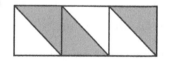

To answer this question, simply match up the shaded regions to identical non-shaded regions. If that doesn't work, then you have your correct answer. Choice C is correct because the two pieces are not identical.

Operations with Fractions

There are some basic rules that you need to know for fractions on the SSAT.

They are:

1. You can multiply or divide the numerator (top number) as long as you multiply or divide the denominator (bottom number) by the SAME number. This allows us to create equivalent fractions – or fractions that are equal in value.

2. If you want to add or subtract fractions, you need to have the same bottom number (or common denominator). Use equivalent fractions to do that. You then add or subtract the top numbers, but keep the same bottom number (common denominator).

3. If you want to multiply fractions, you multiply across the top and then across the bottom (you DON'T figure out a common denominator).

4. If you want to divide fractions, you flip the second fraction and then multiply.

Creating equivalent fractions

The cardinal rule for equivalent fractions is that if you multiply or divide the top by some number, you must also multiply or divide the bottom by the same number in order for the value to remain the same. You can NOT add or subtract the same number from both the top and the bottom and keep the same value, however.

For example:

$$\frac{1}{2} \times \frac{2}{2} = \frac{2}{4}$$

Since we *multiplied* both the numerator (top number) and denominator (bottom number) by the same number, we know that the equation is true.

$$\frac{1}{2} = \frac{2}{4}$$

Another example:

$$\frac{1+2}{2+2} = \frac{3}{4}$$

Since we *added* the same number to the numerator and denominator, the value did not stay the same.

$$\frac{1}{2} \neq \frac{3}{4}$$

Here are some questions that test your ability to create equivalent fractions:

4. If $\dfrac{3}{5} = \dfrac{\square}{35}$, then $\square$ is equal to

    (A) 7
    (B) 14
    (C) 15
    (D) 21
    (E) 33

This question is testing your ability to create equivalent fractions. In examining the denominators (or bottom numbers), we can see that 5 must be multiplied by 7 in order to get 35 as the answer. Since the denominator was multiplied by 7, the numerator (or top number) must also be multiplied by 7. Since $3 \times 7 = 21$, answer choice D is correct.

5. Which shows the fraction $\dfrac{12}{18}$ simplified, or reduced, to its lowest terms?

    (A) $\dfrac{2}{3}$

    (B) $\dfrac{1}{2}$

    (C) $\dfrac{1}{3}$

    (D) $\dfrac{6}{9}$

    (E) $0.\overline{6}$

The key to this question is that the correct answer must be a fraction in its lowest terms. Answer choices A, D, and E all have the same value as $\dfrac{12}{18}$. However, answer choice E is not a fraction at all, so we can eliminate it. Answer choice D is a fraction, but it is not in its lowest terms since the numerator and denominator could both be divided by 3. There is no number greater than 1 that can be divided into both 2 and 3 without a remainder, so answer choice A is correct.

6. $\dfrac{3+3+4}{5+3+7} =$

(A) $\dfrac{1}{3}$

(B) $\dfrac{1}{2}$

(C) $\dfrac{2}{3}$

(D) $\dfrac{7}{13}$

(E) $\dfrac{8}{9}$

The first step in answering this question is to simplify the numerator and the denominator. If we perform the addition, we get $\dfrac{3+3+4}{5+3+7} = \dfrac{10}{15}$. The problem is that $\dfrac{10}{15}$ is not an answer choice. We must simplify. If we divide the numerator and the denominator by 5, we can see that $\dfrac{10 \div 5}{15 \div 5} = \dfrac{2}{3}$. Answer choice C is correct.

To add or subtract fractions

We use equivalent fractions to get the same bottom number, otherwise known as a common denominator. We then add (or subtract) across the top and keep the common denominator as the denominator in our answer.

For example, let's say our problem looks like this:

$$\dfrac{1}{2} + \dfrac{2}{3} = ?$$

We are looking for a number that both denominators go into, or are factors of. The number 6 is a multiple of both 2 and 3, so 6 will be our common denominator. First, we find equivalent fractions with the common denominator.

$$\dfrac{1}{2} \times \dfrac{3}{3} = \dfrac{3}{6}$$

$$\dfrac{2}{3} \times \dfrac{2}{2} = \dfrac{4}{6}$$

We can now add the equivalent fractions. Remember to add only the numerators and keep the denominator.

$$\dfrac{3}{6} + \dfrac{4}{6} = \dfrac{7}{6}$$

We aren't quite done yet. We now have a fraction where the top number is bigger than the bottom number (an improper fraction). To fix this, we can break apart the fraction so that we can see how many "ones" we have and what fraction is left.

$$\frac{7}{6} = \frac{6}{6} + \frac{1}{6}$$

Finally, we can create a mixed number as an answer.

$$\frac{6}{6} + \frac{1}{6} = 1 + \frac{1}{6} = 1\frac{1}{6}$$

To multiply fractions

We can simply multiply across the top and across the bottom.

For example:

$$\frac{1}{2} \times \frac{2}{3} = \frac{2}{6}$$

We then have to simplify the fraction, since both the numerator and denominator can be divided by 2. We use our rule of equivalent fractions (do the same to the top and bottom), only this time we are dividing.

$$\frac{2 \div 2}{6 \div 2} = \frac{1}{3}$$

Our final answer is $\frac{1}{3}$.

Dividing fractions

To divide fractions, we just flip the second fraction and multiply.

For example, let's say our problem was:

$$\frac{2}{3} \div \frac{4}{5}$$

In order to find our answer, we flip the second fraction and multiply, so our problem becomes:

$$\frac{2}{3} \times \frac{5}{4} = \frac{2 \times 5}{3 \times 4} = \frac{10}{12}$$

We aren't quite done yet, we still have to simplify. Since 10 and 12 are both divisible by 2, we divide the top and the bottom by 2.

$$\frac{10 \div 2}{12 \div 2} = \frac{5}{6}$$

Our final answer is $\frac{5}{6}$.

One other thing to keep in mind is order of operations, or PEMDAS. PEMDAS tells us that we perform whichever operation is in parentheses first, then any exponents, then multiplication or division from left to right, and finally addition or subtraction from left to right.

Those are the basics for what you need to know about operations with fractions. That's not so bad, right?

Now let's move on to how these basics will be tested.

Here is how one of these questions could look on the SSAT:

7. $7 \times \left(\frac{1}{3} + \frac{2}{3} \right) =$

    (A) $\frac{7}{6}$

    (B) $\frac{14}{3}$

    (C) $\frac{14}{6}$

    (D) $\frac{14}{9}$

    (E) 7

To solve this problem, we first have to perform the operation in parentheses. If we add $\frac{1}{3} + \frac{2}{3}$, we get 1 as the answer. Our new problem is 7×1, so the answer is 7, or choice E.

Here is another one for you to try:

8. $15\left(\dfrac{6}{9}-\dfrac{2}{3}\right)=$

(A) 0
(B) 1
(C) 3
(D) 5
(E) 15

To solve this problem, first we have to find a common denominator to perform the operation in parentheses. The denominators (9 and 3) are both factors of 9, so we make that our common denominator. We can leave the first fraction alone, but we have to use equivalent fractions to convert the denominator of the second fraction to 9.

$$\dfrac{2}{3}\times\dfrac{3}{3}=\dfrac{6}{9}$$

Now that we have equivalent fractions, we can see that our problem in parentheses is really:

$$\dfrac{6}{9}-\dfrac{6}{9}=0$$

If we substitute in, our problem becomes 15×0, and since anything times zero is zero, the correct answer is choice A.

You may also see questions that ask you to add or subtract with mixed numbers, or numbers that have a whole number part and a fraction part.

The key to questions that ask you to add with mixed numbers is that you often have to simplify an improper fraction, or a fraction where the numerator is greater than the denominator.

-   If you have an improper fraction, you will need to convert it into a mixed number in order to identify the correct answer choice

Here are a couple of examples:

9. $3\dfrac{1}{2} + 4\dfrac{2}{3} =$

(A) 7

(B) $7\dfrac{5}{6}$

(C) 8

(D) $8\dfrac{1}{6}$

(E) $8\dfrac{1}{3}$

One way to approach this problem is to break apart the whole number and fractional parts of each mixed number. Our problem then becomes:

$$3 + \dfrac{1}{2} + 4 + \dfrac{2}{3}$$

Now we can use the commutative property of addition to group the whole numbers and the fractions. We now have:

$$3 + 4 + \dfrac{1}{2} + \dfrac{2}{3}$$

This allows us to add the whole number parts and the fractional parts separately. If we add the whole number portion, we get 7 as the answer for that part of the expression. In order to add the fractions, we need to find a common denominator:

$$\dfrac{1}{2} + \dfrac{2}{3} = \dfrac{3}{6} + \dfrac{4}{6} = \dfrac{7}{6}$$

The problem now is that we have an improper fraction. We need to turn that portion into a mixed number.

$$\dfrac{7}{6} = \dfrac{6}{6} + \dfrac{1}{6} = 1 + \dfrac{1}{6}$$

Now we put the whole number part of the expression together with the fractional part of the expression.

$$7 + 1 + \dfrac{1}{6} = 8\dfrac{1}{6}$$

Answer choice D is correct.

——

Here is another one to try.

10. $3\frac{2}{5} + 1\frac{7}{8} =$

(A) $4\frac{11}{40}$

(B) $4\frac{9}{13}$

(C) $5\frac{1}{8}$

(D) $5\frac{9}{40}$

(E) $5\frac{11}{40}$

Again, we can start by separating the whole number part from the fractional part of each number. This gives us:

$$3 + \frac{2}{5} + 1 + \frac{7}{8}$$

Now we can use the commutative property of addition to group the whole numbers and the fractions to get:

$$3 + 1 + \frac{2}{5} + \frac{7}{8}$$

If we add the whole numbers, we find that the value of that part of the expression is 4. Now we have to find a common denominator in order to add the fractional portion.

$$\frac{2}{5} + \frac{7}{8} = \frac{16}{40} + \frac{35}{40} = \frac{51}{40}$$

The problem now is that we have an improper fraction that needs to be turned into a mixed number.

$$\frac{51}{40} = \frac{40}{40} + \frac{11}{40} = 1 + \frac{11}{40}$$

Now we have to add back in the whole number portion from before.

$$4 + 1 + \frac{11}{40} = 5\frac{11}{40}$$

Answer choice E is correct.

———

———

You may also see questions that ask you to subtract a mixed number from a whole number. One way to approach these problems is to "borrow" from the whole number to create a mixed number.

For example, let's say the problem is:

$$40 - 35\frac{1}{3}$$

We can change 40 into:

$$39 + 1 = 39 + \frac{3}{3} = 39\frac{3}{3}$$

Now we have the problem:

$$39\frac{3}{3} - 35\frac{1}{3} = 4\frac{2}{3}$$

- To subtract a mixed number from a whole number, you can "borrow" from the whole number to create a mixed number

Here are a couple of questions to try:

11. $50 - 8\frac{2}{5} =$

    (A) $41\frac{2}{5}$

    (B) $41\frac{3}{5}$

    (C) $42\frac{2}{5}$

    (D) $42\frac{3}{5}$

    (E) $43\frac{2}{5}$

One way to approach this question is to turn 50 into:

$$49\frac{5}{5}$$

———

Now our problem becomes:

$$49\frac{5}{5} - 8\frac{2}{5}$$

Subtracting the whole number portions gives us 41. Subtracting $\frac{2}{5}$ from $\frac{5}{5}$ leaves us with $\frac{3}{5}$ for the fractional portion of our answer. If we combine these two, we get a final answer of $41\frac{3}{5}$. Answer choice B is correct.

Here is another one to try:

12. $40 - 6\frac{2}{9} =$

    (A) $33\frac{2}{9}$

    (B) $33\frac{7}{9}$

    (C) $34\frac{2}{9}$

    (D) $34\frac{7}{9}$

    (E) $46\frac{2}{9}$

First we have to borrow from the 40, then we can subtract. Here is what the math looks like:

$$40 - 6\frac{2}{9} = 39\frac{9}{9} - 6\frac{2}{9} = 33\frac{7}{9}$$

The correct answer is B.

There may also be questions that test multiplication with fractions. To multiply fractions, we simply multiply across the top and across the bottom.

For example:

$$\frac{1}{2} \times \frac{2}{3} = \frac{2}{6}$$

We then have to simplify the fraction, since both the numerator and the denominator can be divided by 2. We use our rule of equivalent fractions (do the same to the top and bottom).

$$\frac{2 \div 2}{6 \div 2} = \frac{1}{3}$$

Our final answer is $\frac{1}{3}$.

When multiplying fractions, we need to remember that we do NOT find a common denominator. We just multiply across the top and across the bottom. We also need to remember that the word "of" indicates multiplication. Finally, if you have to multiply several fractions, first see if you can cross-cancel to make the math easier.

- Do NOT find a common denominator for multiplying fractions
- The word "of" tells you to multiply
- See if you can cross-cancel

Here are a couple of problems for you to try:

13. Evaluate: $\frac{5}{6} \times \frac{6}{7} \times \frac{7}{8}$

(A) $\frac{1}{2}$

(B) $\frac{5}{8}$

(C) $\frac{18}{21}$

(D) $\frac{35}{21}$

(E) $\frac{8}{5}$

In order to answer this question, we could multiply out and then reduce the answer. However, that is a lot of work with no calculator! Instead, we will cross-cancel. We can cancel the 6's and the 7's. This leaves us with:

$$\frac{5}{\cancel{6}} \times \frac{\cancel{6}}{\cancel{7}} \times \frac{\cancel{7}}{8} = \frac{5}{1} \times \frac{1}{1} \times \frac{1}{8} = \frac{5}{8}$$

Answer choice B is correct.

14. $\frac{3}{5}$ of $\frac{2}{3}$ is equal to which fraction?

(A) $\frac{6}{5}$

(B) 1

(C) $\frac{4}{5}$

(D) $\frac{3}{5}$

(E) $\frac{2}{5}$

To answer this question, we need to remember that the word "of" tells us to multiply. This means that our problem is really:

$$\frac{3}{5} \times \frac{2}{3}$$

Now we cross-cancel the 3's and are left with:

$$\frac{1}{5} \times \frac{2}{1} = \frac{2}{5}$$

Answer choice E is correct.

The next problem type is multiplying a whole number and a fraction.

Here is an example:

$$6 \times \frac{2}{3}$$

The key is to make the whole number into a fraction. The way we do this is just to put the whole number over 1, since that does not change the value of the whole number.

Now the problem looks like this:

$$\frac{6}{1} \times \frac{2}{3}$$

It is now a basic fraction multiplication problem. But before you multiply, notice that you can cross-cancel. The 6 on top and the 3 on the bottom both can be evenly divided by 3, and so the cancellation would look like this:

$$\frac{\overset{2}{\cancel{6}}}{1} \times \frac{2}{\underset{1}{\cancel{3}}} = \frac{4}{1} = 4$$

Here's a problem for you to try:

$$3 \times \frac{11}{15} =$$

15. Which of the following is equal to the above calculation?

(A) $2\frac{1}{5}$

(B) $2\frac{3}{5}$

(C) $2\frac{11}{15}$

(D) $3\frac{1}{5}$

(E) $3\frac{11}{15}$

In order to solve, we have to first put the 3 over 1 so that we are multiplying two fractions. Then we use cross-cancelling, since we don't have a calculator and want to keep the numbers smaller. We are left with an improper fraction, so we have to convert that into a mixed number. The math looks like this:

$$3 \times \frac{11}{15} = \frac{\overset{1}{\cancel{3}}}{1} \times \frac{11}{\underset{5}{\cancel{15}}} = \frac{11}{5} = \frac{5}{5} + \frac{5}{5} + \frac{1}{5} = 2\frac{1}{5}$$

The correct answer is A.

On the SSAT, you might see a problem like the following:

16. All of the following calculations have the same result EXCEPT

   (A) $1 \times \dfrac{1}{5}$

   (B) $2 \times \dfrac{1}{10}$

   (C) $3 \times \dfrac{2}{15}$

   (D) $4 \times \dfrac{1}{20}$

   (E) $5 \times \dfrac{2}{50}$

In order to answer this question, we can use cross-cancelling. If we cross-cancel (and reduce, for answer choice E), then we can see that all of the answer choices are equal to $1 \times \dfrac{1}{5}$ except for choice C. Since this is an EXCEPT question, choice C is the correct answer.

Here is one for you to try on your own:

17. All of the following calculations have the same result EXCEPT

   (A) $1 \times \dfrac{1}{3}$

   (B) $2 \times \dfrac{1}{6}$

   (C) $3 \times \dfrac{1}{9}$

   (D) $4 \times \dfrac{1}{12}$

   (E) $6 \times \dfrac{1}{24}$

In order to solve this one, we just use cross-cancelling. If we do this, we get that all of the answer choices are equal to $1 \times \dfrac{1}{3}$ except for choice E, so choice E is the correct answer.

The way that the SSAT tests division of fractions is pretty straightforward.

Here is how division with fractions is tested on the SSAT:

18. $\dfrac{1}{5} \div \dfrac{1}{5} =$

    (A) 0

    (B) $\dfrac{1}{10}$

    (C) $\dfrac{2}{10}$

    (D) 1

    (E) 10

In order to solve this problem, we just flip the second fraction and multiply. It would look like this:

$$\frac{1}{5} \div \frac{1}{5} = \frac{1}{5} \times \frac{5}{1} = \frac{5}{5} = 1$$

Choice D is correct.

Other problems ask you to perform multiple operations.

Here is an example:

19. Sarah has the following problem:

$$\frac{1}{3} \triangle \frac{1}{5}$$

She should replace the $\triangle$ with which of the following operations if she wants the result to be as small as possible?

    (A) ÷

    (B) ×

    (C) +

    (D) –

    (E) the result would be the same for each of the operations

In order to answer this question, we have to do each of the operations.

We can make a list:

(A) $\dfrac{1}{3} \div \dfrac{1}{5} = \dfrac{1}{3} \times \dfrac{5}{1} = \dfrac{5}{3}$

(B) $\dfrac{1}{3} \times \dfrac{1}{5} = \dfrac{1}{15}$

(C) $\dfrac{1}{3} + \dfrac{1}{5} = \dfrac{5}{15} + \dfrac{3}{15} = \dfrac{8}{15}$

(D) $\dfrac{1}{3} - \dfrac{1}{5} = \dfrac{5}{15} - \dfrac{3}{15} = \dfrac{2}{15}$

(E) the result would be the same for each of the operations – this answer choice is definitely out since we can see that the answers are not the same for each operation

We can clearly see that multiplying gives us the smallest number, so choice B is correct.

Word Problems with Fractions

You may see several word problems with fractions on the SSAT. There are a few common forms of these types of problems, which we will now go through.

The first problem type will tell you what a fraction of something is equal to then ask you to find another amount. For example, they might tell you that $\dfrac{2}{7}$ of a jug holds 3 cups and then ask you how much liquid there would be if the jug was $\dfrac{4}{7}$ full.

The trick to these questions is not to find the full amount and then try to convert back into the desired fraction. Instead, think about what the first fraction must be multiplied by in order to get the second fraction.

- Think about what you have to multiply the first fraction by in order to get the second fraction

Here is what this type of question could look like on the SSAT:

20. If $\dfrac{3}{7}$ of a number is 60, then what is $\dfrac{6}{7}$ of that same number?
(A) 180
(B) 120
(C) 90
(D) 30
(E) 15

To solve this problem, just think about what you have to multiply $\frac{3}{7}$ by in order to get $\frac{6}{7}$. We would have to multiply by 2. So we multiply 60 by 2 and get 120, or answer choice B.

Here is another one to try that requires you to convert from one fraction to another:

21. If $\frac{1}{3}$ of a can of soda contains 12 grams of sugar, then how many grams of sugar are there in the full can of soda?

    (A) 4

    (B) 6

    (C) 12

    (D) 24

    (E) 36

In order to solve this problem, think about what you would have to multiply $\frac{1}{3}$ by in order to get a whole. We have to multiply $\frac{1}{3}$ by 3 in order to get 1. Since we multiplied the fraction by 3, we also multiply the grams of sugar by 3 to get 36. Choice E is correct.

Harder still is when we have to break apart a fraction to find the missing piece.

Here is an example:

22. Charles poured 4 cups into a pitcher and found that it was $\frac{2}{3}$ full. How many cups does the pitcher hold when it is full?

    (A) 2

    (B) 3

    (C) 4

    (D) 6

    (E) 8

For this problem, we have to figure out what fraction needs to be added to make the pitcher full. Since it is $\frac{2}{3}$ full now, another $\frac{1}{3}$ needs to be added. $\frac{1}{3}$ is half of $\frac{2}{3}$, so 2 cups would equal $\frac{1}{3}$ of the pitcher. If we add 2 cups to the 4 cups that were already in the pitcher, it would be full, so the whole pitcher holds 6 cups. Answer choice D is correct.

Here is another one for you to try:

23. A bottle that is $\dfrac{3}{4}$ full contains 15 cups of juice. If the bottle was full, how many cups of juice would it hold?

(A) 10
(B) 12
(C) 15
(D) 18
(E) 20

In order to solve this problem, we have to think about what fraction of the bottle needs to be added in order to make it full. Since it is $\dfrac{3}{4}$ full, we would need to add $\dfrac{1}{4}$ of the bottle in order to make it full. If three parts out of 4 is equal to 15, we divide 15 by 3 to get that one part out of 4, or $\dfrac{1}{4}$, would be equal to 5. We need to add 5 cups of juice in order to fill the pitcher. That means that the whole pitcher could hold 20 cups, and answer choice E is correct.

Another type of word problem requires you to really understand what happens when we convert between mixed numbers and improper fractions.

A mixed number is simply a number that has a whole number part and a fractional part. Here is an example:

$$3\dfrac{1}{5}$$

An improper fraction is just a fraction where the top number (numerator) is bigger than the bottom number (denominator).

One way to convert from a mixed number to an improper fraction is to break the mixed number down into ones and then convert those ones into fractions.

Here is how it would look with our previous example:

$$3\dfrac{1}{5} = 1+1+1+\dfrac{1}{5} = \dfrac{5}{5}+\dfrac{5}{5}+\dfrac{5}{5}+\dfrac{1}{5} = \dfrac{16}{5}$$

This tells us that:

$$3\dfrac{1}{5} = \dfrac{16}{5}$$

On the SSAT, they don't just come out and ask you to convert between the two, however. Here is what a question might look like that tests this skill:

24. How many sixths are there in $3\frac{1}{6}$?

    (A) 1

    (B) 6

    (C) 12

    (D) 18

    (E) 19

To figure out how many total sixths we have in that mixed number, we must rewrite the number in terms of sixths. This means converting it into an improper fraction.

It would look like this:

$$3\frac{1}{6} = 1+1+1+\frac{1}{6} = \frac{6}{6}+\frac{6}{6}+\frac{6}{6}+\frac{1}{6} = \frac{19}{6}$$

This tells us that there are 19 sixths in $3\frac{1}{6}$, so answer choice E is correct.

Here is another one for you to try:

25. How many fourths are there in $2\frac{3}{4}$?

    (A) 12

    (B) 11

    (C) 8

    (D) 3

    (E) 2

First, let's convert that mixed number into an improper fraction:

$$2\frac{3}{4} = 1+1+\frac{3}{4} = \frac{4}{4}+\frac{4}{4}+\frac{3}{4} = \frac{11}{4}$$

This tells us that there are 11 fourths in $2\frac{3}{4}$, so answer choice B is correct.

You may also be given a problem that gives you a real-life situation and asks you to come up with a fractional part. These questions are pretty straightforward, so we will just do a couple of sample problems.

Questions 26-27 are based on the following two classes.

There are 18 girls in Ms. Johnson's class, and there are 12 girls in Mr. Hewitt's class. There are a total of 32 boys in both classes.

26. What fractional part of the students in the two classes are girls?

(A) $\dfrac{1}{2}$

(B) $\dfrac{30}{32}$

(C) $\dfrac{2}{5}$

(D) $\dfrac{16}{33}$

(E) $\dfrac{15}{31}$

There are a total of 62 students if we add the number of boys and the number of girls together. Since 30 of these students are girls, the fractional part that is girls is $\dfrac{30}{62}$. If we divide the numerator and denominator by 2, we can see that $\dfrac{30}{62} = \dfrac{15}{31}$. Answer choice E is correct.

27. What fractional part of the students in the two classes is boys?

(A) $\dfrac{16}{31}$

(B) $\dfrac{32}{30}$

(C) $\dfrac{1}{2}$

(D) $\dfrac{15}{16}$

(E) $\dfrac{30}{62}$

There are 32 boys out of a total of 62 students. This gives us a fractional part of $\dfrac{32}{62}$, which can be simplified to $\dfrac{16}{31}$. Answer choice A is correct.

You may also see word problems that ask you to apply the basic operations in order to solve.

Here are a couple of examples:

28. Marty ate $\dfrac{1}{6}$ of a pizza and Sharon ate $\dfrac{1}{5}$ of a pizza. Together, what fractional part of a pizza did they eat?

(A) $\dfrac{11}{30}$

(B) $\dfrac{1}{30}$

(C) $\dfrac{1}{11}$

(D) $\dfrac{3}{7}$

(E) $\dfrac{1}{3}$

In order to answer this question, we must add together the $\dfrac{1}{6}$ that Marty ate and the $\dfrac{1}{5}$ that Sharon ate. Our problem is therefore $\dfrac{1}{6}+\dfrac{1}{5}=\dfrac{5}{30}+\dfrac{6}{30}=\dfrac{11}{30}$. Answer choice A is correct.

29. Rob had a rope that was 12 inches long. He cut off $2\frac{3}{4}$ inches from the rope. How many inches remained?

(A) 8

(B) $8\frac{1}{4}$

(C) $8\frac{3}{4}$

(D) $9\frac{1}{4}$

(E) $9\frac{3}{4}$

To answer this question, we need to subtract $2\frac{3}{4}$ from 12, which gives us the problem:

$$12 - 2\frac{3}{4}$$

We can use our trick of borrowing a 1 from the 12 to create an improper fraction.

$$11\frac{4}{4} - 2\frac{3}{4} = 9\frac{1}{4}$$

Answer choice D is correct.

Comparing Fractions

Some questions will ask you to compare fractions on the SSAT.

In order to do this, you need to get a common denominator to compare the answer choices to the fraction in the question. Rather than looking for a denominator that all of the answer choices go into, I recommend setting up a different equivalent fraction to compare to each answer choice. These equivalent fractions should have the same denominator as the answer choice so that they can be easily compared.

- Set up an equivalent fraction for each answer choice

Take a look at this example:

30. Which of the following fractions is less than $\frac{1}{4}$?

    (A) $\frac{10}{40}$

    (B) $\frac{4}{3}$

    (C) $\frac{5}{16}$

    (D) $\frac{3}{20}$

    (E) $\frac{7}{24}$

To solve, just make a chart:

Answer choice	Equal to $\frac{1}{4}$	Which is smaller?
(A) $\frac{10}{40}$	$\frac{10}{40}$	Equal
(B) $\frac{4}{8}$	$\frac{2}{8}$	$\frac{1}{4}$
(C) $\frac{5}{16}$	$\frac{4}{16}$	$\frac{1}{4}$
(D) $\frac{3}{20}$	$\frac{5}{20}$	Answer choice!
(E) $\frac{7}{24}$	$\frac{6}{24}$	$\frac{1}{4}$

From the chart, we can see that only choice D is smaller than $\frac{1}{4}$, so choice D is correct.

_____

Here is another one for you to try:

31. Which of the following fractions is greater than $\frac{2}{3}$?

(A) $\frac{8}{12}$

(B) $\frac{7}{14}$

(C) $\frac{7}{9}$

(D) $\frac{11}{18}$

(E) $\frac{1}{6}$

Again, let's create our chart.

Answer choice	Equal to $\frac{2}{3}$	Which is greater?
(A) $\frac{8}{12}$	$\frac{8}{12}$	Equal
(B) $\frac{7}{14}$	14 isn't divisible by 3, so equivalent fractions won't work. But I can see that $\frac{7}{14}$ is equal to one-half, so I know it has to be less than $\frac{2}{3}$.	$\frac{2}{3}$
(C) $\frac{7}{9}$	$\frac{6}{9}$	Answer choice!
(D) $\frac{11}{18}$	$\frac{12}{18}$	$\frac{2}{3}$
(E) $\frac{1}{6}$	$\frac{4}{6}$	$\frac{2}{3}$

We can see that answer choice C is correct.

Now you know how to do well on fraction problems on the SSAT! Be sure to complete the fraction practice set to reinforce your learning.

Fractions Practice Set

1. The figure below shows a rectangle. If Q is the midpoint of side PR, then what fraction of the rectangle is shaded?

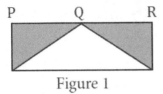

Figure 1

(A) $\dfrac{1}{6}$

(B) $\dfrac{1}{5}$

(C) $\dfrac{1}{4}$

(D) $\dfrac{1}{3}$

(E) $\dfrac{1}{2}$

2. $\dfrac{2}{5} \div \dfrac{2}{5} =$

(A) 0

(B) $\dfrac{4}{10}$

(C) $\dfrac{4}{5}$

(D) 1

(E) 4

3. $16\left(\dfrac{12}{16} - \dfrac{3}{4}\right) =$

(A) 0

(B) $\dfrac{1}{16}$

(C) 1

(D) 15

(E) 16

4. If $\dfrac{3}{7}$ of a number equals 15, then what is $\dfrac{6}{7}$ of that same number equal to?

    (A) 45
    (B) 30
    (C) 15
    (D) 7.5
    (E) 5

5. A jar contains 2 cups of sauce. If it is currently $\dfrac{2}{3}$ full, then how many cups can the jar hold when it is completely full?

    (A) 1
    (B) 2
    (C) 3
    (D) 5
    (E) 6

6. If a type of pudding has 200 calories in a $\dfrac{1}{3}$ cup serving, then how many calories are there in 1-cup serving?

    (A) 100
    (B) 150
    (C) 200
    (D) 400
    (E) 600

7. Which of the following is less than $\dfrac{2}{3}$?

    (A) $\dfrac{6}{9}$

    (B) $\dfrac{11}{15}$

    (C) $\dfrac{8}{16}$

    (D) $\dfrac{13}{18}$

    (E) $\dfrac{15}{21}$

8. How many fifths are there in $4\frac{2}{5}$?

   (A) 22
   (B) 20
   (C) 5
   (D) 4
   (E) 2

9. If $\frac{4}{\Delta} = \frac{20}{30}$, then what is the value of Δ?

   (A) 5
   (B) 6
   (C) 10
   (D) 12
   (E) 15

10. $\frac{3+4+5}{4+5+6} =$

   (A) $\frac{1}{3}$

   (B) $\frac{1}{2}$

   (C) $\frac{3}{4}$

   (D) $\frac{4}{5}$

   (E) $\frac{9}{10}$

11. $4\frac{1}{3} + 5\frac{3}{5} =$

   (A) $8\frac{14}{15}$

   (B) $9\frac{1}{2}$

   (C) $9\frac{3}{5}$

   (D) $9\frac{14}{15}$

   (E) $10\frac{1}{15}$

12. $\dfrac{1}{2} \times \dfrac{2}{6} \times \dfrac{3}{8} \times \dfrac{8}{9}$

Which of the following is equal to the above calculation?

(A) $\dfrac{1}{72}$

(B) $\dfrac{1}{18}$

(C) $\dfrac{2}{9}$

(D) $\dfrac{1}{3}$

(E) $\dfrac{2}{3}$

13. $35 - 6\dfrac{11}{12} =$

(A) $27\dfrac{1}{12}$

(B) $27\dfrac{11}{12}$

(C) $28\dfrac{1}{12}$

(D) $28\dfrac{11}{12}$

(E) $29\dfrac{11}{12}$

14. Which fraction is equal to $\dfrac{2}{3}$ of $\dfrac{1}{2}$?

(A) $\dfrac{1}{3}$

(B) $\dfrac{1}{4}$

(C) $\dfrac{1}{5}$

(D) $\dfrac{2}{5}$

(E) $\dfrac{3}{5}$

15. Which of the following is equal to $4 \times \dfrac{5}{12}$?

    (A) $\dfrac{1}{3}$

    (B) $\dfrac{2}{3}$

    (C) $\dfrac{3}{4}$

    (D) $1\dfrac{1}{3}$

    (E) $1\dfrac{2}{3}$

16. A recipe for bread calls for using $6\dfrac{1}{2}$ cups of flour. Janelle wishes to make a smaller amount, so she will use only half the recommended amount of each ingredient. How much flour should she use?

    (A) 3 cups

    (B) $3\dfrac{1}{4}$ cups

    (C) $3\dfrac{1}{2}$ cups

    (D) $3\dfrac{3}{4}$ cups

    (E) 13 cups

17. A bottle of juice contained 16 ounces of juice. Sandra poured $4\dfrac{1}{3}$ ounces of juice into a glass. How many ounces of juice remained in the bottle?

    (A) $10\dfrac{1}{3}$

    (B) $11\dfrac{1}{3}$

    (C) $11\dfrac{2}{3}$

    (D) $12\dfrac{1}{3}$

    (E) $12\dfrac{2}{3}$

18. All of the following have the same product EXCEPT

(A) $2 \times \dfrac{5}{2}$

(B) $3 \times \dfrac{3}{5}$

(C) $4 \times \dfrac{10}{8}$

(D) $6 \times \dfrac{5}{6}$

(E) $1 \times \dfrac{15}{3}$

Fractions answer key

1. E
2. D
3. A
4. B
5. C
6. E
7. C
8. A
9. B
10. D
11. D
12. B
13. C
14. A
15. E
16. B
17. C
18. B

Percent Problems

Percent problems are really just glorified fraction problems where the denominator is 100.

On the Middle Level SSAT you will have to:

1. Find a percent of a number
2. Use a percent to find a quantity
3. Given a percentage of a number, find a different percentage of the same number
4. Percent increase or decrease

Keep in mind that *per* means "out of " and *cent* means "hundred."

Therefore, *percent* means "out of a hundred."

Find a Percent of a Number

The easiest way to solve percent problems is to use equivalent fractions and cross-multiplying.

Here is the basic setup:

$$\frac{\text{part}}{\text{whole}} = \frac{\text{percent}}{100}$$

For example, let's say that we want to find 20% of 50.

First, we set up the equivalent fraction and plug in what we have been given.

$$\frac{x}{50} = \frac{20}{100}$$

Now we use the principles of equivalent fractions to solve. To get from 50 to 100, we have to multiply by 2. So what number do we have to multiply by 2 in order to get 20? We have to multiply 10 by 2 in order to get 20, so $x = 10$, and 20% of 50 is 10.

Here is a question for you to try:

1. If there are 25 students in a class, but only 15 of them are in the school band, then what percent of the students are in the school band?

    (A) 4%
    (B) 25%
    (C) 50%
    (D) 60%
    (E) 75%

In order to solve this problem, we have to set up a basic equivalent fraction problem:

$$\frac{15}{25} = \frac{x}{100}$$

To get from 25 to 100, we have to multiply the denominator by 4. That means that we also have to multiply the numerator by 4. $15 \times 4 = 60$, so answer choice D is correct.

Here is another problem to try:

2. There are ten fish in an aquarium. If three of the fish are green, what percent of the fish are NOT green?

    (A) 30%
    (B) 40%
    (C) 50%
    (D) 60%
    (E) 70%

The only trick to this question is that the test writers tell you how many fish are green but then ask for the percent of fish that are NOT green. If three fish are green, then seven fish are not green. We can set up a basic equivalent fraction:

$$\frac{7}{10} = \frac{x}{100}$$

To get from 10 to 100, we had to multiply the denominator by 10. That means we also have to multiply the numerator by 10, so we get that 70% of the fish were not green. Answer choice E is correct.

Here is another problem to try:

3. If there are 50 students on a bus and they are all in the fifth grade, what percent of students on the bus are fifth graders?

    (A) 5%
    (B) 25%
    (C) 50%
    (D) 100%
    (E) 110%

    This is kind of a tricky question. We don't actually have to do any calculating! If all of the students on the bus are in fifth grade, then 100% of the students on the bus are fifth graders. Answer choice D is correct.

Another type of problem uses the fact that if we break an item into various components by percent, then those percents must add to 100.

*   The percents must add to 100 if we divide an item into components

Here are a couple of examples:

4. A certain rental company rents out cars, vans, and trucks only. If 12% of its rentals are vans and 21% of its rentals are trucks, what percent of its rentals must be cars?

    (A) 33%
    (B) 50%
    (C) 60%
    (D) 66%
    (E) 67%

    If we add together the percent of van and truck rentals, we can see that vans and trucks make up 33% of rentals. Since the percents must add to 100, we can subtract 33 from 100 and get that 67% of the rentals must be cars. Answer choice E is correct.

5. A solution is composed of 29.4% calcium, 23.5% sulfur, and the rest is water. What percent of the solution is water?

    (A) 52.9%
    (B) 51.9%
    (C) 47.1%
    (D) 46.1%
    (E) 45.9%

    Again, we add together the percents given. Since 29.4 + 23.5 = 52.9, we know that 52.9% of the solution is NOT water. If we subtract this from 100, we get that 47.1% of the solution is water. Answer choice C is correct.

Use a Percent to Find a Quantity

Some questions will ask you to use a percent to find an actual quantity.

We can use the same basic equation:

$$\frac{\text{part}}{\text{whole}} = \frac{\text{percent}}{100}$$

The most basic of this type of question is really just testing whether or not you understand what a percent represents.

Here is an example:

6. The price of a lamp was reduced by 30%. The new price was $30 less than the original price. What was the original price?

    (A) $1

    (B) $10

    (C) $100

    (D) $1,000

    (E) cannot be determined from information given

This question is relatively easy. We just need to rewrite it as equivalent fractions.

$$\frac{\text{part}}{\text{whole}} = \frac{\text{percent}}{100}$$

$$\frac{30}{\text{whole}} = \frac{30}{100}$$

This makes it easy to see that the starting price must have been $100 and answer choice C is correct.

Other questions will ask you to solve for a part or a whole given a percent. Just remember to return to our basic equation.

- If you see the word "percent" or the % symbol, remember to use the equation $\frac{\text{part}}{\text{whole}} = \frac{\text{percent}}{100}$, fill in the information given, and solve

Here are a couple of examples:

7. 12 is 48 percent of

    (A) 24

    (B) 25

    (C) 36

    (D) 48

    (E) 52

In order to answer this question, we use our basic formula:

$$\frac{\text{part}}{\text{whole}} = \frac{\text{percent}}{100}$$

$$\frac{12}{\text{whole}} = \frac{48}{100}$$

We can see that to get from 48 to 12, we divide by 4. This means to get from 100 to the "whole" we also divide by 4. Since $100 \div 4 = 25$, answer choice B is correct.

8. Forty percent of 20 is

   (A) 8
   (B) 20
   (C) 25
   (D) 40
   (E) 80

We will use the same equation, only plugging in for the whole this time and solving for the part.

$$\frac{\text{part}}{\text{whole}} = \frac{\text{percent}}{100}$$

$$\frac{\text{part}}{20} = \frac{40}{100}$$

To get from 100 to 20, we must divide by 5. This means we also divide by 5 to get from 40 to the "part." Since $40 \div 5 = 8$, answer choice A is correct.

You may also see word problems that ask you to use the rules of percents to find a quantity.

The most basic type of problem gives you a total number, a percent, and asks you what quantity that percent would represent.

Here is an example:

9. There are 600 students in a school. Of these students, 67% have a sibling. How many students in the school have a sibling?

   (A) 67
   (B) 267
   (C) 350
   (D) 384
   (E) 402

We can use the basic equation for percents to answer this question.

$$\frac{x}{600} = \frac{67}{100}$$

Since 100 multiplied by 6 is 600, we must also multiply 67 by 6. One way to do this is to use place value.

$$6 \times 67 = 6 \times (60 + 7)$$

Now we can use the distributive property.

$$6 \times (60 + 7) = (6 \times 60) + (6 \times 7) = 360 + 42 = 402$$

Answer choice E is correct.

Trickier is when we are given a percent and the actual quantity it represents and then are asked to find a different quantity. These are hard, so we will do a couple of these.

10. There are 40 red candies in a bowl, which represents 20% of the candies in the bowl. There are also 60 green candies in the dish, which represents 30% of the candies. If the rest of the candies are blue, how many blue candies are in the bowl?

    (A) 50
    (B) 75
    (C) 100
    (D) 125
    (E) 150

One way to solve is to use our percents equation to figure out a total.

$$\frac{40}{\text{total}} = \frac{20}{100}$$

Since we have to multiply 20 by 2 to get 40, we multiply 100 by 2 and can see that there are a total of 200 candies. Since there are 40 red candies, 60 green candies, and the rest of the 200 candies must be blue, there must be 100 blue candies. Answer choice C is correct.

11. 32% of the students (8 students) walked to school today. 56% of the students (14 students) rode the bus. The remainder of the students was driven in a car. How many students were driven in a car?

    (A) 3
    (B) 8
    (C) 12
    (D) 24
    (E) 36

Let's use the number of students who walked to school to figure out how many total students there are.

$$\frac{8 \text{ students}}{\text{total}} = \frac{32}{100}$$

Since we divide 32 by 4 to get 8, we should divide 100 by 4 to get the total number of students. Since $100 \div 4 = 25$, there are 25 total students. Now we can just subtract the students who walked and the students who rode the bus.

$$25 - 8 - 14 = 3$$

There were only 3 students remaining, so 3 students must have been driven in a car, and answer choice A is correct.

There are also some percent questions that deal with money, such as finding a discount. For questions that ask you to figure out a discount, be sure to circle what the question asks for – some questions ask for the amount of the reduction while others asks for the new price.

- For percent discount questions, circle whether the question asks for the discount or the new price

These questions also frequently use the language "about" or "closest to", which means that we can round off.

- If you see "about" or "closest to," remember to round off

Here are a couple of questions to try:

12. A store is having a sale that is 20% off of all purchases. If an item normally costs $24.95, which is closest to its price after the discount?

    (A) $5.00
    (B) $15.00
    (C) $20.00
    (D) $25.00
    (E) $30.00

Since the question asks "which is closest to," we can round off $24.95 to $25.00. Now we can set up our equation.

$$\frac{\text{discount}}{25} = \frac{20}{100}$$

In order to get from 100 to 25, we divide by 4. If we divide 20 by 4, we get that the price was reduced by $5. We aren't done yet, though, since the question asks for the new price and not the discount. The item originally cost about $25 and there was a $5 reduction in price, so the new price is closest to $20.00 and answer choice C is correct.

13. A sweater costs $39.95. The store is having a sale that offers a 25% discount on this item. The discount on the sweater is about what dollar amount?

(A) $2.50
(B) $5.00
(C) $7.50
(D) $10.00
(E) $12.50

Let's set up our equation, remembering to round off $39.95 to $40 since the question uses the word "about."

$$\frac{\text{discount}}{40} = \frac{25}{100}$$

This one is a little trickier because we can't divide 100 by a whole number and get 40. However, we can reduce the fraction on the right.

$$\frac{25 \div 25}{100 \div 25} = \frac{1}{4}$$

Now we can substitute in $\frac{1}{4}$ for $\frac{25}{100}$.

$$\frac{\text{discount}}{40} = \frac{1}{4}$$

Since $4 \times 10 = 40$, we can see that the discount is 1×10, or $10. Answer choice D is correct.

Given a Percentage of a Number, Find a Different Percentage of the Same Number

This problem type should look very familiar to you. It is just like the problem type we covered in the fractions section where they give you one fraction of a number and ask for another fraction of the same number. There is a reason they are so similar – a percentage is just another way to write a fraction!

- These problems are just like the questions that give you one fraction of a number and ask for a different fraction

We will use the same basic technique. Rather than solving for the original number, we will just figure out what they multiplied the original percent by to get the new percent.

- Don't find the original number

Here is an example:

14. If 20% of a number is 15, then what is 40% of the same number?

   (A) 3
   (B) 6
   (C) 15
   (D) 30
   (E) 60

To answer this question, let's think about how we get from 20% to 40%. We multiply by 2, right? So that means we can just multiply 15 by 2 to get 40% of the same number. The correct answer is choice D.

Here is another one for you to try:

15. If 30% of a number is 25, then what is 90% of the same number?

   (A) 75
   (B) 50
   (C) 25
   (D) 10
   (E) 5

Let's think about how we get from 30% to 90%. We multiply by 3. That means that we can just multiply 25 by 3 to get what 90% of that same number would be. Choice A is correct.

Percent Increase or Decrease

You may see a question that asks you to find a percent increase or decrease. Here is the basic formula:

$$\text{percent change} = \frac{\text{positive difference between initial and final quantities}}{\text{initial quantity}} \times 100$$

If we break this into two equations, they are:

$$\text{percent increase} = \frac{\text{final quantity} - \text{initial quantity}}{\text{initial quantity}} \times 100$$

$$\text{percent decrease} = \frac{\text{initial quantity} - \text{final quantity}}{\text{initial quantity}} \times 100$$

For example, let's say there are 10 cars in a parking lot. Five more cars pull into the lot. The number of cars has increased by $\frac{15-10}{10} \times 100 = 50\%$.

Here are a couple of questions to try:

16. At 5 PM, there were 50 people in a restaurant. At 6 PM, there were 75 people in a restaurant. By what percent did the number of people in the restaurant increase between 5 PM and 6 PM?

   (A) 25%

   (B) 50%

   (C) $66\frac{2}{3}$%

   (D) 75%

   (E) $82\frac{1}{2}$%

We can use our basic equation. The initial quantity was 50 and the final quantity was 75.

$$\frac{75-50}{50}\times100 = \frac{25}{50}\times100 = 50\%$$

Answer choice B is correct.

17. In a certain school district, the average class size was 25 students per class in 1990. In 2000, the average class size was 22 students per class. By what percent did the average class size decrease between 1990 and 2000?

   (A) 3%
   (B) 9%
   (C) 12%
   (D) 15%
   (E) 25%

We can use the same equation, only since it is percent decrease we will use initial quantity – final quantity.

$$\frac{25-22}{25}\times100 = \frac{3}{25}\times100 = 12\%$$

Answer choice C is correct.

Now you know what you need in order to ace percent problems! Be sure to complete the percent practice set.

Percent Practice Set

1. If 25% of a number is 16, then what is 50% of the same number?

   (A) 4
   (B) 8
   (C) 16
   (D) 24
   (E) 32

2. There are ten players on the tennis team. Four of these players only play doubles and the rest of the players only play singles. What percent of the players only play singles?

   (A) 100%
   (B) 60%
   (C) 50%
   (D) 40%
   (E) 10%

3. If all 30 kids in a class have returned their permission slips, what percent of the class has returned their permission slips?

   (A) 0%
   (B) 3%
   (C) 30%
   (D) 60%
   (E) 100%

4. If 15% of a certain number is 30, then 30% of the same number is

   (A) 7.5
   (B) 15
   (C) 30
   (D) 60
   (E) 90

5. In a class of 25 students, none of the students did their homework. What percent of the students did their homework?

   (A) 0%
   (B) 20%
   (C) 25%
   (D) 50%
   (E) 100%

6. A paint mixture is made up a blue, green, and yellow paint. If the mixture is 14.7% blue paint and 62.5% green paint, what percent of the mixture must be yellow paint?

   (A) 21.8%
   (B) 22.2%
   (C) 22.8%
   (D) 23.2%
   (E) 77.2%

7. 36 is 20% of

   (A) 7.2
   (B) 18
   (C) 72
   (D) 180
   (E) 360

8. The price of a shirt was reduced by 10%. If the price is now $5 less than the original price, what was the original price of the shirt?

   (A) $100
   (B) $90
   (C) $50
   (D) $40
   (E) $25

9. Sixty percent of 90 is

   (A) 54
   (B) 60
   (C) 72
   (D) 90
   (E) 144

10. 40% of the orchestra students are in 5th grade and 56% of the orchestra students are in 4th grade. The remainder of the students in the orchestra are in 3rd grade. If there are twenty 5th graders in the orchestra, how many 3rd graders are there in the orchestra?

(A) 2

(B) 4

(C) 8

(D) 12

(E) 20

11. A store is having a sale that offers 30% off of all purchases. If a bag normally costs $39.95, its price after the discount is closest to

(A) $27

(B) $28

(C) $28.50

(D) $29

(E) $29.50

12. At the beginning of the school year, there were 20 students in a class. During the school year, 4 more students joined the class. By what percent did the number of students in the class increase?

(A) 15%

(B) 17%

(C) 18%

(D) 20%

(E) 24%

13. A gallon of milk normally costs $3.95. If the store is having a sale that is 15% off all milk, about what will the discount be?

(A) $4.60

(B) $4.00

(C) $3.40

(D) $0.80

(E) $0.60

Answers to Percent Practice Set

1. E
2. B
3. E
4. D
5. A
6. C
7. D
8. C
9. A
10. A
11. B
12. D
13. E

In the ratios section, we will cover:

- Creating equivalent ratios
- Using ratios to determine quantities

A fraction compares a part to the whole. For example, if I have four pieces of paper and one is red and three are green, then I would say that $\frac{1}{4}$ of my paper is red.

- Fractions compare a part to the whole

A ratio, on the other hand, compares one part to another part. For instance, in our above example, the ratio of red to green paper is 1 to 3. This can be written as 1 to 3, 1:3, or $\frac{1}{3}$.

- Ratios compare part to part

Creating Equivalent Ratios

In a lot of ways, we can treat ratios like fractions. If we multiply or divide one part of the ratio by a number, then as long as we multiply or divide the other part of the ratio by the same number the ratios are equivalent.

For example, the ratio of 1 to 3 is equal to the ratio of 3 to 9 since we multiplied both numbers by 3. Just like with equivalent fractions, it doesn't work if we add or subtract the same number.

- We can create equivalent ratios just like we create equivalent fractions

Here is an example of how this could be tested on the SSAT:

1. The ratio of 5 to 9 is equal to the ratio of

   (A) 25 to 81
   (B) 15 to 27
   (C) 10 to 27
   (D) 18 to 10
   (E) 9 to 5

Let's look at the answer choices. To get answer choice A, you would have had to square each number, which means you are not multiplying by the same number, so choice A is out. In choice B, you would have to multiply 5 by 3 to get 15. You would also have to multiply 9 by 3 to get 27. Since you are multiplying by the same number in both cases, answer choice B is correct.

Here is another question to try:

2. There are 48 students and 4 teachers on a fieldtrip. What is the ratio of students to teachers?

    (A) 12:1
    (B) 12:13
    (C) 24:1
    (D) 13:12
    (E) 1:12

With the quantities given, we can write the ratio of students to teachers as 48:4. The trick is that in order to get one of the answer choices, we need to simplify this ratio. If we divide both sides of the ratio by 4, we get an equivalent ratio of 12:1. Answer choice A is correct.

Using Ratios to Determine Quantities

In order to determine actual quantities, we can create equivalent ratios that use the quantity given. For example, let's say the ratio of boys to girls is 3:2 and there are 18 boys. We can set up a ratio that is equivalent to 3:2, substituting in 18 for 3. Since we have to multiply 3 by 6 to get 18, we must multiply 2 by 6 in order to figure out the number of girls. There are 12 girls, since 3:2 is equivalent to 18:12.

- To find actual quantities, set up equivalent ratios

Here are a couple of questions to try:

3. The ratio of red candies to blue candies is 2 to 3. If there are 8 red candies, how many blue candies are there?

    (A) 24
    (B) 18
    (C) 16
    (D) 12
    (E) 6

In order to solve, we need figure out what 2 had to be multiplied by in order to get 8. We had to multiply 2 by 4 to get 8, so we also have to multiply 3 by 4. That tells us that there would be 12 blue candies so choice D is correct.

4. The ratio of cars to trucks in a parking lot is 7:2. If there are 14 trucks in the parking lot, how many cars are there?

(A) 4

(B) 9

(C) 14

(D) 49

(E) 63

We can use equivalent ratios to solve. The trick is that we are given the actual quantity for the second part of the ratio, so we need to make sure we plug into the right place. The ratio of 7:2 must be equivalent to the ratio *# of cars*:14. Since we had to multiply the 2 by 7 in order to get 14, we must multiply 7 by 7 to get the number of cars. Since 7 × 7 = 49, answer choice D is correct.

Here is another example that is a little trickier:

5. The following figure shows a rectangular swimming pool.

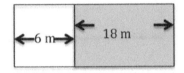

Figure 2

The shaded area is the deep end and the unshaded area is the shallow part. A rope separates the two sections. If the distance from one wall to the rope in the shallow end is 6m (as shown) and the distance from one wall to the rope in the deep end is 18 m (as shown), then what is the ratio of the shallow end to the deep end?

(A) $\frac{6}{24}$

(B) $\frac{1}{3}$

(C) $\frac{3}{1}$

(D) $\frac{3}{18}$

(E) $\frac{3}{4}$

To solve this problem, we have to keep in mind that a ratio is part to part and NOT part to whole. Since the shallow end is 6m and the deep end is 18m, the ratio of the shallow end to the deep end would be $\frac{6}{18}$. This is not an answer choice, however. But remember that just like fractions, ratios can be simplified. We can divide both the numerator and denominator by 6. This leaves us with $\frac{1}{3}$, or answer choice B.

Trickier is when we have ratio problems that ask us to use a total quantity to determine a part. The key here is to create a ratio that includes the total number of parts. For example, let's say we have a question where a salad dressing is 1 part vinegar to 2 parts oil and the question asks how much oil would be in 21 ounces of this salad dressing. We can create a ratio of vinegar:oil:total. We find the total by adding together the parts, so the total in this scenario is 3. Our ratio of vinegar:oil:total is 1:2:3. If there are 21 ounces total, 1:2:3 must be equivalent to vinegar:oil:21. Since we multiply 3 by 7 to get 21 total ounces, we also multiply the other parts of the ratio by 7 and get that there must 7 ounces of vinegar and 14 ounces of oil in 21 ounces of salad dressing.

- If we are given a total quantity, we need to create a ratio that is part:part:total

Here are a couple of questions to try:

6. For a particular brand of chocolate milk, the ratio of milk to chocolate syrup is 11:4. How many ounces of chocolate syrup are needed to make 60 ounces of this chocolate milk?

   (A) 4
   (B) 8
   (C) 15
   (D) 16
   (E) 44

   We can start by creating a ratio of milk:chocolate syrup:total parts, which is 11:4:15 in this case. We are given the total ounces (60), so we can plug in that value and create the ratio milk:chocolate syrup:60. Since we multiplied 15 by 4 to get 60, we should multiply 4 by 4 to get the number of ounces of chocolate syrup. Since $4 \times 4 = 16$, answer choice D is correct.

7. The ratio of girls to boys in a school is 6:5. If there are a total of 220 students in the school, how many boys are there?

   (A) 5
   (B) 6
   (C) 11
   (D) 100
   (E) 110

   We can first create a ratio that includes the total. The ratio of girls:boys:total is 6:5:11. There are 220 total students in the school, and we have to multiply 11 by 20 in order to get 220. Since we multiplied the total part of our ratio (11) by 20, we must also multiply the boy part of our ratio (5) by 20. Since $5 \times 20 = 100$, answer choice D is correct.

You may also see questions that describe a ratio and then ask you for a possible total. For example, the question may state that there are 4 boys for every 5 girls and then ask what could be the total number of children. We should create a ratio that includes a "total" piece again. In this case, the ratio of boys:girls:total is 4:5:9. The trick here is that the total number of children needs to be a multiple of 9, otherwise we would wind up with partial girls and boys. Not good!

- If the question asks for a possible total, create a part:part:total ratio and the total actual quantity must be a multiple of the total part of your ratio

Here are a couple of questions to try:

8. In bouquet of balloons the ratio of white to silver balloons needs to be 3:1. Which of the following could be the total number of balloons in the bouquet?

    (A) 8
    (B) 10
    (C) 21
    (D) 25
    (E) 30

    If we create a ratio that includes the total, we get white:silver:total must be 3:1:4. This means that the total number of balloons must be a multiple of 4. Since 8 is the only answer choice that is a multiple of 4, answer choice A is correct.

9. At a festival, twice as many snowcones were sold as corndogs. Which could be the total number of snowcones and corndogs sold at the festival?

    (A) 20
    (B) 25
    (C) 81
    (D) 100
    (E) 121

    This question does not use the word "ratio", but it is the same kind of problem and we just need to translate "twice as many" into a ratio of 2:1. If we create a ratio of snowcones:corndogs:total, it is 2:1:3. This means that the total number sold must be a multiple of 3. Since 81 is the only multiple of 3 among the answer choices, answer choice C is correct.

Now you know what you need to in order to ace ratio questions! Be sure to complete the practice set to reinforce what you have learned.

Ratios Practice Set

1. If there are 16 red flowers and 10 white flowers, what is the ratio of red to white flowers?

   (A) 5:8
   (B) 8:5
   (C) 10:16
   (D) 10:26
   (E) 16:26

2. The ratio 4 to 9 is equivalent to

   (A) 4 to 13
   (B) 9 to 4
   (C) 16 to 81
   (D) 20 to 36
   (E) 20 to 45

3. A punch is made by mixing lemon juice and apple juice in a ratio of 2 parts lemon juice to 7 parts apple juice. If there are a total of 36 ounces of this punch made, how much lemon juice is in the punch?

   (A) 2 ounces
   (B) 4 ounces
   (C) 6 ounces
   (D) 8 ounces
   (E) 10 ounces

4. The ratio of green to white balloons in an archway is 3:5. If there are 30 green balloons, how many white balloons are there?

   (A) 80
   (B) 50
   (C) 40
   (D) 30
   (E) 18

5. At a cookout, the ratio of hamburgers eaten to hot dogs eaten was 3:4. What could be the total number of hot dogs and hamburgers eaten?

   (A) 9
   (B) 16
   (C) 42
   (D) 48
   (E) 52

6. At an animal shelter, there are three times as many dogs as cats. What could be the total number of dogs and cats at the shelter?

    (A) 8
    (B) 9
    (C) 14
    (D) 18
    (E) 30

Answers to Ratios Practice Set

1. B
2. E
3. D
4. B
5. C
6. A

Decimals

In this section, we will cover the following question types:

- Using place value to determine the value of a decimal
- Performing operations with decimals
- Converting between decimals, fractions, and percents

Using Place Value to Determine the Value of a Decimal

Some questions on the SSAT may ask you to use place value to answer questions.

Keep in mind the following chart.

4	5	7	2	0	8	.	1	9	6	3	4
Hundred thousands	Ten thousands	Thousands	Hundreds	Tens	Ones	Decimal point	Tenths	Hundredths	Thousandths	Ten-thousandths	Hundred-thousandths

The first type of question asks you to use words to describe a decimal. The key is to remember that if the last word ends in "-ths" (tenths, hundredths, thousandths, ten-thousandths, etc), the last digit should fall in that place value.

Here are a couple of examples:

1. Which represents the decimal thirty-two thousand six hundred forty-one hundred thousandths?

   (A) 0.032641
   (B) 0.32641
   (C) 32.641
   (D) 3,264.1
   (E) 320,641

We can start by writing out the number without the decimal. This gives us 32,641. Now we have to remember that the last digit must fall in the hundred thousandths place. In order for this to happen, we must move the decimal five places to the left. We now have 0.32641. Answer choice B is correct.

2. Which choice correctly describes the decimal 0.0205?

   (A) two hundred five hundredths
   (B) two hundred five thousandths
   (C) two thousand five ten-thousandths
   (D) two thousand five hundred ten-thousandths
   (E) two hundred five ten-thousandths

   If we were to move the decimal to the right of the last digit, we would get two hundred five. Now if we move the decimal back to where it was before, we can see that the last digit falls in the ten-thousandths place. Therefore, the value of the decimal is two hundred five ten-thousandths. Answer choice E is correct.

You might also see questions that ask you which decimal has the greatest (or least) value. These are pretty straight-forward so we will just try a couple of questions.

3. Which number has the greatest value?

   (A) 2.0009
   (B) 2.0090
   (C) 2.0019
   (D) 2.0100
   (E) 2.0089

   If we look at the first digit (2), all of the answer choices have 2 in the same place value, so we can't use that to eliminate any choices. Now, if we look to the next place value (tenths), all of the choices have a zero, so we can't use that to eliminate any answer choices. However, if we look at the next place value, we can see that all of the choices except for choice D have zero hundredths. Choice D has one hundredth, which is more than zero, so choice D has the greatest value and is correct.

4. Choose the least of the numbers below.

   (A) 0.0007
   (B) 0.0107
   (C) 0.0017
   (D) 0.1007
   (E) 0.0170

   Let's use the same process for this question. If we look at the first place value to the left (units), all of the choices have zero so we cannot use this to rule anything out. Now if we look at the tenths place, answer choice D has one tenth, but the other choices have zero tenths, so choice D is greater than the other choices and can be eliminated. Now we go to the next place (hundredths). Answer choices B and E have a one in that place, so they have a greater value than choices A and C and can be ruled out. We are down to choices A and C. Since choice C has one thousandth but choice A has zero thousandths, choice A has a lesser value and is the correct answer choice.

You may also see questions that ask you to round. When we round to a certain place, we look at the number to the right of that place value. For example, if we round to the nearest hundredth, we look at the thousandths place. If the digit in the thousandths place is 5 or greater, we round up the hundredths place. If it is less than five, then the hundredths place remains unchanged.

- To round to a certain place value, look to the digit to the right of that place value

Here are a couple of examples for you to try:

5. Round 56.31873 to the nearest hundredth.

    (A) 56.3
    (B) 56.31
    (C) 56.32
    (D) 56. 319
    (E) 56.3187

In the number given, the digit "1" is in the hundredths place. If we look to the right of this digit, there is an "8" in the thousandths place. Since this is 5 or greater, we will round up the hundredths place and the number becomes 56.32. Answer choice C is correct.

6. Which numbers will be equal if they are rounded to the nearest thousandth?

    (A) 4.3582 and 4.3584
    (B) 3.6293 and 3.6295
    (C) 7.0001 and 7.0007
    (D) 3.2989 and 3.2919
    (E) 8.0265 and 7.9999

If we start with answer choice A, when we round the first number to the nearest thousandth it becomes 4.358. When we round off the second number to the nearest thousandth, it becomes 4.358. Since these two numbers are the same when we round to the nearest thousandth, answer choice A is correct.

Performing Operations with Decimals

You may also have questions that ask you to add, subtract, or multiply with decimals.

To add or subtract with decimals, you simply line up the decimals and then perform the operation.

- To add or subtract decimals, just line up the decimal points

For example, let's say we want to add 3.5 and 2.6. The math would look like this:

$$
\begin{array}{r}
3.5 \\
+2.6 \\
\hline
6.1
\end{array}
$$

When you have a decimal point, remember to carry over and borrow like you would with normal addition and subtraction.

- Remember to carry and borrow, just like any other addition or subtraction problem

Here is a basic question for you to answer:

7. Which is equal to 6.7 – 5.3?

    (A) 1.2
    (B) 1.4
    (C) 1.9
    (D) 2.4
    (E) 2.9

If we take away 3 tenths from 7 tenths, we can see that the decimal portion of our answer should be 4 tenths, so answer choice B or D must be correct. If we subtract 5 from 6, we can see that we should have a 1 left over in the units place. Putting the decimal portion together with the units portion, we can see that 1.4, or answer choice B, is correct.

You may see a word problem that requires you to apply the rules of decimals.

Here is an example for you to try:

8. Carl went shopping and bought 4 items. He bought a candy bar that cost $1.25, a sandwich that cost $4.50, an apple that cost $0.75, and a bottle of juice. If he spent a total of $8.25, how much did the bottle of juice cost?

    (A) $1.50
    (B) $1.75
    (C) $2.00
    (D) $2.25
    (E) $2.75

Our first step is to add the values of the items that we do know the costs of:

$1.25 + $4.50 + $0.75 = $6.50

Now we have to subtract the total of the items that we know ($6.50) from the total amount of money that Carl spent:

$8.25 – $6.50 = $1.75

Answer choice B is correct.

Decimal multiplication is pretty straightforward if you remember one rule:

- When multiplying decimals, if you move the decimal point to the right when you begin the problem, you must move it back to the left when you get the answer.

Here are the steps for multiplying decimals:

1. If any of the numbers in your question have decimal points, move the decimal point to the right. Keep track of how many decimal places you moved in total!
2. Multiply these numbers together.
3. Take the answer that you get and then move the decimal place back to the left the same number of spaces that you moved it to the right before multiplying.

Here is an example:

$34 \times 0.03 =$

Step one, move the decimal place to the right – and keep track of the number of spaces moved.

34×3

We moved the decimal point of the second number two spots to the right – we need to remember that. Now we can just perform multiplication with whole numbers.

$34 \times 3 = 102$

In the first step, we moved the decimal two places to the right, so now we move it two places to the left in the final answer.

$34 \times 0.03 = 1.02$

Here is how this concept is tested on the SSAT:

9. If pencils cost $0.15 each at the school store, how much would it cost to buy 8 pencils?

(A) $0.75
(B) $1.05
(C) $1.20
(D) $1.25
(E) $1.35

To solve this problem, we have to move the decimal to two places to the right. This allows us to calculate 15×8 as our multiplication problem. The answer is 120. Now we have to move the decimal back two places to the left. That gives us 1.20 as our final answer, so choice C is correct.

Here is another one for you to try:

10. At a store, each bouncy ball costs $0.69. About how much would it cost to buy 3 bouncy balls at this store?

(A) $2.50
(B) $2.10
(C) $2.00
(D) $1.80
(E) $1.40

Did you see that the question asks "about how much?" The word "about" tells us to round. So we can round the $0.69 to $0.70. The problem is now 0.70×3, so we move the decimal one place to the right so that we can multiply 7×3, which gives us an answer of 21. To get our final answer, we have to move the decimal back one place to the left. This leaves us with 2.1, or choice B.

Here are a couple of questions that are a little trickier. If you are in fifth grade, you might find they are a little too hard. That is fine, just keep in mind that you will only be compared to other fifth graders.

11. Seven tenths of the 400 students in a school study a language other than English. How many students study a language other than English?

(A) 7
(B) 70
(C) 28
(D) 280
(E) 360

In order to answer this question, we have to remember that "of" tells us to multiply. To find seven tenths of 400, we perform the operation 0.7×400. If we move the decimal one place to the right on the first number, we get $7 \times 400 = 2,800$. Now we move the decimal back one place to the left and get 280 as our final answer. Answer choice D is correct.

12. Fourteen hundredths of 500 cats have blue eyes. How many of the cats have blue eyes?

(A) 70
(B) 140
(C) 210
(D) 280
(E) 1,400

We will again translate into an equation, remembering that "of" tells us to multiply. We now have 0.14×500. Since $14 \times 500 = 7,000$ and we had to move the decimal point two places to the right, we move the decimal back to the left two places and get 70 as our answer. Answer choice A is correct.

Converting Between Decimals, Fractions, and Percents

You may see some questions that ask you to convert between fractions, decimals, and percents. When see these questions, you can use place value to convert decimals into fractions. For example, the number 0.4 represents four tenths or $\frac{4}{10}$, and the number 0.25 represents twenty-five hundredths or $\frac{25}{100}$. For percents, remember that a percent is just a fraction with 100 as a denominator. For example, 30% is equal to $\frac{30}{100}$.

- You can use place value to turn a decimal into a fraction
- Remember that a percent is just a fraction with 100 as the denominator

Here are a couple of examples for you to try. Keep in mind that these questions are challenging, particularly if you are in fifth grade. Just remember that you are only compared to students your age.

13. Which of the following shows the numbers in order from least to greatest?

(A) $0.2, \frac{1}{3}, 0.3, \frac{3}{11}$

(B) $\frac{1}{3}, 0.2, \frac{3}{11}, 0.3$

(C) $\frac{1}{3}, \frac{3}{11}, 0.2, 0.3$

(D) $0.2, 0.3, \frac{1}{3}, \frac{3}{11}$

(E) $0.2, \frac{3}{11}, 0.3, \frac{1}{3}$

Let's start with the easier comparisons. Since it is easy to see that 0.2 is less than 0.3, we can use that to rule out. In this question, however, all of the answer choices show this relationship correctly. Now let's compare 0.3 to $\frac{3}{11}$. We can convert 0.3 into $\frac{3}{10}$, and $\frac{3}{11}$ is less than $\frac{3}{10}$, so we know that the correct answer must have $\frac{3}{11}$ listed before 0.3. We can rule out choices A and D. Now we can compare 0.3 and $\frac{1}{3}$. We can turn 0.3 into $\frac{3}{10}$. In order to compare $\frac{3}{10}$ to $\frac{1}{3}$, however, they need to have either the same numerator or the same denominator. If we multiply $\frac{1}{3}$ by $\frac{3}{3}$, it is clear that $\frac{1}{3} = \frac{3}{9}$. Since $\frac{3}{10}$ is less than $\frac{3}{9}$, 0.3 needs to come before $\frac{1}{3}$ in the list. Answer choices B and C can be eliminated. Only answer choice E remains, and it is the correct answer.

14. 54% is closest to which fraction?

(A) $\dfrac{1}{2}$

(B) $\dfrac{6}{11}$

(C) $\dfrac{3}{5}$

(D) $\dfrac{7}{11}$

(E) $\dfrac{10}{17}$

This is a very hard question. The question asks which one comes closest so we will have to estimate. First, let's turn 54% into $\dfrac{54}{100}$. Now we will have to convert the answer choices into equivalent fractions. Not all of the denominators are factors of 100, however, so we will need to try to find denominators that are close to 100.

(A) $\dfrac{1\times50}{2\times50} = \dfrac{50}{100}$

(B) $\dfrac{6\times9}{11\times9} = \dfrac{54}{99}$

(C) $\dfrac{3\times20}{5\times20} = \dfrac{60}{100}$

(D) $\dfrac{7\times9}{11\times9} = \dfrac{63}{99}$

(E) $\dfrac{10\times6}{17\times6} = \dfrac{60}{102}$

Since $\dfrac{54}{99}$ is very close in value to $\dfrac{54}{100}$, answer choice B is correct.

Now you know how to do well on decimal problems on the SSAT. Be sure to complete the decimals practice set to reinforce your learning.

Decimals Practice Set

1. If each eraser costs $0.19, then about how much would it cost to buy 9 erasers?

   (A) $1.50
   (B) $1.80
   (C) $1.85
   (D) $1.90
   (E) $2.10

2. Round 300.0419 to the nearest thousandth.

   (A) 300.05
   (B) 300.1
   (C) 300.042
   (D) 300.42
   (E) 300.40

3. Which represents the decimal four hundred sixty-two thousandths?

   (A) 400.062
   (B) 400.62
   (C) 0.462
   (D) 0.0462
   (E) 0.4062

4. In the number 863,219 which digit has the least value?

   (A) 1
   (B) 2
   (C) 3
   (D) 8
   (E) 9

5. Lily bought three boxes of raisins that cost $0.89 each. If she paid with a $5 bill, how much change did she receive?

   (A) $2.33
   (B) $2.67
   (C) $2.70
   (D) $3.00
   (E) $3.22

6. Which is equivalent to 9 – 4.55?

   (A) 3.45
   (B) 3.55
   (C) 4.35
   (D) 4.45
   (E) 4.55

7. Three-fifths of the students in a class have birthday in April, May or June. If there are 30 students in the class, how many do NOT have a birthday in April, May, or June?

   (A) 12
   (B) 15
   (C) 18
   (D) 20
   (E) 24

8. 81% is closest to which fraction?

   (A) $\dfrac{9}{13}$

   (B) $\dfrac{9}{11}$

   (C) $\dfrac{10}{11}$

   (D) $\dfrac{10}{13}$

   (E) $\dfrac{9}{10}$

9. Which of the following shows the numbers in order from least to greatest?

   (A) 0.2, 0.3, 25%, $\dfrac{1}{3}$

   (B) 0.3, 25%, 0.2, $\dfrac{1}{3}$

   (C) 0.2, 0.3, $\dfrac{1}{3}$, 25%

   (D) $\dfrac{1}{3}$, 0.3, 25%, 02

   (E) 0.2, 25%, 0.3, $\dfrac{1}{3}$

10. Which pair of numbers would be equal if rounded to the nearest tenth?

    (A) 9.082 and 9.049

    (B) 6.521 and 6.625

    (C) 4.3511 and 4.449

    (D) 3.026 and 3.206

    (E) 5.2 and 5.257

Decimals Practice Set

1. B
2. C
3. C
4. E
5. A
6. D
7. A
8. B
9. E
10. C

Average Problems

Average problems on the SSAT aren't so bad because they fall into very predictable categories.

The types of problems you will see include:

1. Questions that use the basic definition of an average
2. Consecutive number average problems
3. Weighted average problems
4. Questions that don't use the word *average* but can be solved with the concepts of averages

Average problems on the SSAT use the following equation:

$$\frac{\text{sum of numbers}}{\text{number of numbers}} = \text{average}$$

Sometimes you will have to manipulate the equation to get:

$$\text{sum of numbers} = \text{number of numbers} \times \text{average}$$

Questions that Use the Basic Definition of an Average

In general, to find an average of numbers, we add together the numbers and then divide by the number of numbers.

For example:

Let's say we are given the numbers 3, 6, and 18 and need to find their average.

Here is what the math would look like to find the average:

$$\frac{3+6+18}{3} = \frac{27}{3} = 9$$

On the SSAT, you are not likely to be asked just to find the average of three numbers, however. The problems will include many other words so that not every student will answer these questions correctly. Just follow carefully and look out for words like NOT.

- Follow average questions closely and look out for details that could trip you up

Here is what these average questions could look like on the actual SSAT:

1. Jean is thinking of two numbers whose average is equal to half of the average of 10 and 22. Which of the following could be the two numbers that Jean is thinking of?

   (A) 2 and 20
   (B) 4 and 18
   (C) 5 and 11
   (D) 9 and 11
   (E) 15 and 17

The trick to this question is that it is a multi-step problem, and we have to not stop before we are done. First, we have to find the average of 10 and 22. The math would look like this:

$$\frac{10+22}{2} = \frac{32}{2} = 16$$

Now we know that the average of 10 and 22 is 16. We can't stop here and find an answer choice that averages to 16, however. We need to find an answer choice where the average of the two numbers is half of 16, or 8.

Now let's find the averages for those answer choices:

(A) $\frac{2+20}{2} = \frac{22}{2} = 11$

(B) $\frac{4+18}{2} = \frac{22}{2} = 11$

(C) $\frac{5+11}{2} = \frac{16}{2} = 8$

(D) $\frac{9+11}{2} = \frac{20}{2} = 10$

(E) $\frac{15+17}{2} = \frac{32}{2} = 16$

We can see that only answer choice C gives us an average of 8, so that is our correct answer. We can also see that 5 and 11 are respectively each half of 10 and 22. It makes sense then that the average of 5 and 11 would be half the average of 10 and 22.

Here is another one for you to try:

2. Of the following pairs of numbers, which pair does NOT have an average equal to one-third the average of 9 and 21?

(A) 4 and 6
(B) 3 and 7
(C) 1 and 9
(D) 14 and 16
(E) 2 and 8

To answer this question, we first need to find the average of 9 and 21. The math would look like this:

$$\frac{9+21}{2} = \frac{30}{2} = 15$$

Now, we have to remember to take one-third of that average. One-third of 15 is 5, so we are looking for an answer choice that gives us an average that is NOT 5. The only answer choice that does not give us an average of 5 is choice D. This is the correct answer. Answer choice D gives us an average of 15, not 5.

Consecutive Number Average Problems

Sometimes they will give you an average for consecutive whole numbers, consecutive odd numbers, or consecutive even numbers.

You should rejoice when you see these problems – as long as you know the problem type, consecutive number average problems are very easy.

The only potential trick is forgetting what kind of numbers they are using (consecutive, consecutive even, or consecutive odd) or forgetting whether they are asking for the smallest number or the greatest number. Circle what kind of numbers they are looking for and what they are asking for and you will be just fine.

- Circle what kind of numbers are being used (consecutive, consecutive even, or consecutive odd)
- Circle what they are asking for (smallest or greatest number)

Here is an example of how this question could look on the SSAT:

3. The average of three consecutive odd numbers is 11. What is the smallest number?

(A) 9
(B) 10
(C) 11
(D) 12
(E) 13

First of all, did you remember to circle "consecutive odd" and "smallest number?" Good. Consecutive number problems are pretty easy – the average is the middle number. The strategy for this is to draw a blank for each number. Insert the average in the middle blank and find what they are looking for.

For the above example:

1. Draw a blank for each number: ____   ____   ____
2. Insert the average in the middle: ____   _11_   ____
3. Find what they are looking for: _9_   _11_   ____

Since the smallest number is 9, answer choice A is correct.

Here is another one for you to try:

4. If the average of five consecutive whole numbers is 12, what is the largest one?

    (A) 7
    (B) 10
    (C) 12
    (D) 14
    (E) 17

For this problem, we draw out five slots and put 12 in the middle. We then fill in the other slots like so:

_____   _____   _12_   _13_   _14_

From this, it is clear to see that 14 is the largest number, so answer choice D is correct.

Weighted Average Problems

Sometimes you have to find a total average given the average of a couple of groups. What you need to do is use the following equation to find the sum of each group:

sum of group = number of numbers × average

Then use the average equation again to find the total average.

$$\frac{\text{sum of group 1 + sum of group 2}}{\text{total number of numbers}} = \text{overall average}$$

This is called a weighted average. You don't need to remember this term – you just need to know NOT to add the two averages together and divide by 2.

Here is an example of how this is tested on the SSAT:

5. The average length of four kittens is 20 inches. The average length of a different set of two kittens is 14 inches. What is the average length of all six kittens?

    (A) 14
    (B) 15
    (C) 16
    (D) 18
    (E) 20

To solve this problem, we first have to figure out the sum of all the lengths. If we multiply 4 times 20, we get that the sum of the lengths of the kittens that are 20 inches long is 80 inches. Then, to find the sum of the kittens that are 14 inches long, we multiply 2 times 14 to get 28. Now we add 80 and 28. This tells us that the sum of the lengths of all the kittens in 108. If we divide that sum by the total number of kittens (6), we get that the average length is 18 inches, or choice D.

Sometimes we have to do even more steps. Some problems require us to change some of the numbers and find a new average.

Here is how this looks on the SSAT:

6. The average price of three dolls is $18. The price is reduced by $3 for two of these dolls. What is the new average price for these three dolls?

    (A) $18
    (B) $17
    (C) $16
    (D) $15
    (E) $14

We can treat this as a weighted average problem. To make it easy, we can say that we now have one doll that is $18 and two dolls that are $15. (These may not actually be the prices, but they will give us the correct sum.) We have to find the sum of their prices. There are two dolls that cost $15, so the sum of the prices for those two dolls is $30. Then we add in the doll that remained $18. This tells us that altogether the three dolls cost $48. We divide $48 by 3, since there are three dolls, and find that the new average price is $16. Answer choice C is correct.

Those were tricky, so let's try another one:

7. At the beginning of the year, the average mass of four students was 48 kilograms. By the end of the year, two students had each gained 4 kilograms and the other two students had not gained or lost any weight. What was the average mass of the four students at the end of the year (in kilograms)?

   (A) 48
   (B) 49
   (C) 50
   (D) 51
   (E) 52

In this problem, we can just say that each student had a mass of 48 kg to begin with. This may not be accurate, but what matters is that the sum of their masses gives us 48 kg as an average. At the end of the year, we now have two students with a mass of 48 kg and two students with a mass of 52 kg. We need to do a weighted average. Here is what the math looks like:

$$\frac{\text{sum of group 1} + \text{sum of group 2}}{4} = \frac{(2 \times 48) + (2 \times 52)}{4} = \frac{96 + 104}{4} = \frac{200}{4} = 50$$

This tells us that the new average weight of the group is 50 kg. Choice C is correct.

Questions that Don't Use the Word "Average" But Can Be Solved With the Concepts of Averages

You may see problems that use the word *sum* that allow us to use the concepts of averages.

Let's take a look at the following problem:

8. The sum of five consecutive numbers is 105. What is the largest number?

   (A) 19
   (B) 20
   (C) 21
   (D) 22
   (E) 23

We can use what we learned from consecutive number average problems. When the numbers are consecutive, the middle number will also be the average. To find the average (and the middle number) we have to calculate the following:

$$\text{average} = \frac{\text{sum}}{\text{number of numbers}} = \frac{105}{5} = 21$$

———

Now we can draw out five slots (since we have five numbers), and put the average in the middle:

_____ _____ __21__ _____ _____

From here, we just fill in consecutive numbers to get:

<u>19</u> <u>20</u> <u>21</u> <u>22</u> <u>23</u>

We can see that 23 is the largest number so choice E is correct.

Here is another one for you to try:

9. If the sum of three consecutive odd numbers is 45, then what is the smallest number?

(A) 11
(B) 13
(C) 14
(D) 15
(E) 17

Since it is a consecutive number problem, we know that the middle number is also the average. To find the average, we divide the sum by 3, since that is the number of numbers. That tells us that the average, as well as the middle number, is 15. Now, did you remember that they wanted consecutive odd numbers? That means that our numbers must be 13, 15, and 17. They are asking for the smallest number, so choice B is correct.

Another type of problem doesn't require you to use *average*, but it does require you to use *sum*. It is also not that different from the problems that we did earlier where some members of a group increased in size or weight, but others did not. So we will cover them here – even if they aren't strictly average problems.

Here is an example:

10. If the sum of the ages of four children is 18, what will be the sum of their ages three years from now?

(A) 32
(B) 30
(C) 26
(D) 24
(E) 22

The trick to this question is that we can't just add four years to 18 and be done with it. Each child will be three years older, and there are 4 children, so the sum of their ages will actually increase by 12. The correct answer is B.

———

Here is another one for you to try:

11. The sum of the weights of three children is 118 pounds. If two of those children gain 4 pounds each and the third child's weight remains the same, then what is the sum of their new weights, in pounds?

    (A) 118
    (B) 122
    (C) 124
    (D) 125
    (E) 126

    For this problem, we have to keep in mind that there were 2 children who each gained 4 pounds. This means that the overall sum would increase by 8, not just 4. That means we have to add 8 to 118 in order to get 126, or answer choice E.

Another type of problem that doesn't use the word *average* but we can use the average principles for is rate problems. These problems are some of the most difficult, so if they seem very hard, don't spend too much time on them.

Keep in mind that when they give a rate in terms of miles per hour, what that gives us is the average distance traveled in a one-hour block.

Let's take a look at how this could be tested on the SSAT:

12. Kim competed in a triathlon, a race with 3 parts. First, she swam a mile at the rate of 2 miles per hour. Then, she ran 12 miles at the rate of 6 miles per hour. Then she rode 20 miles on her bike at the rate of 30 miles per hour. How long did it take her to complete the entire triathlon?

    (A) 34 minutes
    (B) 1 hour 30 minutes
    (C) 2 hour 52 minutes
    (D) 3 hours
    (E) 3 hours 10 minutes

    This problem is a doozy, so let's break it down into pieces. In the first segment of the race, she swam a mile. Since her rate was 2 miles per hour, it would have taken her half an hour to swim 1 mile, or 30 minutes. In the next segment, she ran 12 miles. Since her speed was 6 miles per hour, it would have taken her 2 hours, or 120 minutes, to complete the running segment. Then she rode her bike for 20 miles. Since she was going at the rate of 30 miles per hour, we have to use a proportion to solve. Since 20 miles is $\frac{2}{3}$ of 30 miles, it would have taken her $\frac{2}{3}$ of an hour, or 40 minutes.

    If we add all the minutes together, we get $30 + 120 + 40 = 190$. Now the trick is that we have to convert this back into hours and minutes. Since $190 = 60 + 60 + 60 + 10$, we know that 190 minutes equals 3 hours and 10 minutes. Choice E is correct.

Keep in mind that this is a VERY challenging question. If you get it right, that's great. But you will be among the few that do! Schools are looking at your percentile scores, so if you felt that this question was way over your head, it probably won't affect your percentile score.

Now you know how to do well on average problems on the SSAT. Be sure to complete the average practice set that starts on the following page.

Average Problems Practice Set

1. If the average of five consecutive even numbers is 22, what is the smallest number?

    (A) 17
    (B) 18
    (C) 20
    (D) 22
    (E) 27

2. If the sum of three consecutive even numbers is 60, then what is the smallest of these numbers?

    (A) 18
    (B) 19
    (C) 20
    (D) 21
    (E) 22

3. The average height for three students was 46 inches. If two of the students each grew 3 inches and the third student's height did not change, then what is their new average height, in inches?

    (A) 50
    (B) 49
    (C) 48
    (D) 47
    (E) 46

4. Of the following pairs of numbers, which pair has an average that is twice the average of 6 and 14?

    (A) 5 and 15
    (B) 4 and 16
    (C) 18 and 21
    (D) 3 and 5
    (E) 12 and 28

5. Lucy is thinking of two numbers whose average is half the average of 5 and 11. Which of the following pairs could NOT be the numbers that Lucy is thinking of?

    (A) 1 and 7
    (B) 2 and 6
    (C) 3 and 5
    (D) 7 and 8
    (E) 4 and 4

6. When three children added their ages together, they got 19 as the sum. What will be the sum of their ages four years from now?

    (A) 60
    (B) 55
    (C) 40
    (D) 31
    (E) 24

Challenge problem:

7. Julian and Tommy ran in a 6-mile race. Julian ran the first 4 miles at 10 miles per hour. He then walked the rest of the race at 4 miles per hour. Tommy jogged the first 3 miles at 6 miles per hour. He then walked the rest of the race at 3 miles per hour. Who won the race and by how many minutes did he win?

    (A) The two boys finished at the same time
    (B) Tommy won by 36 minutes
    (C) Tommy won by 12 minutes
    (D) Julian won by 12 minutes
    (E) Julian won by 36 minutes

8. Harry took 3 tests, and his average score on those 3 tests was 80. If he scored a 88 on his fourth test, what was his average score on all 4 tests?

    (A) 82
    (B) 84
    (C) 85
    (D) 86
    (E) 88

9. In a throwing contest, Marcos throws 3 balls. The average distance that the first two balls went was 55 meters. He has one more ball to throw. If he wants his average distance thrown to be at least 60 meters, what is the minimum distance he must throw the third ball, in meters?

    (A) 65
    (B) 68
    (C) 70
    (D) 72
    (E) 75

Answers to Average Problems Practice Set

1. B
2. A
3. C
4. E
5. D
6. D
7. E
8. A
9. C

Solving Equations & Inequalities

On the SSAT Middle Level, solving equations will be tested in several ways. The problem types include:

- Basic solving for a variable
- Solving for a variable and then finding another value
- Plugging in for a variable
- Setting up an equation to fit a story
- Solving for overlapping groups
- Creating and using inequalities
- Made-up functions

Basic Solving for a Variable

The basic goal of solving equations is to get a variable by itself – or to isolate it.

There are two basic rules for isolating a variable:

1. Use PEMDAS (order of operations), but in reverse
2. Do the opposite operation in each step

Here is a basic example:

$x + 2 = 4$

In each step, notice that we do the *opposite* operation in order to simplify the equation. The left side has *addition*, so we must *subtract*.

$$x + 2 = 4$$
$$\underline{-2 \quad -2}$$
$$x = 2$$

The problem is solved, the value of x is 2.

Here is another example:

$$\frac{1}{2}x = 7$$

The left side has division by 2 so we must multiply by 2.

$$\frac{1}{2}x = 7$$
$$\times 2 \quad \times 2$$
$$x = 14$$

The problem is solved. The value of x is 14.

Finally, here is an example that puts it all together and requires us to use PEMDAS in reverse:

$$3m + 7 = 13$$

If we reverse the order of PEMDAS, we have to take care of addition/subtraction first, remembering to perform the opposite operation.

$$3m + 7 = 13$$
$$-7 \quad -7$$
$$3m = 6$$

Now we take care of multiplication/division. Since m is multiplied by 3, we will do the opposite and divide by 3.

$$3m = 6$$
$$\div 3 \quad \div 3$$
$$m = 2$$

Here is an example of how these problems could look on the SSAT:

1. If $Q + 7 = 7$, then Q is equal to

    (A) 0

    (B) $\frac{1}{7}$

    (C) 1

    (D) 7

    (E) 14

In this question, we want to get Q by itself. Currently, Q has a 7 added to it. To get rid of that 7, we have to do the opposite, or subtract 7 from both sides. That leaves us with $Q = 0$, so answer choice A is correct.

Here is another one for you to try:

2. If $6 \times 2 \times N = 12$, then $N =$

 (A) 0

 (B) $\dfrac{1}{12}$

 (C) 1

 (D) 6

 (E) 12

In order to solve, we have to simplify the left side of the equation to $12 \times N$ and then get N by itself. N is multiplied by 12, so we have to do the opposite and divide both sides by 12. If we do that, we get $N = 1$, so answer choice C is correct.

You may have noticed that these questions test basic identities: any number multiplied by 1 is itself, and any number with 0 added to it is still the same number.

•   Problems with variables are often testing identities

Sometimes the problems get a little trickier. As long as you stick to reverse PEMDAS and do the opposite to isolate a variable, you will be just fine.

Here is an example:

3. If $8 \times R + 2 = 5$, then $R =$

 (A) $\dfrac{3}{8}$

 (B) $\dfrac{6}{8}$

 (C) 2

 (D) 8

 (E) 16

To solve, first we have to see if there is anything added or subtracted. There is a 2 added to the side with the variable, so we subtract that from both sides and get $8 \times R = 3$. Now we have an 8 that is multiplied by the variable, so we divide both sides by 8 and get $R = \dfrac{3}{8}$, so answer choice A is correct.

You may also see questions that use a shape instead of a variable. We can solve these problems just like there is a variable, using the same rules.

•   A shape in an equation is just another way to represent a variable

———

———

Here is an example:

4. If $300 + 700 + 70 = 1,000 + \Delta$, then what is the value of Δ?

   (A) 7
   (B) 70
   (C) 700
   (D) 930
   (E) 1,070

   Our first step is simplify the left side of the equation, which gives us 1,070 on the left side of the equal sign. Therefore, we know that $1,000 + \Delta = 1,070$. If we subtract 1,000 from both sides, it is clear that Δ must be equal to 70. Answer choice B is correct.

You may also see a question with a decimal. Just follow the same rules.

Here is an example:

5. If $\dfrac{X}{100} = 0.78$, then what is the value of X?
   (A) 0.0078
   (B) 0.078
   (C) 0.78
   (D) 7.8
   (E) 78

   In this question X is initially divided by 100. In order to isolate X, we need to do the opposite and multiply both sides by 100. To multiply 0.78 by 100, we move the decimal two places to the right. The result is 78, so answer choice E is correct.

You may also see questions that ask you to solve for a variable in an expression with negative numbers.

Here is an example:

6. In the equation $34 - (-3x) = -5$, what is the value of x?

   (A) −13
   (B) −11
   (C) −3
   (D) 11
   (E) 13

   Our first step is to simplify the left part of the equation. Since subtracting a negative number is the same as adding a positive number, the equation becomes $34 + 3x = -5$. Now, we need to subtract 34 from both sides. Since $-5 - 34 = -39$, our equation is now $3x = -39$. Finally, we divide both sides by 3. Since a negative number divided by a negative number is a positive number, $x = -13$. Answer choice A is correct.

———

Solving for a Variable and then Finding Another Value

These questions ask you to solve for a variable and then use that value to solve another problem.

These aren't hard, you just have to remember to complete all the steps. It is very easy to solve for the variable and then choose that as your answer choice. To get around that, be sure to circle what they are asking for.

- Circle what the question is asking for

Here is what these questions look like on the SSAT:

7. If $T + 8 = 8$, then $T + 16 =$

    (A) 0
    (B) 1
    (C) 4
    (D) 8
    (E) 16

If $T + 8 = 8$, then T must equal zero. If we plug in zero for T in the second equation, then we get $0 + 16 = 16$, so choice E is correct.

Here is another one for you to try:

8. If $300 + h = 600$, then $500 + h =$

    (A) 300
    (B) 400
    (C) 600
    (D) 800
    (E) 1,000

To solve the first equation, we have to subtract 300 from both sides in order to get h by itself. This gives us $h = 300$. We aren't done yet, though. The question asks us for $500 + h$, so we have to plug in 300 for h and solve. We get $500 + 300 = 800$, so answer choice D is correct.

Sometimes these problems also mix operations.

Here is an example:

9. If $5 \times T = 35$, what does $5 + T$ equal?

    (A) 0

    (B) $\dfrac{1}{7}$

    (C) 1

    (D) 7

    (E) 12

First we have to solve for T. If we divide both sides of the first equation by 5, then we get $T = 7$. The question asks for $5 + T$, however, so we have to keep going. If we substitute in 7 for T, we get $5 + 7 = 12$, so answer choice E is correct.

You may also see questions that describe a variable situation in words and require you to come up with your own equations.

Here are a couple of examples:

10. When a number is multiplied by 5, the result is 30. If that same number was multiplied by 3, what would the result be?

    (A) 6

    (B) 18

    (C) 24

    (D) 28

    (E) 30

The first part of the question could be translated into the equation $n \times 5 = 30$. If we solve for n, we can see that its value is 6. The question does not ask for the value of the number, however, but rather for what the value of that number multiplied by 3 is. Since $6 \times 3 = 18$, answer choice B is correct.

11. What is 3 more than two times V if $V = 16$?

    (A) 18

    (B) 19

    (C) 34

    (D) 35

    (E) 80

We need translate "3 more than two times V" into an algebraic expression. "3 more than" becomes $3 +$ and "two times V" becomes $2 \times V$. If we put the pieces together, our expression is $3 + 2 \times V$. Now we substitute in 16 for V and get $3 + 2 \times 16$. Now we use PEMDAS to simplify: $3 + 2 \times 16 = 3 + 32 = 35$. Answer choice D is correct.

Plugging In for a Variable

You may also see a question where you are given an expression with a variable and a value for that variable, and then you need to substitute in to find the value of the entire expression. These questions often require you to use the rules of negative numbers or exponents. One important rule for these questions is that if we have a number next to variable (for example, $3y$), then we multiply the number times the variable. Similarly if we have a variable next to a variable, we multiply the two variables together. For example, ab means to multiply the value of a times the value of b.

- A variable next to a number (for example, $4x$) tells us to multiply the number by the value of the variable
- A variable next to a variable (for example, xy) tells us to multiply the values of the variables

Here are a couple of examples:

12. If $a = 7$ and $b = 2$, then what is the value of $a^2 - 4b$?

   (A) 6
   (B) 10
   (C) 22
   (D) 41
   (E) 49

   To answer this question, we substitute in the given values for the variables. If we do this, we get $a^2 - 4b = 7^2 - 4(2) = 49 - 8 = 41$. Answer choice D is correct.

13. If $x = -6$ and $y = 5$, what is the value of $y - x$?

   (A) -11
   (B) -1
   (C) 1
   (D) 4
   (E) 11

   If we substitute in the given values, our expression becomes $5 - (-6)$. Now we need to remember that subtracting a negative number is like adding a positive number. If we simplify, the expression becomes $5 + 6$, which is equal to 11. Answer choice E is correct.

Setting Up an Equation to Fit a Story

You may also see questions that give you a situation and then ask you to determine which equation best describes that situation. These questions have variables in the answer choices, so we will use our strategy of plugging in our numbers to see what works.

- Remember that if there are variables in the answer choices we can plug in our own number and see what works

---

Since we practiced this problem type in the strategies section, we will just do a couple of practice problems here.

14. For a hiking trip, Suzanne needs to buy 3 water bottles for each of her friends plus herself. If Suzanne is hiking with x friends, which expression shows how many water bottles she must buy?

(A) $4x$

(B) $4 + x$

(C) $3x$

(D) $3 + x$

(E) $3(1 + x)$

Using our strategy of plugging in our own numbers, let's say that $x = 5$, meaning that Suzanne is hiking with 5 friends. Since she needs water bottles for 5 friends plus herself, she needs water bottles for a total of 6 people. If there are 3 water bottles per person, she will need 18 water bottles. 18 is our target. Now we will plug in 5 for x in each answer choice and see which one gives us 18 as an answer.

(A) $4x = 4(5) = 20$

(B) $4 + x = 4 + 5 = 9$

(C) $3x = 3(5) = 15$

(D) $3 + x = 3 + 5 = 8$

(E) $3(1 + x) = 3(1 + 5) = 3(6) = 18$

Answer choice E gives us 18 when we plug in 5 for x so it is the correct answer choice.

15. Allison has 5 more t-shirts than Bruce. Bruce has 6 fewer t-shirts than Morris. If Allison has m t-shirts, than how many t-shirts does Morris have?

(A) $11 - m$

(B) $11 + m$

(C) $1 + m$

(D) $1 - m$

(E) $m - 1$

Let's begin by saying $m = 10$, or that Allison has 10 t-shirts. This means that Bruce has 5 t-shirts, since Allison has 5 more t-shirts than Bruce. If Bruce has 6 fewer t-shirts than Morris, then in this scenario Morris has 11 t-shirts. 11 is our target when we plug in 10 for m.

(A) $11 - m = 11 - 10 = 1$

(B) $11 + m = 11 + 10 = 21$

(C) $1 + m = 1 + 10 = 11$

(D) $1 - m = 1 - 10 = -9$

(E) $m - 1 = 10 - 1 = 9$

Since only answer choice C results in 11 when we plug in 10 for m, answer choice C is the correct answer.

Solving for Overlapping Groups

Another type of problem that you will see is when you are given the values for overlapping line segments. While these questions may look like geometry questions, they can be solved by setting up equations and using the concepts of algebra to solve.

To solve these problems:

- Mark all the information given on the drawing
- Set up equations so that you can see how all the parts are related

Here is what these questions look like on the test:

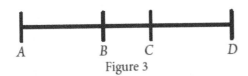

Figure 3

16. In figure 3 above, the distance between B and D is 12. The distance between A and C is also 12. If the distance between C and D is 8, what is the distance between A and B?

(A) 6

(B) 7

(C) 8

(D) 10

(E) 12

To solve this equation, the first step is to mark information given. Our picture now looks something like this:

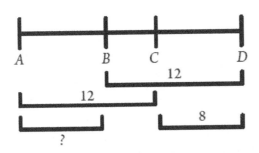

This allows us to set up some equations and solve. We can see that:

$$\overline{BC} + \overline{CD} = 12$$

Since we know that $\overline{CD} = 8$, we can solve to get that $\overline{BC} = 4$. We can also see that:

$$\overline{AB} + \overline{BC} = 12$$

Since we now know that $\overline{BC} = 4$, we can solve to get $\overline{AB} = 8$. Since the question asks for the length of $\overline{AB}$, we know that answer choice C is correct.

Here is another one for you to try:

(It might look scary, but it is really just the same type of problem)

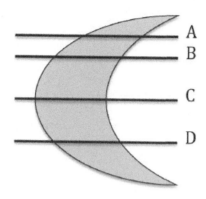

Figure 4

17. In Figure 4, the shaded region is divided by lines *A*, *B*, *C*, and *D*. The shaded area between lines *A* and *C* is 25 square yards. The area of the shaded region between lines *B* and *D* is 30 square yards. If the area of the shaded region between lines *C* and *D* is 15 square yards, then what is the area, in square yards, of the shaded region between *A* and *B*?

(A) 10
(B) 15
(C) 20
(D) 25
(E) 35

First, mark the areas on your picture. From that, you can see that:

$$AC = AB + BC = 25$$

We can also see that:

$$BC + CD = BD$$

Since we are given that the area between *C* and *D* is 15 and that the area between *B* and *D* is 30, it is not hard to figure out that the area between *B* and *C* is also 15.

Now we can plug this back into our first equation and solve:

$$AB + BC = 25$$
$$AB + 15 = 25$$
$$AB = 10$$

Since *AB* is equal to 10, answer choice A is correct.

Here is another one for you to try:

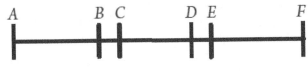

Figure 3

18. In Figure 3, $\overline{AC} = 4$ cm, $\overline{BE} = 6$ cm, and $\overline{DF} = 4$ cm. If $\overline{BC}$ and $\overline{DE}$ are both equal to 1 cm, then what is the total length, in cm, of segment $\overline{AF}$?

(A) 10
(B) 11
(C) 12
(D) 13
(E) 14

Our first step is to set up equations that break apart the segments into pieces.

$$\overline{AC} = \overline{AB} + \overline{BC} = 4$$
$$\overline{BE} = \overline{BC} + \overline{CD} + \overline{DE} = 6$$
$$\overline{DF} = \overline{DE} + \overline{EF} = 4$$

Now we can use the fact that $\overline{BC}$ and $\overline{DE}$ are both equal to 1 to solve for the other segments.

$$\overline{AC} = \overline{AB} + \overline{BC} = \overline{AB} + 1 = 4, \text{ therefore } \overline{AB} = 3$$
$$\overline{BE} = \overline{BC} + \overline{CD} + \overline{DE} = 1 + \overline{CD} + 1 = 6, \text{ therefore } \overline{CD} = 4$$
$$\overline{DF} = \overline{DE} + \overline{EF} = 1 + \overline{EF} = 4, \text{ therefore } \overline{EF} = 3$$

Now let's look at the whole segment AF. We can rewrite it as a sum of its parts:

$$\overline{AF} = \overline{AB} + \overline{BC} + \overline{CD} + \overline{DE} + \overline{EF}$$

Now let's plug in what we know:

$$\overline{AF} = \overline{AB} + \overline{BC} + \overline{CD} + \overline{DE} + \overline{EF} = 3 + 1 + 4 + 1 + 3 = 12$$

Answer choice C is correct.

Creating and Using Inequalities

Sometimes you will see a word problem that uses the language "greater than" or "less than." These words let you know that you need to set up an inequality using the "<" or ">" sign.

- If you see "greater than" or "less than," use "<" or ">" sign

Once you set up an inequality, you can solve using the same rules that you use for solving equations.

Here is an example of a problem that asks you to set up an inequality and then solve:

19. If $B + 7$ is greater than 10, then which of the following could NOT be B?

(A) 2

(B) $3\frac{1}{2}$

(C) 4

(D) 5

(E) $5\frac{1}{2}$

If we set up the inequality, it would look like this:

$$B + 7 > 10$$

If we subtract 7 from both sides in order to get B by itself, we wind up with:

$$B > 3$$

Since B must be greater than 3, choice A could NOT work, so it is the correct answer.

Here is another one for you to try:

20. If four times a number is greater than 12, then all of the following could be the number EXCEPT

(A) 0

(B) $3\frac{1}{2}$

(C) 4

(D) $5\frac{1}{2}$

(E) 6

Let's start by setting up an inequality, using N to represent our number:

$4 \times N > 12$

Now we divide both sides by 4 in order to get N by itself. That leaves us with:

$N > 3$

Since the number has to be greater than 3, answer choice A could NOT be the number, so that is the correct answer.

Sometimes you will have to set up an inequality and then manipulate that inequality.

Let's look at this example:

21. If $Q + 3$ is less than 5, then $3 \times Q$ MUST be less than

(A) 2
(B) 3
(C) 4
(D) 5
(E) 6

First, let's set up our inequality and solve:

$Q + 3 < 5$
$Q < 2$

Now we have to multiply both sides by 3 since we want to know what $3 \times Q$ is less than.

$3 \times Q < 3 \times 2$
$3 \times Q < 6$

Answer choice E is correct.

Here is one for you to try:

22. If $3 \times T$ is greater than 15, then $6 + T$ MUST be greater than

(A) 9
(B) 10

(C) 11

(D) $11\dfrac{1}{2}$

(E) 12

———

Let's set up our inequality and solve for the variable:

$$3 \times T > 15$$

$$T > 5$$

Now we have to find what $6 + T$ is greater than, so we add 6 to both sides. This gives us:

$$T + 6 > 5 + 6$$

$$T + 6 > 11$$

This tells us that $T + 6$ must be greater than 11, so answer choice C is correct.

You may also see questions where an inequality is given in the problem and must be applied. The key to these questions is to set the variable equal to the number that it is greater than (or less than), solve, and then choose the answer that is greater than (or less than) what you solved for.

Here are a couple of examples:

23. If $Y < 7$, then which of the following could be equal to three times Y?

    (A) 20

    (B) 21

    (C) 22

    (D) 23

    (E) 24

If we plug in 7 for the variable, we get $3 \times 7 = 21$. This tells us that if the variable was equal to 7, three times the variable would be 21. However, since the variable is less than 7, the final answer must be less than 21. Answer choice A is correct.

24. If $B > 4$, then which could be the value of $5B - 2$?

    (A) 15

    (B) 16

    (C) 17

    (D) 18

    (E) 19

Let's substitute in 4 for B. This gives us $5B - 2 = 5(4) - 2 = 18$. If B was equal to 4, then the result would be 18. However, since B is greater than 4, the result must be greater than 18. Answer choice E is correct.

Did you notice something about these questions? In order for them to work as multiple-choice questions, if it is a "less than" expression then the least answer choice must be correct, and if it is a "greater than" expression then the greatest answer choice must be correct.

- For this question type, "less than" means the least answer choice is correct and "greater than" means the greatest answer choice is correct

Finally, let's look at a doozy of a question. (If you are in fifth or sixth grade and can't even figure out what the question is asking, remember that percentile is what matters and percentile scores only compare you to other students your age.)

25. If K is greater than one, then which of the following could be equal to $10 \times K$?

I. $\dfrac{1}{3}$

II. 3.5

III. 12

(A) I only
(B) II only
(C) III only
(D) I and II only
(E) II and III only

The trick to this problem is that when we divide the number in the answer choice by 10, the result has to be greater than 1 since K is greater than 1. If we divide $\dfrac{1}{3}$ by 10, we get $\dfrac{1}{30}$, which is definitely not greater than 1, so I is out. If we divide 3.5 by 10, we get 0.35, which is also less than 1, so II is out. If we divide 12 by 10, we get 1.2, which is greater than 1. So only III works. Answer choice C is correct.

Made-up Functions

You may also see questions with very funny symbols in them. You are not supposed to know what these symbols mean. The test writer is just creating a function, or telling you what operations to perform.

For example, let's say the question says $*m* = m + 5$. The question then might ask you what the value of $*7*$ is. We use the given function $*m* = m + 5$ and substitute in 7 for m on both sides. Therefore $*7* = 7 + 5 = 12$.

Here are a couple of questions for you to try:

26. If $\rightarrow b = 2b + 6$, what is the value of $\rightarrow 5$?

(A) 5
(B) 10
(C) 11
(D) 16
(E) 18

In order to solve, we just substitute in 5 for b, which gives us $\rightarrow 5 = 2(5) + 6 = 16$. Answer choice D is correct.

27. If $k \cdots m = k^2 - m^2$, then what is the value of $5 \cdots 4$?

    (A) 1

    (B) 9

    (C) 16

    (D) 25

    (E) 41

Again, we have to substitute in to the given function. Since 5 comes before the dots and k comes before the dots, we will plug in 5 for k and 4 for m. This gives us $5 \cdots 4 = 5^2 - 4^2 = 25 - 16 = 9$. Answer choice B is correct.

Now you know the basics for solving equations and inequalities on the SSAT. Be sure to complete the solving equations and inequalities practice set.

Solving Equations & Inequalities Practice Set

1. If $J + 7 = 7$, then $J =$

   (A) 0
   (B) 17
   (C) 1
   (D) 7
   (E) 14

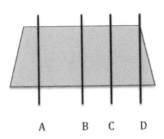

A   B C D

Figure 7

2. The shaded polygon in Figure 7 is divided by lines A, B, C, and D. The area of the shaded region between A and C is 40, and the area of the shaded region between B and D is 35. If the area between B and C is 15, what is the area of the shaded region between A and D?

   (A) 40
   (B) 45
   (C) 50
   (D) 55
   (E) 60

3. If R is less than 7, then $3R + 6$ could be

   (A) 26
   (B) 27
   (C) 28
   (D) 29
   (E) 30

4. If $P + 3$ is greater than 8, then $4 \times P$ MUST be greater than

   (A) 44
   (B) 20
   (C) 21
   (D) 25
   (E) 30

5. If $20 \times R = 20$, then $20 - R =$

   (A) 0
   (B) 1
   (C) 19
   (D) 20
   (E) 21

6. If $6 \times K + 5 = 10$, then $K =$

   (A) 0

   (B) $\dfrac{5}{6}$

   (C) $\dfrac{6}{5}$

   (D) $\dfrac{15}{6}$

   (E) 44

7. If $300 + b = 600$, then $600 + b =$

   (A) 0
   (B) 200
   (C) 300
   (D) 900
   (E) 1,200

8. Three short pipes are joined together to make one long pipe. Originally, each shorter piece of pipe was 10 feet long. When the pipes are joined together, however, the ends must overlap one another by one foot where they are connected. What is the length of the final, longer pipe?

   (A) 30 feet
   (B) 29 feet
   (C) 28 feet
   (D) 26 feet
   (E) 25 feet

9. If $10 \times L$ is less than one, then which of the following could be L?

I.   3

II. $\dfrac{1}{2}$

III.   0

(A) I only
(B) I and II only
(C) II and III only
(D) III only
(E) None of the above

10. If four times a number is greater than twelve, then all of the following could be the number EXCEPT

(A) 5

(B) $4\dfrac{1}{2}$

(C) 4

(D) $3\dfrac{1}{2}$

(E) 3

11. Margo had d dollars. She gave 3 dollars to Frank, and then he had 2 dollars more than Margo. How many dollars did Frank have before Margo gave him the money?

(A) $d - 1$
(B) $d + 1$
(C) $d - 4$
(D) $d + 4$
(E) $2d$

12. If $\dfrac{m}{10} = 5.73$, then what is the value of $10m$?

(A) 0.0573
(B) 0.573
(C) 5.73
(D) 57.3
(E) 573

———

13. What is the value of $j^2 - 2jk$ if $j = 6$ and $k = 4$?

   (A) −36
   (B) −12
   (C) 0
   (D) 12
   (E) 24

14. If $Z = 14$, what is four less than three times Z?

   (A) 10
   (B) 18
   (C) 38
   (D) 42
   (E) 46

15. What is the value of N if $-6 - N = -8$?

   (A) −14
   (B) −6
   (C) −2
   (D) 2
   (E) 14

16. If $\#x\# = x^2 - 4x$, then what is the value of $\#8\#$?

   (A) −16
   (B) 0
   (C) 16
   (D) 32
   (E) 64

Answers for Solving Equations & Inequalities Practice Set

1. A
2. E
3. A
4. B
5. C
6. B
7. D
8. C
9. D
10. E
11. C
12. E
13. B
14. C
15. D
16. D

Word Problems

The phrase "word problems" strikes fear into the hearts of many students. On the SSAT, it doesn't have to!

Word problems on the SSAT tend to actually be very predictable. Identify the type of problem and you are halfway there.

The types of word problems that you are most likely to see on the SSAT are:

1. Multi-step word problems
2. Questions that ask you to form groups
3. Overlapping groups problems
4. Comparing individuals questions
5. Proportion (rate) problems

Some of these question types are really very easy, some of them are harder. As you work through these different problem types, think about how you can identify them on the actual test.

- *Think about what makes each problem type unique*

Multi-step Word Problems

The trick to this type of problem is not that the calculations are super hard, but rather that there are a lot of steps to follow. The key is to underline the information that you need to solve. For example, a problem may say, "Jack's family had a garage with four vehicles in it." We don't need to know that it was a garage or that the garage belonged to Jack's family. We do need to know that there were four vehicles, so that is what we underline.

- *Underline information needed to solve*

If you get stuck, ask yourself if you have used all the numbers given. If not, then think about how you could use that information. The SSAT generally does not give you numbers in a problem that you do not need to use in order to solve. Also, if you can't figure out how to use information, start at the end of the problem and process the information as you move back to the beginning of the problem.

How to get unstuck:

- Use all numbers given in problem
- Start at the end of the question and work backwards

Here is what these questions look like on the SSAT:

1. Jane bought four packages of donut holes which each contained 15 donut holes. She ate two donut holes on the way to school. When she got to school, she gave three donut holes to each of her classmates. She had four donut holes left over. How many classmates does Jane have?

   (A) 15
   (B) 16
   (C) 18
   (D) 30
   (E) 45

To solve this problem, you first need to figure out how many donut holes she had to begin with. She had 4 packs of 15 each. The word "of" tells us to multiply, so we multiply 4×15, which gives us a total of 60 donut holes. She then ate 2 of them, so she had only 58 left. If you were to divide by 3 at this point, you wouldn't get an even number of students. So we have to go back and see what we missed. And we have to start at the end. If we look at the end of the problem, we can see that she had 4 donut holes left over. So she didn't divide 58 donut holes among her classmates, she divided 54 donut holes among her classmates. So we divide 54 by 3 and get that she had 18 classmates. Choice C is correct.

Here is one for you to try:

2. At the beginning of the year, Sam bought 3 boxes of pencils. Each of these boxes contained 18 pencils. He used 4 new pencils each week of school up until the holiday break. If he had 10 pencils that had not been used when the holiday break began, then how many weeks were there between the start of school and the holiday break?

   (A) 10
   (B) 11
   (C) 12
   (D) 13
   (E) 14

To solve, let's first figure out how many pencils he started with. He had 3 boxes of 18, so we multiply 3×18 in order to get 54. Now we have to subtract off 10 since he had 10 pencils left at the end. That means that he used 44 new pencils. Since he used 4 pencils a week, we divide 44 by 4 and find that there were 11 weeks of school, so answer B is correct.

Another type of problem requires us to find a total and then divide.

Here is how it looks on the SSAT:

3. A certain restaurant charges $50 for a room rental and then $6 per attendee to host a party. If 10 guests come to a party and they share the cost equally, then how much should each person pay?

    (A) $6
    (B) $8
    (C) $10
    (D) $11
    (E) $20

    Our first step is to figure out what the total cost of the party would be. It would cost $50 for the room rental but we also have to add the cost of the guests. Since there are 10 guests and each guest costs $6, then the total cost just for the guests would be $60. If we add in the room rental, the total cost would be $110. Since there are ten people sharing the cost equally, we divide $110 by 10 to get that each person would have to pay $11. Answer choice D is correct.

Here is another one for you to try:

4. To run in a race costs $16 for the first family member and $4 for each additional family member. If four family members all run in a race and split the cost equally, then how much would each person pay?

    (A) $16
    (B) $12
    (C) $10
    (D) $7
    (E) $4

    If four family members ran, they would have to pay $16 for the first person and then a total of $12 for the next three people. This adds up to a total of $28. If we divide this equally among the four people, we get that each person would pay $7. Answer choice D is correct.

The next one is a little harder. Just remember to underline what is needed and to write down your work as you go. The more steps that a problem has, the more important it is to write down your work!

5. A baseball team plays 30 games in their season. So far, they have lost 12 games and won 5. How many of their remaining games must they win in order to win more than half of their games this season?

    (A) 9
    (B) 10
    (C) 11
    (D) 13
    (E) 15

First of all, let's figure out how many games they have to win in total. Since there are 30 games, they must win 15 of them in order to win half their games. However, the problem says that they want to win MORE than half their games. So they must win 16 games. They have already won 5, so they have to win 11 more in order to reach their goal. Answer choice C is correct.

Questions that Ask You to Form Groups

Some questions will give you some rules about groups and then ask you about how many groups can be formed. Pay attention to the rules as well as whether they are asking for the number of groups possible, the least number of groups possible, or the greatest number of groups possible.

- Underline the rules for groups
- Circle it if they ask for the least number of groups or greatest number of groups

Here is how the questions could look on the test:

6. There are 15 people waiting in line at a restaurant. If there can be no more than 5 people at a table and no two tables can have the same number of people seated at them, what is the smallest number of tables needed to seat all 15 people?

    (A) 8
    (B) 10
    (C) 3
    (D) 2
    (E) 5

Let's start with plugging in answer choice D since it is the smallest. If we had two tables, one could have 5 people and one could have 4 people since no two tables can have the same number of people. This adds up to 9 people, so choice D does not work. Now let's try choice C since it is the next smallest answer choice. If we had 5 people at one table, 4 people at the next table, and 3 people at the last table, that would only add up to 12 people, which is not enough. Now we try choice E. The first table would have 5 people, the next table would have 4 people, the next table would have 3 people, the next table would have 2 people, and the last table would have 1 person. This adds up to 15, so choice E is correct.

Here is another one for you to try:

7. There are 20 students on a field trip. They need to divide into groups. If each group must have at least 3 students but no more than 6, what is the largest number of groups that the students can form?

    (A) 4
    (B) 3
    (C) 7
    (D) 6
    (E) 8

Since we are looking for the largest number of groups, we want to make each group as small as possible. However, the problem tells us that we can't have less than three students in each group. Let's start with choice E since it is the largest. If we had 8 groups, then we wouldn't have enough students for each group to have at least 3 students (we would need 24 students to form 8 groups), so choice E is out. Now we try choice C and run into the same problem (we would need 21 students to form 7 groups). We don't have enough students so that each group would have at least 3 people. If we try choice D, we would have enough students for each group to have at least 3 people, so choice D is correct.

Here is an even harder one. It is not tricky but there are a lot of steps.

8. At Sunrise Elementary, there are 4 fifth-grade classes, each with 20 students in the class. The whole fifth grade is going on a field trip and there are 3 buses. If every student must ride a bus and the number of students on any bus cannot outnumber the number of students on another bus by more than 1, what is the greatest number of fifth-grade students that can ride on any one bus?

(A) 80
(B) 60
(C) 27
(D) 26
(E) 20

Our first step is to figure out how many fifth-grade students there are. If we multiply 4×20, then we get that there are a total of 80 students. Now we have to divide the number of students by the number of buses. If we divide $80 \div 3$, we get that there are 26.6666 students per bus. But we can't have a partial person! This means that one bus would have 26 students and the other two buses would each have 27 students, since there was a remainder of 2. The question asks what is the greatest number of students on any one bus, so choice C is correct.

Overlapping Groups Problems

There are two types of these questions:

1. Questions that give us two groups that overlap and ask by how much they overlap
2. Questions that give us two groups and one group fits inside the other group

The first type of question tells us how many people belong to two different groups and then tells us how many total people there are. If we add the two groups together, it is greater than the total number of people, so there must be some overlap in the two groups.

To solve these problems:

- Add the two groups together.
- From this number subtract the total number of people.
- This gives us the correct answer choice, or how many people belong to both groups.

Here is how the question can look on the SSAT:

9. In an elementary school, 400 students own a bike and 350 students own a scooter. If a total of 700 students own either a bike or a scooter or both, how many students must own both a bike and a scooter?

    (A) 0
    (B) 50
    (C) 75
    (D) 100
    (E) 300

    To solve this problem, first we add the two groups together. That gives us 750 students. However, there are only 700 students who own either a bike or a scooter. If we subtract 700 from 750, we get that 50 students must own both a bike and a scooter, so answer choice B is correct.

Here is another one for you to try:

10. In a recent poll, 500 people were found to have either a brother or a sister or both. If 300 of these people had a brother and 350 of these people had a sister, then how many people have both a brother and a sister?

    (A) 50
    (B) 100
    (C) 150
    (D) 200
    (E) 300

    If we add 300 and 350, we get 650. We then subtract 500 from this number and get 150. This means that 150 people must have both a brother and a sister, so choice C is correct.

The second type of overlapping groups questions gives us two groups and one group fits entirely inside of the other group. We have to use the difference between the two groups to see how many people are in that in between group.

Here is an example:

11. In a certain class, 14 students travel at least 2 miles to get to school. In the same class, 5 students travel 5 miles or more to get to school. How many students in this class travel at least 2 miles but less than 5 miles to get to school?

    (A) 19
    (B) 14
    (C) 12
    (D) 9
    (E) 7

    Since 14 students travel at least 2 miles, this group would include students that travel 5 miles or more. To find out how many students travel more than 2 miles but less than 5 miles, we subtract the "5 miles or more" group from the "at least 2 miles" group. This gives us 14 − 5 = 9, so answer choice D is correct.

Here is another one to try:

12. In a class of 21 students, all of the students missed at least one question on a test. If 16 students missed three or more questions, how many students missed one or two questions?

(A) 5
(B) 6
(C) 9
(D) 16
(E) 21

The whole group is 21 students, and this includes the group that missed three or more questions. To find just the group that missed one or two questions, we have to subtract off the students who missed three or more. This gives us 21 − 16 = 5, so answer choice A is correct.

Comparing Individuals Questions

Comparing individuals questions give you several comparisons, and you have to sort out an order for the whole group. For example, the question might describe who is taller than whom, or who is older than whom, and so on. The trick to these is simply to draw out the orders given.

- Make a simple drawing for comparison

Here is an example:

13. In a bicycle race, George finished 3 meters behind Carl. Sarah finished ahead of George but behind Hal. Lori finished 5 meters ahead of George. Who came in LAST?

(A) Sarah
(B) George
(C) Carl
(D) Lori
(E) Cannot be determined

The trick to this question is to draw it out:

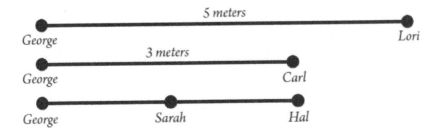

From this we can see that George always comes in last. We can't tell who came in first, or the order of the other bikers, but George always finishes last, so choice B is correct.

Here is another question to try:

14. Chuck is older than Lance but younger than Milo. Taylor is older than both Chuck and Lance. Who is the THIRD oldest?

    (A) Chuck
    (B) Lance
    (C) Milo
    (D) Taylor
    (E) Cannot be determined

Let's go ahead and draw it out:

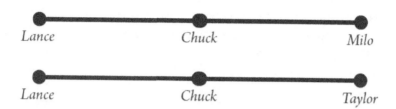

From this drawing, we can see that both Milo and Taylor are older than Chuck. We can't tell who is oldest, but the question does not ask for that. We can tell that Chuck is the third oldest, however, so choice A is correct.

Proportion (Rate) Problems

These questions often use the word *rate*. They can also use the words *per* or *for each*.

- Look out for the words *rate*, *per*, and *for each*

These questions are asking you to set up equivalent fractions, or proportions.

Here is an example:

15. When a school goes on a field trip, they need 2 chaperones for each group of 15 students. If there are a total of 105 students going on a field trip, then how many chaperones do they need?

    (A) 7
    (B) 9
    (C) 14
    (D) 15
    (E) 30

In order to solve this problem, we set up equivalent fractions:

$$\frac{2 \text{ chaperones}}{15 \text{ students}} = \frac{x \text{ chaperones}}{105 \text{ students}}$$

Now we have to solve for x. To get from 15 to 105, we have to multiply by 7. Since we multiplied the denominator by 7, we also have to multiply the numerator by 7. This gives us $2 \times 7 = 14$, so answer choice C is correct.

Here is another one to try. It is a little trickier, but just remember to keep in mind what they are asking for.

16. Suzy works at a museum where she is supposed to give out 3 brochures for every 10 people who come through the door. She started the day with 200 brochures. If 150 people came through the door that day, how many brochures should she have had remaining when the museum closed?

   (A) 30
   (B) 45
   (C) 150
   (D) 155
   (E) 200

First we need to figure out how many brochures she should have handed out. We can use equivalent fractions to do that:

$$\frac{3 \text{ brochures}}{10 \text{ visitors}} = \frac{x \text{ brochures}}{150 \text{ visitors}}$$

We had to multiply the denominator by 15 to get from 10 to 150. This means that we have to multiply the numerator by 15 as well. That tells us that 45 brochures were given out. We aren't done yet, though, since we need to know how many brochures were remaining. We need to do $200 - 45 = 155$, to get that there were 155 brochures left over, so answer choice D is correct.

Some rate questions require you to convert between minutes and hours. Just remember to do the conversion.

   1 hour = 60 minutes

Here is one for you to try:

17. Jim runs four laps every six minutes. At this rate, how many laps does Jim run in one hour?

   (A) 10
   (B) 24
   (C) 40
   (D) 54
   (E) 60

To solve this problem, set up equivalent fractions:

$$\frac{4 \text{ laps}}{6 \text{ minutes}} = \frac{x \text{ laps}}{1 \text{ hour}}$$

The problem here is that we are using minutes and trying to get to hours. Let's convert that one hour into 60 minutes:

$$\frac{4 \text{ laps}}{6 \text{ minutes}} = \frac{x \text{ laps}}{60 \text{ minutes}}$$

To get from 6 to 60, we multiply by 10. So we must also multiply the numerator by 10. That gives us $4 \times 10 = 40$ laps, so answer choice C is correct.

Here is another problem that requires us to convert between minutes and hours:

18. Bill took a 6-mile bike ride. He rode the first mile in 4 minutes. If he continued to ride at the same rate, what fractional part of an hour did it take for him to ride the entire six miles?

(A) $\dfrac{1}{6}$

(B) $\dfrac{1}{5}$

(C) $\dfrac{2}{5}$

(D) $\dfrac{1}{2}$

(E) $\dfrac{3}{4}$

First we have to figure out how many minutes his ride took using equivalent fractions:

$$\frac{1 \text{ mile}}{4 \text{ minutes}} = \frac{6 \text{ miles}}{x \text{ minutes}}$$

We had to multiply the numerator by 6 to get to 6 miles, so we must also multiply the denominator by 6 as well. This gives us that the whole ride took 24 minutes. Now we have to figure out what part of an hour is 24 minutes. We can set up a fraction and then reduce:

$$\frac{24 \text{ minutes}}{60 \text{ minutes}} = \frac{24 \div 12}{60 \div 12} = \frac{2}{5}$$

Answer choice C is correct.

Now you know what you need to answer word problems on the SSAT. Be sure to complete the word problems practice set!

Word Problems Practice Set

1. At the batting cage, 18 buckets had more than 14 balls in each bucket. If 10 of those buckets had at least 16 balls in each bucket, then how many buckets had exactly 15 balls in them?

    (A) 4
    (B) 6
    (C) 8
    (D) 9
    (E) 11

2. Carol is shorter than Jim but taller than Mallory. If Harold is taller than both Carol and Mallory, who is the tallest?

    (A) Carol
    (B) Jim
    (C) Mallory
    (D) Harold
    (E) Cannot be determined

3. Sharon took a 4-mile jog. If she jogged the first mile in 9 minutes and then continued at the same rate, what fraction of an hour did her jog take?

    (A) $\dfrac{1}{3}$

    (B) $\dfrac{2}{5}$

    (C) $\dfrac{7}{12}$

    (D) $\dfrac{3}{5}$

    (E) $\dfrac{4}{5}$

4. A golfer is playing 18 holes. She has won 7 holes and lost 3 holes. What is the greatest number of holes that she can lose on the rest of the course and still win more holes than her opponent?

    (A) 4
    (B) 5
    (C) 7
    (D) 8
    (E) 9

5. Lisa bought three packs of gum that each contained 15 pieces of gum. She chewed one piece of gum and then gave each of her friends 3 pieces each. She had two pieces of gum left at after this. How many friends did Lisa give three pieces of gum to?

   (A) 14
   (B) 15
   (C) 17
   (D) 20
   (E) 32

6. A carriage ride costs $12 for the first two people and $4 more for each additional person. If four people go on a carriage ride together and split the cost equally, how much would each person pay?

   (A) $4
   (B) $5
   (C) $6
   (D) $12
   (E) $20

7. At a high school, there are 3 homeroom classes, each with 15 students in it. These classes need to divide themselves among 4 lunch tables. If the number of students sitting at any lunch table cannot outnumber the number of students sitting at another lunch table by more than one, what is the least number of students that could be sitting at any one table?

   (A) 1
   (B) 2
   (C) 9
   (D) 11
   (E) 12

8. Josh planted 600 trees on 5 acres. He was only supposed to plant 15 trees per acre, however. How many trees should he remove?

   (A) 525
   (B) 500
   (C) 300
   (D) 150
   (E) 75

9. A car wash can clean 3 cars every 10 minutes. At this rate, how many cars can the car wash clean in one hour?

   (A) 3
   (B) 10
   (C) 18
   (D) 30
   (E) 60

10. In a long jump competition, George jumped 2 meters further than Frances. Corrie jumped further than George, but not as far as Megan. If Kim jumped 3 meters further than Frances, but not as far as Corrie, who jumped the THIRD farthest?

    (A) George
    (B) Corrie
    (C) Megan
    (D) Kim
    (E) Cannot be determined

11. A machine stamps 300 notebook covers every 12 minutes. At that rate, how long will it take the machine to stamp 1,050 notebook covers?

    (A) 36 minutes
    (B) 42 minutes
    (C) 60 minutes
    (D) 1 hour 6 minutes
    (E) 1 hour 10 minutes

Answers to Word Problems Practice Set

1. C
2. E
3. D
4. B
5. A
6. B
7. D
8. A
9. C
10. D
11. B

Geometry

On the SSAT, the geometry section deals mostly with angles and shapes and their measurements.

In this section, we will cover:

- Definition of a polygon and how to find its perimeter
- Area of rectangular shapes
- Cube or prism questions
- Angles
- Triangles and their properties
- Circles

Polygons

The root *poly* means "many," so a *polygon* is a many-sided shape. Remember that a circle is not considered a polygon.

- Triangles, rectangles, pentagons and hexagons are examples of polygons

You won't need to define a polygon on the test, but you will need to be able to recognize one.

Perimeter

The *perimeter* of a polygon is the measurement of the outside of a polygon. You find the perimeter of a polygon by adding up the lengths of all the sides.

- The formula for the perimeter is $P = s + s + s + ...$, depending on how many sides the polygon has.

For example, if the lengths of the sides of a rectangle are 4, 6, 4, and 6, the perimeter is $P = 4 + 6 + 4 + 6 = 20$.

- If you are given just the length and the width of a rectangle, multiply each by 2 and then add those numbers together to find the perimeter

On the test you may be given all the measurements needed to calculate the perimeter. However, the test writers might also give you the perimeter and ask you to calculate side lengths.

Here is an example of how these concepts may be tested:

1. If the perimeter of a square is 4 cm, then what is the length of each side?
    (A) 4 cm
    (B) 3 cm
    (C) 2 cm

    (D) 1 cm

    (E) $\frac{1}{2}$ cm

    We know that a square has four sides that are all the same length. This means that we can divide 4 cm by 4 sides, and we get that each side is 1 cm long. Answer choice D is correct.

Here is another problem for you to try:

2. If the perimeter of a triangle whose sides are all the same length is 2 cm, then what is the length of each side?

    (A) 3 cm

    (B) 2 cm

    (C) $\frac{2}{3}$ cm

    (D) $\frac{1}{2}$ cm

    (E) $\frac{1}{3}$ cm

    This problem is a little trickier because the length of each of the sides is not a whole number. There are three equal sides, so we have to divide 2 cm into three equal pieces. We get $\frac{2}{3}$ cm for each side. Answer choice C is correct.

Sometimes the test writers may give you a figure where not all of the side lengths are given and then ask you to find the perimeter. In this case, you first have to find missing side lengths.

*   If the SSAT gives you a figure with side lengths and asks for the perimeter, first check to make sure that you have all the side lengths and solve for any side lengths that you do not have

Here is what these perimeter problems look like on the SSAT:

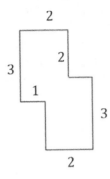

3. All angles in the figure above are right angles. What is the perimeter of the figure?

    (A) 11
    (B) 12
    (C) 13
    (D) 14
    (E) 16

The trick to this problem is that not all the sides are given. To find the perimeter of the figure, we first have to figure out some of the side lengths. From the bottom horizontal pieces, we can add the segment lengths to figure out that the width of the figure is 3, since 1 + 2 = 3. This means that the unlabeled segment near the top right has to be 1. From the right side of the figure, we can add the segment lengths to figure out that the height of the figure is 5, since 3 + 2 = 5, so we can see that the unlabeled segment on the lower left must be 2. Now we add all of our segment lengths together to get 16, or choice E.

Here is an example of a problem that asks you to use the idea of perimeter – even though the word "perimeter" does not even show up in the question:

4. Kyle is winding a piece of string around pegs on a pegboard, as shown below. Kyle starts at A and winds the string in a clockwise direction (as shown). If the string is 87 cm long, then the string will run out just after passing which peg?

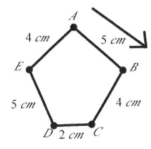

    (A) A
    (B) B
    (C) C
    (D) D
    (E) E

To solve this problem, we first have to figure out what the perimeter of the figure is. If we add the sides together, we get 4 + 5 + 4 + 2 + 5 = 20 cm. Since the string is 87 cm long, we know that it must go around the board more than once. If it goes around once, then 20 cm has been used up, if it goes around twice, then 40 cm has been used. From this, we can see that one more time would give us 60 cm and then another full rotation would get us to 80 cm. This tells us that the string passed point A at 80 cm, and there are now 7 cm left. This 7 cm would allow Kyle to pass point B, but does not provide enough string to get to point C. Therefore, the string will run out just after passing peg B, and answer choice B is correct.

Area of Rectangular Shapes

The area of a rectangle is the amount of space taken up by the inside of the shape.

- The formula for the area of a rectangle is $A = l \times w$, where l is the length and w is the width.

If you have a rectangle that is 4 inches by 6 inches, we can calculate the area to be $A = 4 \times 6 = 24$ square inches.

Remember that a square is a special rectangle.

- The formula for the area of a square is $A = s \times s = s^2$, where s is the length of one side.

Area problems tend to show up at the end of the math section. Remember that most students do not answer these last questions correctly and that the score that matters is your percentile, which only compares you to other students your age. So do your best on these problems, but don't sweat it too much if they seem over your head! Particularly if you are in 5th or 6th grade.

Here is an example of how these concepts may be tested:

5. In Figure 2, *MNOP* is a square and *MQRP* is a rectangle. If the length of *PR* is 10 and the length of *NQ* is 3, then what is the area of square *MNOP*?

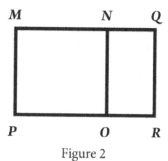

Figure 2

(A) 7
(B) 10
(C) 28
(D) 49
(E) 100

The first step for this problem is to figure out what the length is of one side of the square. We know that the length of *PR* must be the same as the length of *MQ*. This means that the length of *MQ* must be 10. We also know that the length of *NQ* is 3. If we subtract the length of *NQ* from the length of *MQ*, we get that the length of *MN* must be 7. Since the area of the square is equal to the side of a length squared (or multiplied by itself), we know that the area of square *MNOP* must be 49, or answer choice D.

Here is another example of an area problem on the SSAT:

6. The large square in Figure 3 has four smaller squares within it. The area of each smaller square is 5. What is the area of the shaded region?

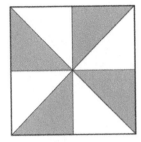

Figure 3

(A) 5

(B) $7\frac{1}{2}$

(C) 10

(D) $\frac{1}{2}$

(E) 15

Each of the shaded triangles takes up half of a small square. We know that the area of each small square is 5, so the area of each triangle must be $2\frac{1}{2}$. There are four of the shaded triangles, so we multiply 4 times $2\frac{1}{2}$, which gives us 10. Answer choice C is correct.

Cubes and prisms

There are not a lot of prism and cube problems on the Middle Level SSAT, but you may see some. Think of a rectangular prism as being the shape of your standard cardboard box. A cube is a rectangular prism whose sides are all the same length and width (think of dice).

You don't need to know a lot of complicated formulas for volume on the SSAT. You may need to know the volume of a cube, however.

The volume of a cube is always calculated as $V = s^3$, where s is the length of one of the sides.

A classic problem involves fitting small cubes into a larger cube.

Here is an example:

7. The small cube below is 1 inch on all sides. How many cubes of this size would be required to fill a larger cube that is 2 inches on all sides?

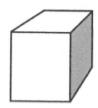

    (A) 2
    (B) 4
    (C) 8
    (D) 16
    (E) 32

Technique 1: Think of the cube having to be doubled in all 3 dimensions. It must be twice as wide, twice as long, and twice as high. Therefore, the 2-inch cube will be 8 times as big, and thus would need 8 smaller cubes. Answer choice C is correct.

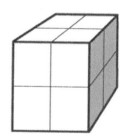

Technique 2: Another way to think of the problem is to compare the volumes of the two cubes. The volume of the small cube is $1 \times 1 \times 1 = 1 \text{ in}^3$. The volume of the 2-inch cube is $2 \times 2 \times 2 = 8 \text{ in}^3$. The larger cube has 8 times the volume of the smaller cube. Again, answer choice C is correct.

Use whichever technique feels easier to you.

Some problems require you to visualize how 3-D objects can fit together.

Here is another example of a problem that requires you to fit smaller cubes with a larger prism.

8. The figure below shows a block that is made up of smaller cubes. How may cubes were needed to make this block?

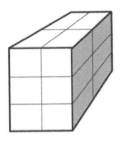

(A) 6
(B) 8
(C) 10
(D) 12
(E) 14

For this question, we have to be able to picture the blocks that we can not see. We can count that the front layer has six blocks in it. We can then see that there are two of these layers going back. This means that we can multiply $6 \times 2 = 12$ to get the total number of blocks. Answer choice D is correct.

Here is an example of a problem that you need to be able to see things in 3-D in order to solve:

9. In Figure 5, a rectangular wooden block is shown with dimensions. If Ally cut the block into two rectangular blocks of exactly the same size and shape, which of the following could be the dimensions of each of the smaller wooden blocks, given in centimeters?

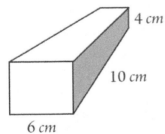

4 cm

10 cm

6 cm

Figure 5

(A) $6 \times 10 \times 2$
(B) $6 \times 5 \times 2$
(C) $3 \times 5 \times 2$
(D) $3 \times 5 \times 4$
(E) $3 \times 10 \times 2$

The key to solving this problem is being able to visualize the different ways that the block could be cut. The most obvious way to cut the block would be the slice it right down the middle on the 10 cm side. This would give us two blocks, each with the dimensions of 6 × 5 × 4. The problem is that this is not an answer choice. So we have to think of how else the block could be cut. To get an answer choice, we actually have to picture slicing the block sideways, or cutting the 4 cm side in half. This gives us two blocks with dimensions 6 × 10 × 2, so answer choice A is correct.

Angles

An angle is where 2 lines or line segments meet.

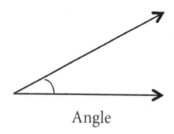

Angle

Here are some important facts about angles:

- A right angle has 90°
- A straight angle has 180°
- Opposite angles are equal

A right angle looks like this:

We designate a right angle like this:

The little box is the symbol to tell you that the angle measure is 90°, which is a right angle.

A straight angle is just a straight line. So why does it have an angle measure of 180°? Well, here is the straight line:

Now, put a line down the middle:

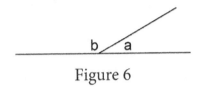

Now you see that it is made up of 2 right angles, each measuring 90°, so the total is 180°.

- Remember, a straight angle has 180°

Here is an example of how this could be tested on the SSAT:

Figure 6

10. In the figure above, angle *a* measures 50°. What is the measure of angle *b*?

(A) 40°
(B) 50°
(C) 100°
(D) 130°
(E) Cannot be determined

A straight angle has 180°, so $a + b = 180°$.

If we plug in what is given and solve, we get:

$$50 + b = 180°$$
$$b = 130°$$

Answer choice D is correct.

Now let's look at opposite angles:

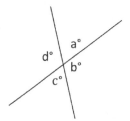

Angles *a* and *c* are opposite angles and are equal to each other. Angles *b* and *d* are also equal to one another.

Here is how this concept could be tested on the SSAT:

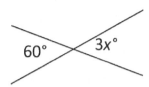

Figure not drawn to scale

11. In the figure above, what is the value of *x*?

    (A) 15
    (B) 20
    (C) 50
    (D) 60
    (E) 180

We know that opposite angles are equal, so we know that $3x = 60$. If we solve for *x*, we get that it is equal to 20, or answer choice B.

Triangles

There are several types of triangles:

- An equilateral triangle has all 3 sides equal, and all 3 angles are the same.
- An isosceles triangle has 2 equal sides and the angles opposite those sides are equal.
- A right triangle has one 90° angle, which is called a right angle. The sum of the other 2 angles is 90°.

Another important fact about triangles is this:

- The sum of the 3 angles in any triangle is always 180°.

Here is how these concepts could be tested on the SSAT:

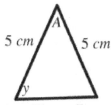

Figure 7

12. In the triangle in Figure 7, the measure of angle A is 80 degrees. What is the angle measure of y in degrees?

(A) 40
(B) 45
(C) 50
(D) 80
(E) It cannot be determined from the information given.

We can identify this triangle as an isosceles triangle because we are given two sides of the same length. The angles opposite these sides are equal. Since we know that the sum of the angles in a triangle equals 180 degrees, we can determine the value of y, eliminating answer choice E. The sum of the two unknown angles is 180° – 80° = 100°. Divide this by 2 and $\frac{100°}{2} = 50°$. The correct answer is choice C.

Here is another one for you to try:

13. In Figure 8 below, what is the value of w?

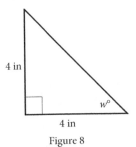

Figure 8

(A) 15°
(B) 30°
(C) 45°
(D) 90°
(E) Cannot be determined

To answer this question, you first need to recognize that we are dealing with an isosceles right triangle. Any time we see a triangle with two sides that are the same length, it almost always means that we will need to use the fact that this makes the triangle isosceles. If a triangle is isosceles, this means that the two angles opposite the congruent sides will also be congruent. We know that the angles in a triangle add up to 180°, and since one of the angles is 90°, then the remaining two angles must add up to 90°. Since these two angles are also equal to one another, we simply divide 90° by 2 and get that each angle is 45°. Answer choice C is correct.

Area of a Triangle

The area of a triangle is the space inside a triangle. The formula is $A = \frac{1}{2}bh$. In a right triangle, like the one below, this formula is easy to use.

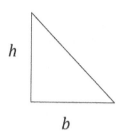

When the triangle is not a right triangle, you have to draw in the height as shown in the triangles below.

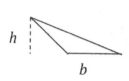

The same formula is used here, although you may need to determine the height from other information given about the triangle.

- The formula for area of a triangle is $A = \frac{1}{2}bh$.

Here is an example of how these concepts may be tested:

14. What is the area of the shaded region if *ABCD* is a square?

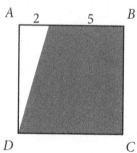

(A) 7
(B) 14
(C) 42
(D) 49
(E) It cannot be determined from the information given.

Although all the dimensions of the shaded region are not given, we can use the information about the square and the triangle to solve this problem, so choice E can be eliminated. First, find the area of the square. The length of $\overline{AB}$ is $2 + 5 = 7$. The area of a square is $A = s^2$, so the area of square $ABCD$ is $A = s^2 = 7^2 = 49$. Since the area we are looking for is smaller than this, we can eliminate choice D. Next, calculate the area of the triangle. We know that $\overline{AD} = \overline{AB}$, so the area of the triangle is $A = \frac{1}{2}bh = \frac{1}{2}(2)(7) = 7$. Now, subtract the area of the triangle from the area of the square to find the area of the shaded region, $A = 49 - 7 = 42$. The correct answer is choice C.

Circles

On the Middle Level SSAT, you basically need to be able to use the concepts of radius and diameter. The radius is the distance from the center to the edge of the circle. The diameter is the distance straight across the circle, going through the center. The diameter is twice the radius.

- Radius = distance from center of circle to any point on circle
- Diameter = distance straight across a circle, through the center
- Diameter = 2 × radius

Here is an example of a question that tests these concepts:

15. Figure 9 shows a circle with a radius of 5. Which of the following could NOT be the length of a line segment that lies completely within the circle?

Figure 9

(A) 11
(B) 10
(C) 8
(D) 5
(E) 4

The longest line segment that will fit completely inside a circle is the diameter. In this circle, the diameter is 10. That means that any line segment that is longer than 10 would not fit entirely within the circle. Answer choice A is correct.

Here is another example of a question that tests the concept of diameter:

16. Fifteen baseballs are packed in a box as shown in Figure 10. Every ball touches another ball or the side of the box in four spots. The diameter of each baseball is 3 inches. Which of the following is possible for the length and width of the box?

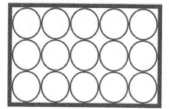

Figure 10

(A) 3 in × 5 in
(B) 6 in × 10 in
(C) 6 in × 12 in
(D) 9 in × 12 in
(E) 9 in × 15 in

The diameter of each ball is 3 inches. Since there are 5 balls across, we know that one side of the box must be at least 15 inches. There are 3 balls going up and down, so we know that the other side of the box needs to be at least 9 inches. Answer choice E is correct.

Now you know what you need in order to crush the geometry questions on the SSAT! Be sure to complete the geometry practice set that follows.

Geometry Practice Set

1. In Figure 1 to the right, what is the value of x?

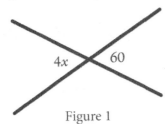

Figure 1

(A) 8
(B) 15
(C) 20
(D) 30
(E) 60

2. The cube in Figure 2 is 2 inches on all sides. How many cubes of this size would be required to fit into a larger cube that is 4 inches on all sides?

Figure 2

(A) 8
(B) 16
(C) 32
(D) 64
(E) 128

3. In the triangle to the side, what is the value of x?

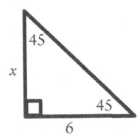

(A) 4
(B) 6
(C) 8
(D) 10
(E) Cannot be determined

4. What is the area of the quadrilateral *ABCD* in Figure 3?

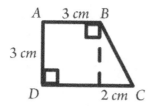

Figure 3

(A) 11 cm²
(B) 12 cm²
(C) 15 cm²
(D) 27 cm²
(E) Cannot be determined

5. If the perimeter of a square is 5 inches, what is the length of each side?

(A) $\frac{1}{5}$ inch

(B) $\frac{1}{2}$ inch

(C) 1 inch

(D) $1\frac{1}{4}$ inches

(E) $1\frac{1}{2}$ inches

6. Lance is winding a string around the pegboard in Figure 4. He starts at P and winds the string in the counter clockwise direction (as shown). If the string is 60 cm long, Lance will run out of string directly after passing which peg?

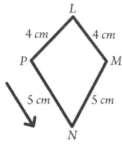

Figure 4

(A) L
(B) M
(C) N
(D) P
(E) Cannot be determined

7. The square in Figure 5 has 4 smaller squares within it, as shown. If the area of each of the smaller squares is 5, then what is the area of the shaded region?

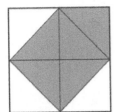

Figure 5

(A) 4
(B) 5
(C) 7.5
(D) 10
(E) 12.5

8. The wooden block in Figure 6 is to be cut into 8 equally sized cubes. What will be the dimensions of each of these cubes?

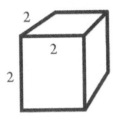

Figure 6

(A) $8 \times 8 \times 8$
(B) $2 \times 2 \times 2$
(C) $2 \times 2 \times 1$
(D) $2 \times 1 \times 1$
(E) $1 \times 1 \times 1$

Answers to Geometry Practice Set

1. B
2. A
3. B
4. B
5. D
6. C
7. E
8. E

Visualization Problems

On the SSAT, you may have to visualize what COULD be.

There are a few different problem types that require you to do this. In this section we will cover:

- Converting 3-D drawings to 2-D
- Questions that require you to think of possibilities
- Looking for patterns

Sometimes you have to see beyond what is on the paper, and you have to think and visualize, and sometimes use your pencil, in order to get the problem right.

The key to these problems is to NOT just jump on the first answer that looks right! These problems stretch your thinking and often the quick answer that you jump on is not the right one.

For these problems, you ALWAYS will look at all 5 answer choices before you answer the question

Converting 3-D Drawings to 2-D

One type of problem that you should be familiar with is the 3-D (3 dimensional) to 2-D (2 dimensional) type. You are given a 3-D object and you have to decide what a part of it looks like in 2-D.

Here is an example of what this type of problem looks like:

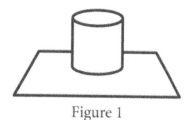

Figure 1

1. A cylindrical container of oatmeal with a flat bottom rests on a piece of paper, as shown in Figure 1 above. Which of the following best represents the set of points where the container touches the paper?

(A)

(B)

(C)

(D)

(E)

Think about the bottom of a flat cylindrical container such as an oatmeal box or a container of salt. Imagine setting it on a piece of paper. First, you know that where it touches the paper it will be a circle. This eliminates choices A and E. You can eliminate choice C because it is only half a circle. So now look at B and D. Answer B might be your first quick choice, and it is wrong! The bottom of the container is perfectly flat, so it touches the paper at the circle, PLUS all the points inside the circle, too. Therefore, the correct answer is D.

Here is another one for you to try:

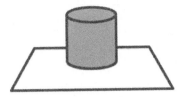

Figure 2

2. A cylindrical plastic cup is placed upside down on a piece of paper so that only its rim touches the paper, as shown in Figure 2. Which of the following shows all the points at which the cup touches the piece of paper?

    (A) ⬭

    (B) ⬬

    (C) ◯

    (D) ⬤

    (E) ⨆

To solve this problem, we have to think about what a cup would look like in two dimensions. In Figure 2, it looks like the rim would be an oval, but that is only because it is a 3-D drawing showing depth. In two dimensions, the rim of the cup would actually be a circle, so we know it has to be choice C or D. Now, we have to make sure that we use all the information given in the problem. The problem tells us that only the rim of the cup touches the piece of paper, so choice C is correct.

Questions that Require You to Think of Possibilities

The next type of problem deals with visualizing limits and considering ALL of the possibilities of what can happen. Sometimes it is a word problem and sometimes it is a picture problem. The rules for this type of problem are:

1. Use your pencil AND your brain! Draw the problem out.

2. Read every word of the problem. There are hints about how to answer it.

3. Consider EVERY answer choice and think before you mark your answer.

———

Let's try an example:

3. A cow is tied to a fencepost in the middle of a 60-foot fence. The rope is 20 feet long. What are the size and shape of his grazing area?

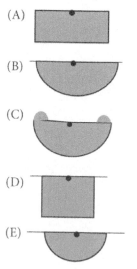

(A)

(B)

(C)

(D)

(E)

Get your pencil out for this one! Draw the post and the fence, and then draw the rope.

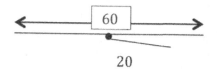

20

Now, act like a hungry cow. You are at the end of the rope. If you keep the rope tight, the pattern will be circular, so choices A and D are eliminated. Notice that the rope is shorter than the length of half the fence, so the cow can't get around the fence to graze on the other side, so choice C is out. This leaves choices B and E. If you quickly picked choice B, then you made the fatal decision for this type of problem! Notice that choice B allows the cow to eat almost to the very end of the 60-foot fence, whereas choice E restricts her from being too close to the end of the fence. The rope is 20 feet long, so the cow can't get very close to the end of the fence and choice E is correct.

———

Here is another one for you to try:

4. If points *A* and *B* were connected in the following figures, in which answer choice would a rectangle and a triangle be formed?

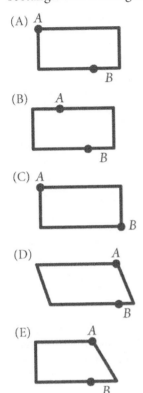

(A) A
       B

(B) A
       B

(C) A
       B

(D) A
       B

(E) A
       B

For this question, get out your pencil and connect *A* and *B* on each drawing. You also need to pay close attention to the question. The question tells us that we have to create a rectangle AND a triangle. The only answer choice that creates both a rectangle and a triangle when you connect *A* and *B* is choice E, so that is the correct answer choice.

Looking for Patterns

The third type of problem that requires visualization involves patterns. A simple example is to see what happens if you turn a shape upside down. See what happens when you turn this triangle upside down:

becomes

That was easy. Now see what happens when you turn a shape upside down and then flip it sideways:

becomes

It's a little bit harder now!

The key to this type of problem is to do some self-talk. Ask yourself: "How does the first item become the second item, and what steps did they take to get there?" Then talk to yourself about it! For the pie shape above, there are TWO things that were done to it. First, they turned it upside down, so that the empty part was on the bottom right. Then they flipped it sideways, so then the empty part was flipped from the bottom right to the bottom left.

Here is an example of what a pattern question may look like on the SSAT:

5.

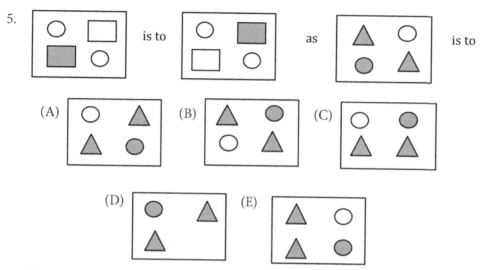

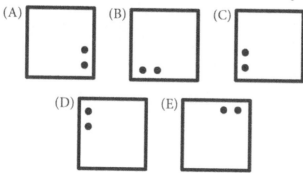

This problem checks to see that your brain can see the pattern when something is changed. In the pattern introduced in the question, the circles didn't change shape, position, or shading. The only thing that changed was that the shaded rectangles switched position. So do the same thing to the new figure. Keep the shaded triangles where they are, and then switch the 2 circles so that the shaded circle is now on the upper right. Answer choice B is the correct one.

Here is another one for you to try:

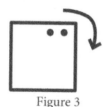

Figure 3

6. The square card in Figure 3 has had two holes punched in it, as shown. If the card is rotated in a clockwise direction, as shown, which of the following could NOT be what the card looks like?

(A)   (B)   (C)

(D)   (E)

This question asks us to figure out what a figure would look like if we rotated it. The easiest thing to do is to pick up the paper and actually rotate it. What does the figure look like if you rotate the paper 90 degrees? What does it look like if you rotate it 180 degrees? If you do this, you can see that no matter how far you rotate the figure, you are not going to be able to get answer choice C. Since we are looking for the one that does NOT work, answer choice C is the correct answer.

Now you know the basics for visualization problems. The best way to get better at these problems is to practice them, so be sure to complete the visualization practice set.

Visualization Practice Set

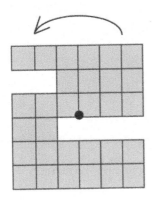

1. Given the figure above, if it rotates a quarter turn in the counterclockwise direction, which of the following would be the result?

(A)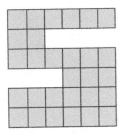

(B)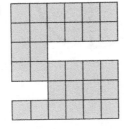

(C)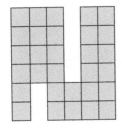

(D)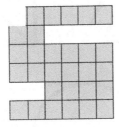

(E)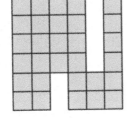

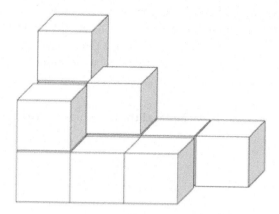

2.   Given the figure above, how many small cubes were used to create this figure?

   (A) 7
   (B) 8
   (C) 9
   (D) 10
   (E) 11

3.   Which of the following figures could be drawn without either lifting the pencil or retracing?

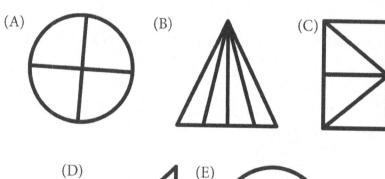

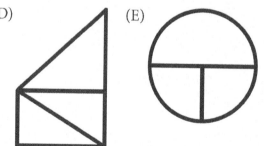

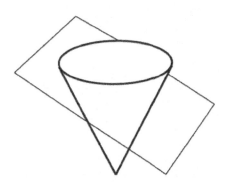

4. A plane slices through the cone-shaped object as shown above. What is the shape of the figure where the cone and the plane intersect?

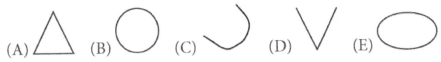

(A)   (B)   (C)   (D)   (E)

Answers to Visualization Practice Set

1. A
2. E
3. D
4. E

On the SSAT you will encounter several types of graphs that you will have to answer questions about. You may see a line graph, a bar graph, or a circle graph.

In this section we will cover:

1. Basic line graph and bar graph questions
2. More complex bar graphs
3. Circle graphs

The good news is that you will not have complicated math to do. The bad news is that you will have to read each question very carefully. That is the key to succeeding with these problems.

Common phrases and what they mean:

- "How many more…" means subtract
- "What percent of…" means find a percent
- "What is the difference…" means subtract
- "What fraction of…" means find a fraction
- "The greatest increase is…" means subtract
- "The combined total of…" means add

Basic Line Graph and Bar Graph Questions

The trick to these question types is to read the question carefully. There are often two or three questions that go with the same graph, and they sometimes look a lot alike. The key is to look for the differences in the questions.

Here is an example of a line graph problem on the SSAT:

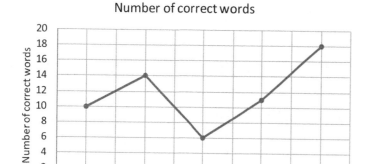

Number of correct words

1. Elena is studying vocabulary word lists. Each day she studies a new word list, and each night she takes a test to see how many words she has learned that day. Her results for last week are shown in the graph above. During which 2-day period did the largest change in number of correct words occur?

   (A) Monday to Tuesday
   (B) Tuesday to Wednesday
   (C) Wednesday to Thursday
   (D) Thursday to Friday
   (E) None of these

Notice that the question is about change. It doesn't ask about improvement, so even a negative answer will be possible. Let's look at each period:

- Monday to Tuesday: 10 to 14, so the change is 4
- Tuesday to Wednesday: 14 to 6, so the change is 8
- Wednesday to Thursday: 6 to 11, so the change is 5
- Thursday to Friday: 11 to 18, so the change is 7

The greatest change is from Tuesday to Wednesday so answer choice B is correct.

Here is another question that uses the same graph:

2. The number of words learned on Wednesday is how many times the number of words learned on Friday?

   (A) 18
   (B) 6
   (C) 3
   (D) $\frac{1}{3}$
   (E) $\frac{1}{6}$

The first thing that you need to note about this question is that it is asking for how many times and not how many more. This means that we are looking for what we need to multiply the words learned on Friday by in order to get the words learned on Wednesday. On Friday, Elena learned 18 words and on Wednesday she learned 6 words. In order to get from 18 to 6, you have to multiply 18 by $\frac{1}{3}$, so answer choice D is correct.

The next type of graph you will see is a bar chart, where the height of the bar shows how many times something happened or how many there are of some category.

Here is an example of a bar chart question:

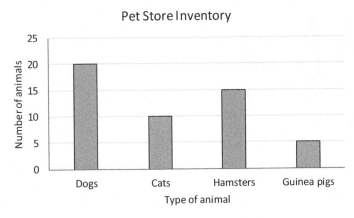

3. The owner of a small pet store performs an inventory of the animals in his store. The results are summarized in the bar graph above. How many more dogs were in the pet store than guinea pigs?

    (A) 3
    (B) 5
    (C) 10
    (D) 15
    (E) 20

To answer this question, we have to figure out how many dogs and how many guinea pigs were in the store when the inventory was performed. If we look at the bar chart, we can see that there were 20 dogs in the store and 5 guinea pigs. Since it is a "how many more" question, we find the difference between 20 and 5, which is 15. Answer choice D is correct.

More Complex Bar Graphs

One type of bar graph that you may see has bars that compare the same thing at different times.

Here is an example of how you may see this type of bar graph question on the SSAT:

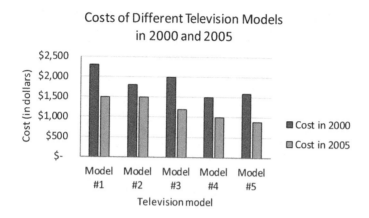

4. The original price of which model was reduced by one-third between 2000 and 2005?

    (A) Model #1

    (B) Model #2

    (C) Model #3

    (D) Model #4

    (E) Model #5

In order to solve this question, we have to multiply each of the model prices in 2000 by one-third and then subtract that from the price in 2000. The answer choice that gives us the 2005 value when we subtract one-third from the 2000 price is the correct answer. If we take the 2000 price ($1500) of Model #4 and multiply by one-third, we get that the price should be reduced by $500. If we reduce $1500 by $500, then we get $1000, which is the 2005 price of Model #4. This means that answer choice D is correct.

Here is another one to try using the same graph of television model prices:

5. The television model that cost the least in 2005 was what price in 2000?

    (A) $900

    (B) $1000

    (C) $1200

    (D) $1500

    (E) $1600

The trick to this question is just to keep track of the details. This is a multi-step problem. First we have to figure out which television model cost the least in 2005. Then we have to figure out what the same television cost in 2000. If we look at the gray bars, we can see that Model #5 cost the least in 2005. If we look at the black bar for the same model, we can see that Model #5 cost $1600 in 2000, so answer choice E is correct.

Another type of bar graph that you may see breaks down the bars into fractional pieces.

Here is an example of how you might see this type of graph on the SSAT:

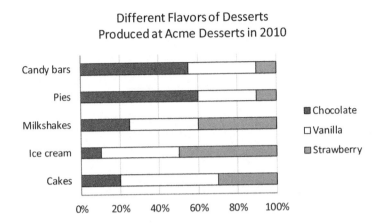

**Different Flavors of Desserts
Produced at Acme Desserts in 2010**

6. The fractional part of the cakes produced by Acme Desserts in 2010 that were vanilla was

(A) $\frac{1}{5}$

(B) $\frac{3}{10}$

(C) $\frac{1}{2}$

(D) $\frac{7}{10}$

(E) $\frac{4}{5}$

To solve this question, we first have to figure out what percent of the cakes produced were vanilla. The white bar represents vanilla cakes. It starts at 20% and then goes until 70%. If we find the difference between the two, we can see that 50% of the cakes produced were vanilla. Since 50% is equal to $\frac{1}{2}$, answer choice C is correct.

Here is another one to try:

7. What fractional part of the milkshakes produced by Acme Desserts in 2010 was strawberry?

   (A) $\dfrac{1}{5}$

   (B) $\dfrac{3}{10}$

   (C) $\dfrac{2}{5}$

   (D) $\dfrac{3}{5}$

   (E) $\dfrac{7}{10}$

If we look at the graph, we can see that the lighter gray part of the bar for milkshakes (the lighter gray portion represents strawberry milkshakes) takes up 40% of the bar. Another way to write 40% is $\dfrac{40}{100}$. If we reduce $\dfrac{40}{100}$ then we get $\dfrac{2}{5}$ and answer choice C is correct.

Circle Graphs

Circle graph problems are relatively straightforward on the SSAT. Generally, these problems ask you to translate from a percent or fraction into a circle graph, or vice versa.

Here are the basic benchmarks that you should know:

$\dfrac{1}{4} = 25\% =$

$\dfrac{1}{2} = 50\% =$

$\dfrac{3}{4} = 75\% =$

Here is an example of a problem like those you might see on the SSAT testing circle graphs:

8. Gregory wants to make a circle graph showing the percentage of tennis matches that he has won. This season, he has won 4 matches and lost 4 matches. Which circle graph shows this correctly?

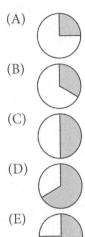

(A)

(B)

(C)

(D)

(E)

In order to answer this question, we first have to figure out what fraction or percent of his matches he won. Since he won 4 matches and lost 4 matches, he won half of his matches. Answer choice C correctly represents him winning half of his matches.

The best way to ace the graph questions is through practice. Be sure to complete the graphs practice set.

Graphs Practice Set

Questions 1-2 refer to the following graph.

1. During which of the following two-month periods did Matt's Shop sell the most bicycles?

    (A) January and February
    (B) February and March
    (C) March and April
    (D) April and May
    (E) May and June

2. In August, ten fewer than twice the number of bikes sold in April were sold. How many bikes were sold in August?

    (A) 15
    (B) 25
    (C) 40
    (D) 50
    (E) 60

Questions 3-4 refer to the following graph.

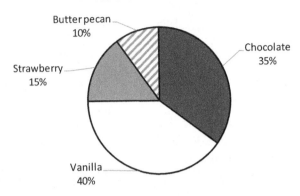

Ice Cream Preferences

Butter pecan
10%

Chocolate
35%

Strawberry
15%

Vanilla
40%

3. A total of 300 people were asked their favorite ice cream. The results are summarized in the circle graph above. How many people preferred chocolate ice cream?

    (A) 35
    (B) 45
    (C) 105
    (D) 120
    (E) Cannot be determined

4. How many more people preferred vanilla than butter pecan?

    (A) 30
    (B) 60
    (C) 90
    (D) 120
    (E) 150

Questions 5-6 refer to the following graph.

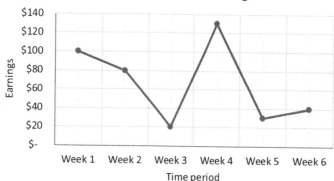

Rachel's Part-time Job Earnings

5. Rachel has a part-time job helping her neighbor with chores and errands. Each week she keeps track of her earnings, and the earnings for her first 6 weeks of work are displayed in the line graph. How much total money did Rachel earn in Weeks 3 and 4?

(A) $20
(B) $65
(C) $110
(D) $120
(E) $150

6. Comparing Rachel's Week 3 earnings to her Week 2 earnings, we would say that

(A) They are $\frac{1}{4}$ as much

(B) They are $\frac{1}{3}$ as much

(C) They are half as much
(D) They are twice as much
(E) They are four times as much

Answers to Graph Practice Set

1. A
2. D
3. C
4. C
5. E
6. A

Tips for the Writing Sample

When you take the SSAT, you will be asked to complete a writing sample. You will be given 25 minutes and two pages to write your response. Your writing sample will NOT be scored. Rather, a copy of it will be sent to the schools that you apply to.

You will be given a choice between two creative writing prompts. The creative prompts might look like "story starters" that a teacher may have used in your school. The test writers will give you a starting sentence and you take it from there.

Here are some examples of what these questions could look like:

- A strange wind blew through town on that Thursday night.
- I thought long and hard before slowly opening the door.
- I had never been in an experience quite like this before.

Plan for the Writing Sample

To approach the writing sample, follow this four step plan:

Step 1: Choose Topic
- Go with the prompt that creates a bigger "spark" in your mind

Step 2: Plan
- Take just a couple of minutes and plan, it will be time well spent
- Be sure to know what your problem is and how it will be resolved

Step 3: Write
- Break your writing into paragraphs – don't do a two page blob
- Remember to start new paragraphs for dialogue and to break up long descriptions
- Write legibly – it does not have to be perfect and schools know that you are writing with a time limit, but if the admissions officers can't read what you wrote, they can't judge it

Step 4: Edit / Proofread

- Save a couple of minutes for the end to look over your work

- You won't be able to do a major editing job where you move around sentences and rewrite portions

- Look for where you may have left out a word or misspelled something

- Make your marks simple and clear – if you need to take something out, just put a single line through it and use a carat to insert words that you forgot

The writing sample is not graded, but the schools that you apply to do receive a copy.

What are schools looking for?

Organization

There should be structure to your story. There needs to be a problem, which builds to a climax, and then a resolution. Since you only have two pages and 25 minutes to get this done, you should know your problem before you begin to write. The biggest mistake that students make is not knowing their resolution before they begin to write. They can't drop clues as they write because they don't know where the story is going! What happens is that students write themselves into a corner and then have to do something that makes no sense in order to get their characters out of a real bind.

Word choice

Use descriptive language. Don't describe anything as "nice" or "good." Describe specifically why something is nice or good. Good writing shows us and DOESN'T tell us.

Creativity and development of ideas

It is not enough just to be able to fit your writing into the form that you were taught in school. These prompts are designed to show how you think. This is your chance to shine! With these creative prompts, this is your chance to come up with unique ideas.

The writing sample is a place for you to showcase your writing skills. It is just one more piece of information that the admissions committee will use in making their decisions.

Answer Sheet

This book includes one full-length practice test. The answer sheet for the test is on the next two pages.

Section 1: Quantitative		
1 (A) (B) (C) (D) (E)	10 (A) (B) (C) (D) (E)	19 (A) (B) (C) (D) (E)
2 (A) (B) (C) (D) (E)	11 (A) (B) (C) (D) (E)	20 (A) (B) (C) (D) (E)
3 (A) (B) (C) (D) (E)	12 (A) (B) (C) (D) (E)	21 (A) (B) (C) (D) (E)
4 (A) (B) (C) (D) (E)	13 (A) (B) (C) (D) (E)	22 (A) (B) (C) (D) (E)
5 (A) (B) (C) (D) (E)	14 (A) (B) (C) (D) (E)	23 (A) (B) (C) (D) (E)
6 (A) (B) (C) (D) (E)	15 (A) (B) (C) (D) (E)	24 (A) (B) (C) (D) (E)
7 (A) (B) (C) (D) (E)	16 (A) (B) (C) (D) (E)	25 (A) (B) (C) (D) (E)
8 (A) (B) (C) (D) (E)	17 (A) (B) (C) (D) (E)	
9 (A) (B) (C) (D) (E)	18 (A) (B) (C) (D) (E)	

Section 2: Reading Comprehension		
1 (A) (B) (C) (D) (E)	15 (A) (B) (C) (D) (E)	29 (A) (B) (C) (D) (E)
2 (A) (B) (C) (D) (E)	16 (A) (B) (C) (D) (E)	30 (A) (B) (C) (D) (E)
3 (A) (B) (C) (D) (E)	17 (A) (B) (C) (D) (E)	31 (A) (B) (C) (D) (E)
4 (A) (B) (C) (D) (E)	18 (A) (B) (C) (D) (E)	32 (A) (B) (C) (D) (E)
5 (A) (B) (C) (D) (E)	19 (A) (B) (C) (D) (E)	33 (A) (B) (C) (D) (E)
6 (A) (B) (C) (D) (E)	20 (A) (B) (C) (D) (E)	34 (A) (B) (C) (D) (E)
7 (A) (B) (C) (D) (E)	21 (A) (B) (C) (D) (E)	35 (A) (B) (C) (D) (E)
8 (A) (B) (C) (D) (E)	22 (A) (B) (C) (D) (E)	36 (A) (B) (C) (D) (E)
9 (A) (B) (C) (D) (E)	23 (A) (B) (C) (D) (E)	37 (A) (B) (C) (D) (E)
10 (A) (B) (C) (D) (E)	24 (A) (B) (C) (D) (E)	38 (A) (B) (C) (D) (E)
11 (A) (B) (C) (D) (E)	25 (A) (B) (C) (D) (E)	39 (A) (B) (C) (D) (E)
12 (A) (B) (C) (D) (E)	26 (A) (B) (C) (D) (E)	40 (A) (B) (C) (D) (E)
13 (A) (B) (C) (D) (E)	27 (A) (B) (C) (D) (E)	
14 (A) (B) (C) (D) (E)	28 (A) (B) (C) (D) (E)	

Section 3: Verbal

1 (A) (B) (C) (D) (E)	21 (A) (B) (C) (D) (E)	41 (A) (B) (C) (D) (E)
2 (A) (B) (C) (D) (E)	22 (A) (B) (C) (D) (E)	42 (A) (B) (C) (D) (E)
3 (A) (B) (C) (D) (E)	23 (A) (B) (C) (D) (E)	43 (A) (B) (C) (D) (E)
4 (A) (B) (C) (D) (E)	24 (A) (B) (C) (D) (E)	44 (A) (B) (C) (D) (E)
5 (A) (B) (C) (D) (E)	25 (A) (B) (C) (D) (E)	45 (A) (B) (C) (D) (E)
6 (A) (B) (C) (D) (E)	26 (A) (B) (C) (D) (E)	46 (A) (B) (C) (D) (E)
7 (A) (B) (C) (D) (E)	27 (A) (B) (C) (D) (E)	47 (A) (B) (C) (D) (E)
8 (A) (B) (C) (D) (E)	28 (A) (B) (C) (D) (E)	48 (A) (B) (C) (D) (E)
9 (A) (B) (C) (D) (E)	29 (A) (B) (C) (D) (E)	49 (A) (B) (C) (D) (E)
10 (A) (B) (C) (D) (E)	30 (A) (B) (C) (D) (E)	50 (A) (B) (C) (D) (E)
11 (A) (B) (C) (D) (E)	31 (A) (B) (C) (D) (E)	51 (A) (B) (C) (D) (E)
12 (A) (B) (C) (D) (E)	32 (A) (B) (C) (D) (E)	52 (A) (B) (C) (D) (E)
13 (A) (B) (C) (D) (E)	33 (A) (B) (C) (D) (E)	53 (A) (B) (C) (D) (E)
14 (A) (B) (C) (D) (E)	34 (A) (B) (C) (D) (E)	54 (A) (B) (C) (D) (E)
15 (A) (B) (C) (D) (E)	35 (A) (B) (C) (D) (E)	55 (A) (B) (C) (D) (E)
16 (A) (B) (C) (D) (E)	36 (A) (B) (C) (D) (E)	56 (A) (B) (C) (D) (E)
17 (A) (B) (C) (D) (E)	37 (A) (B) (C) (D) (E)	57 (A) (B) (C) (D) (E)
18 (A) (B) (C) (D) (E)	38 (A) (B) (C) (D) (E)	58 (A) (B) (C) (D) (E)
19 (A) (B) (C) (D) (E)	39 (A) (B) (C) (D) (E)	59 (A) (B) (C) (D) (E)
20 (A) (B) (C) (D) (E)	40 (A) (B) (C) (D) (E)	60 (A) (B) (C) (D) (E)

Section 4: Quantitative

1 (A) (B) (C) (D) (E)	10 (A) (B) (C) (D) (E)	19 (A) (B) (C) (D) (E)
2 (A) (B) (C) (D) (E)	11 (A) (B) (C) (D) (E)	20 (A) (B) (C) (D) (E)
3 (A) (B) (C) (D) (E)	12 (A) (B) (C) (D) (E)	21 (A) (B) (C) (D) (E)
4 (A) (B) (C) (D) (E)	13 (A) (B) (C) (D) (E)	22 (A) (B) (C) (D) (E)
5 (A) (B) (C) (D) (E)	14 (A) (B) (C) (D) (E)	23 (A) (B) (C) (D) (E)
6 (A) (B) (C) (D) (E)	15 (A) (B) (C) (D) (E)	24 (A) (B) (C) (D) (E)
7 (A) (B) (C) (D) (E)	16 (A) (B) (C) (D) (E)	25 (A) (B) (C) (D) (E)
8 (A) (B) (C) (D) (E)	17 (A) (B) (C) (D) (E)	
9 (A) (B) (C) (D) (E)	18 (A) (B) (C) (D) (E)	

Practice Test

Writing Sample

The writing sample is a way for schools to learn a little more about you. Below are two possible writing topics. Please choose the topic that you find most interesting. Fill in the circle next to the topic you choose and then use this page and the next to write your essay.

(A) The room was very quiet until…

(B) It was hard to imagine, but…

Complete your writing sample on this page and the next. You have 25 minutes to complete this section.

CONTINUE TO THE NEXT PAGE

STOP

Section 1: Quantitative

25 questions
30 minutes

Directions: Each problem is followed by five answer choices. Solve each problem and then decide which answer choice is best.

1. Which of the following is closet to the result of 34.5 – 6.2?

   (A)   29
   (B)   32
   (C)   33
   (D)   35
   (E)   42

2. If a flower is randomly selected from a bouquet, the probability that it is red is $\frac{1}{3}$. If there are 42 flowers in the bouquet, how many of them are red?

   (A)   6
   (B)   7
   (C)   12
   (D)   14
   (E)   15

3. If $12N + 7 = 7$, then what is the value of N?

   (A)   –12
   (B)   –7
   (C) $-\frac{1}{12}$
   (D)   0
   (E)   1

CONTINUE TO THE NEXT PAGE

4. Levi brought 4 dozen cookies to share with his teammates. He gave each teammate 3 cookies and had 9 cookies left over. How many teammates does he have?

   (A)   7
   (B)   9
   (C)   10
   (D)   12
   (E)   13

5. If the perimeter of triangle *DEF* (shown below) is 24, then what is the length of segment *DE*?

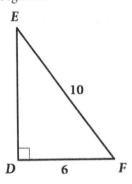

   (A)   4
   (B)   7
   (C)   8
   (D)   16
   (E)   18

6. What is the result of 5.6 – 1.7 + 3.5?

   (A)   0.4
   (B)   3.9
   (C)   5.3
   (D)   6.2
   (E)   7.4

CONTINUE TO THE NEXT PAGE

7. Tashina created the structure below by stacking cubes on top of or next to one another. If there are no gaps between the cubes, then how many cubes did Tashina use to create this structure?

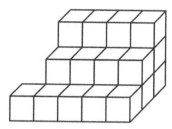

(A)   25
(B)   26
(C)   28
(D)   30
(E)   31

8. Alexandra left her house and rode her bike for 36 minutes. She then rested for 15 minutes. It took her 41 minutes to ride back to her house. If she arrived back at her house at 9:52 AM, what time did she leave for her bike ride?

(A)   8:14 AM
(B)   8:18 AM
(C)   8:20 AM
(D)   8:30 AM
(E)   8:45 AM

9. Which is the value of $0.8 \times \dfrac{1}{2}$?

(A) $\dfrac{1}{5}$

(B) $\dfrac{2}{5}$

(C) $\dfrac{3}{10}$

(D) $\dfrac{4}{5}$

(E)   4

CONTINUE TO THE NEXT PAGE

10. Lowell ate $\frac{1}{5}$ of a pie and Jasmine ate $\frac{1}{4}$ of a pie. What fraction of the pie remained uneaten?

   (A) $\frac{1}{3}$

   (B) $\frac{9}{20}$

   (C) $\frac{3}{5}$

   (D) $\frac{3}{4}$

   (E) $\frac{11}{20}$

11. How many numbers between 0 and 20 are prime?

   (A) 2
   (B) 7
   (C) 8
   (D) 9
   (E) 11

12. Which is $\frac{45}{60}$ written in decimal form?

   (A) 0.75
   (B) 0.90
   (C) 1.33
   (D) 2.50
   (E) 7.50

13. What is the value of $3,000 - 50 + 1$?

   (A) 2,499
   (B) 2,501
   (C) 2,949
   (D) 2,950
   (E) 2,951

CONTINUE TO THE NEXT PAGE

14. If $h = 3$ and $j = 5$, then what is the value of $15 + 3(j - h)$?

(A) 9
(B) 21
(C) 36
(D) 49
(E) 54

15. If $\dfrac{2}{7}$ of a number is equal to 6, what is the value of $\dfrac{6}{7}$ of the same number?

(A) 2
(B) 12
(C) 18
(D) 21
(E) 25

16. If $5 - 2m = 19$, then what is the value of m?

(A) −15
(B) −12
(C) −7
(D) 7
(E) 12

17. If the area of a rectangle is 64 square inches, and the side lengths in inches are integers, then what is one possible perimeter?

(A) 40 inches
(B) 48 inches
(C) 54 inches
(D) 64 inches
(E) 72 inches

18. The diagonal of a rectangle is 20 inches and the length of the rectangle is 16 inches. What is the width of this rectangle, in inches?

(A) 6
(B) 8
(C) 9
(D) 10
(E) 12

CONTINUE TO THE NEXT PAGE

19. If the area of a circle is between 60π and 70π square inches, which could be the diameter of the circle, in inches?

$(A = \pi r^2)$

(A) 8
(B) 16
(C) 18
(D) 20
(E) 25

20. Daryl bought a television that was on sale for 20% off of the original price. If the sale price was $480, what was the original price of the television?

(A) $96
(B) $384
(C) $576
(D) $600
(E) $634

21. The data in the histogram below shows how many pages students read during a read-a-thon. How many more students read fewer than 60 pages than read at least 60 pages?

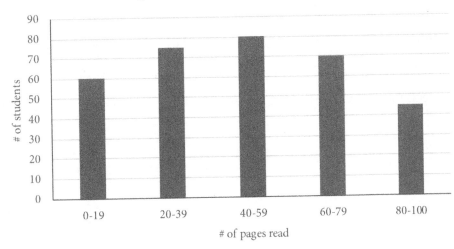

Pages read during read-a-thon

(A) 10
(B) 15
(C) 75
(D) 80
(E) 100

CONTINUE TO THE NEXT PAGE

22. If the sum of three consecutive numbers is 63, what is the greatest of these integers?

    (A)   20
    (B)   21
    (C)   22
    (D)   23
    (E)   25

23. If $4m$ is greater than 8, then $4 + m$ must be greater than

    (A)   6
    (B)   7
    (C)   8
    (D)   9
    (E)   12

24. If Clorinda can shape 1 cookie in 45 seconds, how many cookies can she shape in one hour at this rate?

    (A)   20
    (B)   40
    (C)   60
    (D)   80
    (E)   100

25. The height of triangle X is 2 times the height of triangle Y. The base length of triangle X is $\frac{1}{4}$ the base length of triangle Y. If the area of triangle Y is B square inches, then which expression represents the area of triangle X, in square inches?

    (A) $\frac{1}{4}B$

    (B) $\frac{1}{2}B$

    (C) $2B$
    (D) $4B$
    (E) $8B$

STOP

Section 2: Reading Comprehension

40 questions
40 minutes

Directions: Read each passage in this section carefully and answer the questions that follow. Choose the best answer based on the passage.

CONTINUE TO THE NEXT PAGE

Very few animals can glow in the dark. Among animals that live on land, only parrots and some types of scorpions are known to exhibit fluorescence, or the ability to absorb light of one wavelength and then reemit light of another wavelength. There are more ocean animals that can fluoresce. These include some types of fish and sharks, corals, and one species of sea turtle. There Line 5 are also ocean creatures that exhibit bioluminescence, which is different from fluorescence because it requires no outside light source.

Until recently, there were no amphibians known to exhibit fluorescence. This changed when it was discovered that the South American polka dot tree frog can fluoresce. In lighted conditions, this tree frog is a mix of greens, yellow and reds. If the lights are dimmed, however, the polka 10 dot tree frog will begin to glow green and blue. The discovery of fluorescence in this tree frog is particularly exciting because it led to the detection of new types of molecules in the frog's skin. These newly described molecules are extraordinarily bright. They provide 18% of the visible light that a full moon emits, which is enough light for a related species of frog to see by.

The discovery of fluorescence in the polka dot tree frog opens a world of possibilities. There 15 are another 250 species of tree frogs that have skin that is like that of the polka dot tree frog. There might be a whole world of fluorescent tree frogs that scientists have yet to discover.

1. It can be inferred from the passage that most amphibians are

(A) usually a mix of different colors
(B) on the list of endangered species
(C) not known to exhibit fluorescence
(D) contain a molecule unique to amphibians
(E) the only type of animals that exhibit fluorescence

2. Based on information in the passage, it can be concluded that most ocean animals do not exhibit fluorescence because

(A) they are not amphibians
(B) only land animals exhibit fluorescence
(C) they do not have an outside light source
(D) they are only capable of bioluminescence
(E) their skin lacks a molecule that can absorb and then emit light of a different wavelength

3. The author suggests that fluorescence is

(A) caused by more than one type of molecule
(B) not an area of interest to enough scientists
(C) most likely present in many types of tree frogs
(D) more common in land animals than ocean animals
(E) does not require exposure to an outside light source for all animals

4. According to the passage, in daylight conditions the South American polka dot tree frog

(A) glows brightly
(B) appears to be green, yellow, and red
(C) absorbs the full spectrum of different colors
(D) is hard to spot because it hides from predators
(E) can turn green and blue in order to blend into surroundings

5. The passage is primarily concerned with

(A) describing a newly discovered molecule
(B) describing an exciting scientific discovery
(C) explaining why so few animals exhibit fluorescence
(D) encouraging scientists to study tree frogs more closely
(E) convincing readers of the importance of preserving the habitat of the South American polka dot tree frog

CONTINUE TO THE NEXT PAGE

As the evening fell it began to get very cold, and the growing twilight seemed to merge into one dark mistiness the gloom of the trees, oak, beech, and pine, though in the valleys which ran deep between the spurs of the hills, as we ascended through the Pass, the dark firs stood out here and there against the background of late-lying snow. Sometimes, as the road was cut through the pine

Line 5 woods that seemed in the darkness to be closing down upon us, great masses of greyness, which here and there bestrewed the trees, produced a peculiarly weird and solemn effect, which carried on the thoughts and grim fancies engendered earlier in the evening, when the falling sunset threw into strange relief the ghost-like clouds which amongst the Carpathians seem to wind ceaselessly through the valleys. Sometimes the hills were so steep that, despite our driver's haste, the horses

10 could only go slowly. I wished to get down and walk up them, as we do at home, but the driver would not hear of it. "No, no," he said; "you must not walk here; the dogs are too fierce"; and then he added, with what he evidently meant for grim pleasantry—for he looked round to catch the approving smile of the rest—"and you may have enough of such matters before you go to sleep." The only stop he would make was a moment's pause to light his lamps.

6. The tone of the passage can best be described as

(A) ironic
(B) annoyed
(C) enthusiastic
(D) ominous
(E) startled

7. As used in line 6, the word "solemn" is closest in meaning to

(A) threatening
(B) exciting
(C) listless
(D) ancient
(E) gloomy

8. It can be inferred that this passage most likely takes place

(A) in a small village
(B) at the end of winter
(C) on the outskirts of a city
(D) during the holiday season
(E) at the beginning of autumn

9. Which of the following sensory images is most important to this passage?

(A) the sight of the horses
(B) the sound of barking dogs
(C) the sight of the ghost-like clouds
(D) the smell of the oak, beech, and pine trees
(E) the sound of horse hooves on the road

10. The author uses all of the following to emphasize the sense of gloom EXCEPT the

(A) trees
(B) setting sun
(C) speed of the horses
(D) driver of the carriage
(E) other passengers in the carriage

11. It can be concluded from the passage that the narrator

(A) is afraid of dogs
(B) is traveling to a new job
(C) is going to meet a stranger
(D) does not regularly travel through the Carpathians
(E) regrets his decision to ride with this particular driver

CONTINUE TO THE NEXT PAGE

This passage was produced by the National Park Service.

By the Act of March 1, 1872, Congress established Yellowstone National Park in the Territories of Montana and Wyoming "as a public park or pleasuring-ground for the benefit and enjoyment of the people" and placed it "under exclusive control of the Secretary of the Interior." The founding of Yellowstone National Park began a worldwide national park movement. Today more than 100

Line 5 nations contain some 1,200 national parks or equivalent preserves.

In the years following the establishment of Yellowstone, the United States authorized additional national parks and monuments, many of them carved from the federal lands of the West. These were also administered by the Department of the Interior, while other monuments and natural and historical areas were administered by the War Department and the Forest Service of the

10 Department of Agriculture. No single agency provided unified management of the varied federal parklands.

On August 25, 1916, President Woodrow Wilson signed the act creating the National Park Service, a new federal bureau in the Department of the Interior responsible for protecting the 35 national parks and monuments then managed by the department and those yet to be established.

15 This "Organic Act" states that "the Service thus established shall promote and regulate the use of the Federal areas known as national parks, monuments and reservations…by such means and measures as conform to the fundamental purpose of the said parks, monuments and reservations, which purpose is to conserve the scenery and the natural and historic objects and the wild life therein and to provide for the enjoyment of the same in such manner and by such means as will

20 leave them unimpaired for the enjoyment of future generations."

The National Park System of the United States now comprises more than 400 areas covering more than 84 million acres in 50 states, the District of Columbia, American Samoa, Guam, Puerto Rico, Saipan, and the Virgin Islands. These areas are of such national significance as to justify special recognition and protection in accordance with various acts of Congress.

12. The passage suggests that before 1872
   (A) there were no national parks in the United States
   (B) the Department of the Interior did not exist
   (C) national parks were administered primarily by the War Department
   (D) national parks were popular in countries other than the United States
   (E) most of the land in the western United States was controlled by the federal government

13. According to the passage, the National Park Service
   (A) operates without support from Congress
   (B) became separate from the Department of the Interior
   (C) now includes the Forest Service of the Department of Agriculture
   (D) is responsible for all federal lands in the West
   (E) took over management of parks and monuments from several different agencies

14. Based on information in the passage, all of the following are true about the National Park Service EXCEPT it
   (A) created Yellowstone National Park
   (B) is part of the Department of the interior
   (C) protects lands identified as significant by Congress
   (D) was established while Woodrow Wilson was president
   (E) has a mission of preserving American lands for future generations

CONTINUE TO THE NEXT PAGE

15. The primary purpose of the fourth paragraph is to

(A) transition to a new topic
(B) describe various national parks
(C) explain why the National Park Service was founded
(D) emphasize how important national parks have become since Yellowstone was founded
(E) conclude a discussion of the significance of the establishment of the Department of the Interior

16. Which title best reflects the main idea of this passage?

(A) Why National Parks Should Be Created
(B) Yellowstone: America's First National Park
(C) A Brief History of United States National Parks
(D) Agencies Working Together in the United States
(E) The Importance of Preserving Scenery and Historic Sites

This poem was written by Nora May French.

BETWEEN TWO RAINS

IT is a silver space between two rains;
The lulling storm has given to the day
An hour of windless air and riven grey;
The world is drained of color; light remains.
Line 5   Beyond the curving shore a gull complains;
Unceasing, on the bastions of the bay,
With gleam of shields and veer of vaporing spray
The long seas fall, the grey tide wars and wanes.
It is a silver space between two rains:
10   A mood too sweet for tears, for joy too pale—
What stress has swept or nears us, thou and I?
This hour a mist of light is on the plains,
And seaward fares again with litten sail
Our laden ship of dreams adown the sky.

17. "Wanes" (line 8) most nearly means

(A) stops
(B) lessens
(C) pulls
(D) lingers
(E) budges

18. The poem mentions all of the following EXCEPT

(A) the sea
(B) ships
(C) sailors
(D) rain
(E) light

19. The author's tone can be described as

(A) reflective and hopeful
(B) sarcastic and angry
(C) defeated and pessimistic
(D) resigned and optimistic
(E) playful and humorous

20. The author of this poem is primarily concerned with

(A) sharing an experience she once had
(B) contrasting two very different storms
(C) describing the sea when a storm has ended
(D) discussing the dangers of an unpredictable sea
(E) comparing the time between two storms to the fragility of dreams

CONTINUE TO THE NEXT PAGE

This letter was written by merchant George Horace Lorimer to his son.

Dear Pierrepont: The cashier has just handed me your expense account for the month, and it fairly makes a fellow hump-shouldered to look it over. When I told you that I wished you to get a liberal education, I didn't mean that I wanted to buy Cambridge. Of course the bills won't break me, but they will break you unless you are very, very careful.

Line 5   I have noticed for the last two years that your accounts have been growing heavier every month, but I haven't seen any signs of your taking honors to justify the increased operating expenses; and that is bad business—a good deal like feeding his weight in corn to a scalawag steer that won't fat up.

I haven't said anything about this before, as I trusted a good deal to your native common-sense
10   to keep you from making a fool of yourself in the way that some of these young fellows who haven't had to work for it do. But because I have sat tight, I don't want you to get it into your head that the old man's rich, and that he can stand it, because he won't stand it after you leave college. The sooner you adjust your spending to what your earning capacity will be, the easier they will find it to live together.

15   The only sure way that a man can get rich quick is to have it given to him or to inherit it. You are not going to get rich that way—at least, not until after you have proved your ability to hold a pretty important position with the firm; and, of course, there is just one place from which a man can start for that position with Graham & Co. It doesn't make any difference whether he is the son of the old man or of the cellar boss—that place is the bottom. And the bottom in the office end of this business is a seat at the mailing-desk, with eight dollars every Saturday night.

21. According to the passage, the author's son can expect to

(A) finish his education soon
(B) inherit wealth from his father
(C) receive no more money from his father
(D) be called back home to work in his father's company
(E) be promoted in his father's company only after proving himself

22. The author considers which of the following to contribute to foolish behavior?

(A) receiving money that was not earned
(B) trying to become wealthy too quickly
(C) holding an important position in a firm
(D) spending too much money while attending college
(E) starting work at the mailing-desk at your father's company

23. The author describes himself as "hump-shouldered" in the first sentence in order to

(A) show how angry he is
(B) accentuate his disappointment
(C) describe his own physical deterioration
(D) warn his son that he will no longer pay his bills
(E) emphasize how exhausted he is made by his son's behavior

24. According to the passage, the son should spend less money while in school in order to

(A) show respect for his father
(B) have money saved up for when he graduates
(C) prevent the father from running out of money
(D) adjust to the lifestyle he can afford after graduation
(E) prove to his father that he deserves an important position at his father's company

CONTINUE TO THE NEXT PAGE

25. Which of the following best states the main idea of this passage?

    (A) People should not expect to spend more money than they earn.
    (B) It is a bad idea for children to work for their parents' businesses.
    (C) All employees should start at the level of working at the mailing-desk.
    (D) Students should be expected to earn spending money while in college.
    (E) Many parents send too much money to their children attending college.

The development of the drug penicillin is one of the greatest achievements of modern medicine. Before penicillin, doctors often had to simply wait and hope when a patient had an infection caused by bacteria. Cuts and scratches could turn into untreatable blood infections. Doctors did not have a reliable medicine that could kill bacteria.

Line 5   The development of this important drug was by chance. In 1928, Alexander Fleming was working as a Professor of Bacteriology at St. Mary's Hospital in London. He was studying Staphylococcus, a bacteria that causes sore throats, boils, and abscesses. On September 3, he returned from a holiday and observed that something unusual had happened in one of his petri dishes. He was growing colonies, or groups of bacteria, on special plates called petri dishes. Most of

10   his petri dishes were covered with colonies of the Staphylococcus bacteria. On one dish, however, he observed a spot where no colonies were growing. In this spot, he noticed that a mold was growing. This mold was later identified as Penicillum notatum. This mold produces a substance that stops the growth of many different types of bacteria, including some that cause disease.

The idea that mold could stop the growth of bacteria was not new. In ancient Egypt, people

15   were known to apply moldy bread to infected wounds as a cure. However, the discovery of the Penicillum notatum mold in a laboratory was an important step in developing the drug penicillin.

26. This passage was most likely intended as

    (A) praise for a little known scientist
    (B) a lesson about the wisdom of ancient cultures
    (C) a warning about the development of new drugs
    (D) information about an important scientific advance
    (E) an advertisement for St. Mary's Hospital

27. The author apparently considers the development of penicillin the result of

    (A) years of hard work
    (B) unclean conditions
    (C) a fortunate coincidence
    (D) a careful study of history
    (E) scientists working together

28. According to the passage, all of the following are true about penicillin EXCEPT that it

    (A) kills some bacteria
    (B) was first developed in Egypt
    (C) was created after a mold was observed
    (D) revolutionized how doctors treat infections
    (E) was the outcome of work done by Fleming

29. The passage implies that Alexander Fleming

    (A) had a long career
    (B) profited from penicillin
    (C) made careful observations
    (D) was respected by his peers
    (E) was not well-known during his lifetime

30. This passage is primarily about

    (A) unusual uses of mold
    (B) the work of Alexander Fleming
    (C) how a treatment was developed
    (D) treatment of bacterial infections
    (E) differences between penicillin and other drugs

CONTINUE TO THE NEXT PAGE

Dr. Flossie Wong-Staal was born as Yee Ching Wong in China in 1947. In 1952, her family fled the communist government in China. They settled in Hong Kong, where she chose the English name Flossie for herself. In Hong Kong, she began her science education in a school run by English nuns. This early exposure to science would lead her to a career in molecular biology. Her work in
Line 5 this field would change the world.

Dr. Wong-Staal went to college at the University of California, Los Angeles, otherwise known as UCLA. She then continued her education at UCLA by earning a PhD in molecular biology. After she received her PhD, she went to work in a lab studying cancer cells at the National Institutes of Health. Her work there focused on viruses that cause cancer, both in animals and humans.
10 Working at this lab led to her studying the Human Immunodeficiency Virus, or HIV.

In 1984, Dr. Wong-Staal was the first person to map, or identify, the genes of the HIV virus. It was this mapping that allowed a diagnostic test to be developed. This diagnostic test would prove crucial to slowing the spread of the HIV virus. Once infected people were aware that they had the virus, they could take certain actions to prevent the disease from being spread to new people. This
15 test also allowed blood banks to begin screening for the virus. This stopped patients who needed to receive blood from donors from being infected with HIV. After her work with HIV, Dr. Wong-Staal continued researching viruses, looking for cures, treatments, and vaccines for some of the world's most deadly diseases.

31. The author's main purpose is to

(A) describe the achievements of a talented scientist
(B) illustrate the importance of scientific experiments
(C) convince readers to pursue a career in the sciences
(D) share an experience common to recent immigrants
(E) demonstrate the importance of a new diagnostic test

32. As used in line 13, "crucial" most nearly means

(A) ideal
(B) uncertain
(C) rapid
(D) unrelated
(E) essential

33. The passage implies that before the work of Dr. Wong-Staal

(A) genes had not yet been mapped
(B) viruses were not well understood
(C) vaccines for viruses had not yet been invented
(D) patients who received blood transfusions risked HIV infection
(E) the link between cancer and viruses had not yet been discovered

34. This passage is probably taken from a

(A) fictional account
(B) scientist's journal
(C) medical supply catalog
(D) book about influential scientists
(E) notice about possible treatments

CONTINUE TO THE NEXT PAGE

During World War II, many American men went to fight as soldiers in Europe and Asia. They left jobs that needed to be filled in order for the country to operate. The demand for workers also increased greatly because of the need for more manufacturing. Materials like uniforms, weapons, and munitions needed to be produced for the war effort. American women entered the workforce

Line 5 in numbers never before seen to fill these job vacancies. Between 1940 and 1945, the percent of women who worked outside the home increased from 27 percent to almost 37 percent. Women were also allowed to work in industries that had only allowed male employees previously. For example, before the war, less than 1 percent of workers in the aviation industry were female. By 1943, however, more than 310,000 women worked in the aviation industry, making up 65% of its

10 workforce.

Government officials knew that the participation of women in the workforce in the United States would be important for achieving victory in the war overseas. An advertising campaign was started to encourage women to work in factories that produced war goods. One campaign featured "Rosie the Riveter." Rosie was based on workers at munitions factories, where weapons and

15 ammunition were made. Posters featured Rosie with her hair pulled back under a red bandanna, a tenacious look on her face, and her fist raised to show power and strength. Her portrait became one of the most widely recognized images from World War II.

35. According to the passage, before World War II, women

(A) did not work outside the home
(B) were not featured in advertisements
(C) did not work in the munitions industry
(D) were not encouraged to work outside the home
(E) were rarely hired to work in the aviation industry

36. Which of the following is a synonym for the word "tenacious" (line 16)?

(A) relaxed
(B) determined
(C) pleasant
(D) feeble
(E) puzzled

37. The passage mentions all of the following aspects of World War II EXCEPT

(A) which countries were at war
(B) where American soldiers fought
(C) workers in the aviation industry
(D) the shortage of workers in America
(E) government advertising campaigns

38. The passage suggests that the aviation industry during World War II

(A) was replaced by the munitions industry
(B) was largely moved to overseas factories
(C) would have had trouble operating without female workers
(D) could not fill all of the orders that troops overseas required
(E) was the focus of a large advertising campaign run by the government

39. The passage says "Rosie the Riveter" was

(A) based on a single person
(B) used to encourage male soldiers
(C) used to recruit workers in the aviation industry
(D) a symbol of peace during World War II
(E) one of the most remembered images of World War II

40. This passage is mainly about

(A) female images during a major conflict
(B) the shortage of workers during World War II
(C) the treatment of women during World War II
(D) a group of workers during World War II
(E) advertising campaigns of the United States government

STOP

Section 3: Verbal

60 questions
30 minutes

This section has two types of questions – synonyms and analogies.

Synonyms

Directions: Each question has a word in all capital letters and then five answer choices that are in lower case letters. Choose the answer choice that has the word (or phrase) that is closest in meaning to the word that is in capital letters.

1.   WITHER:

    (A)   droop
    (B)   shovel
    (C)   loan
    (D)   navigate
    (E)   discard

2.   RUBBISH:

    (A)   strand
    (B)   container
    (C)   cabinet
    (D)   batch
    (E)   debris

3.   SUFFICIENT:

    (A)   enough
    (B)   superior
    (C)   limited
    (D)   firm
    (E)   helpful

4.   PERPLEX:

    (A)   ease
    (B)   confuse
    (C)   notify
    (D)   forbid
    (E)   sprawl

5.   SCURRY:

    (A)   grunt
    (B)   advertise
    (C)   bustle
    (D)   sweat
    (E)   handle

6.   PORTION:

    (A)   dwelling
    (B)   formula
    (C)   removal
    (D)   segment
    (E)   expression

CONTINUE TO THE NEXT PAGE

7. RIVAL:

   (A) opponent
   (B) freedom
   (C) team
   (D) scout
   (E) pair

8. ELEVATE:

   (A) convert
   (B) depart
   (C) mend
   (D) raise
   (E) accept

9. DODGE:

   (A) sort
   (B) trample
   (C) invade
   (D) harness
   (E) avoid

10. ASSOCIATE:

   (A) reputation
   (B) colleague
   (C) excursion
   (D) product
   (E) press

11. DIVINE:

   (A) mature
   (B) imaginary
   (C) splendid
   (D) bold
   (E) natural

12. COUNTERFEIT:

   (A) possibility
   (B) sorrow
   (C) information
   (D) happiness
   (E) fake

13. BUCKLE:

   (A) pronounce
   (B) find
   (C) spend
   (D) hammer
   (E) collapse

14. PRECISE:

   (A) naïve
   (B) exact
   (C) reasonable
   (D) absolute
   (E) willing

15. CONTAMINATE:

   (A) pollute
   (B) sink
   (C) flutter
   (D) manufacture
   (E) preserve

16. IMMERSE:

   (A) refine
   (B) overpower
   (C) submerge
   (D) detour
   (E) elect

17. AUTHENTIC:

   (A) drowsy
   (B) reserved
   (C) fortunate
   (D) genuine
   (E) humble

18. SURLY:

   (A) familiar
   (B) grumpy
   (C) relaxed
   (D) normal
   (E) tired

CONTINUE TO THE NEXT PAGE

19. DUPLICATE:

(A) copy
(B) value
(C) export
(D) create
(E) notify

20. LAVISH:

(A) extravagant
(B) thrilling
(C) gloomy
(D) radiant
(E) impolite

21. REPEAL:

(A) harbor
(B) announce
(C) allow
(D) link
(E) cancel

22. IMPLY:

(A) compile
(B) flatter
(C) affirm
(D) suggest
(E) tackle

23. VACATE:

(A) leave
(B) wander
(C) beat
(D) hesitate
(E) persuade

24. AMPLIFY:

(A) take
(B) crease
(C) increase
(D) steal
(E) wiggle

25. TEMPORARY:

(A) straight
(B) abrupt
(C) recent
(D) brief
(E) sincere

26. TUMULT:

(A) sentiment
(B) effort
(C) uproar
(D) memory
(E) ability

27. ILLOGICAL:

(A) reckless
(B) senseless
(C) clever
(D) jealous
(E) forgotten

28. FLUCTUATE:

(A) rely
(B) summon
(C) waver
(D) identify
(E) gain

29. MALIGN:

(A) govern
(B) insult
(C) divide
(D) panic
(E) separate

30. JEOPARDIZE:

(A) focus
(B) depart
(C) threaten
(D) seek
(E) marvel

CONTINUE TO THE NEXT PAGE

Analogies

Directions: Identify the relationships between the words. Then choose the answer choice that best finishes the sentence.

31. Parrot is to bird as

    (A) toucan is to feathers
    (B) crocodile is to reptile
    (C) walrus is to manatee
    (D) snake is to skin
    (E) hamster is to cage

32. Hamburger is to meat as

    (A) salad is to dressing
    (B) pancake is to breakfast
    (C) pie is to crust
    (D) cheese is to milk
    (E) chicken is to barbeque

33. Knife is to cut as

    (A) shawl is to cool
    (B) whisk is to blend
    (C) steam is to boil
    (D) basket is to gather
    (E) guide is to direct

34. Closet is to clothes as

    (A) roof is to shingles
    (B) lawn is to grass
    (C) ice is to rink
    (D) pantry is to food
    (E) pane is to window

35. Petal is to flower as

    (A) leaf is to tree
    (B) tulip is to bulb
    (C) wreath is to door
    (D) boundary is to state
    (E) motto is to advertisement

36. Medicine is to heal as

    (A) wharf is to sail
    (B) stride is to walk
    (C) award is to compete
    (D) crystal is to shine
    (E) stitch is to join

37. Knowledge is to learning as

    (A) experience is to doing
    (B) description is to attempting
    (C) streak is to crumbling
    (D) confidence is to avoiding
    (E) ability is to locating

38. Buckle is to belt as

    (A) cuff is to pants
    (B) handle is to pot
    (C) cover is to seal
    (D) faucet is to tap
    (E) latch is to gate

39. Pack is to wolves as

    (A) llama is to alpaca
    (B) gaggle is to geese
    (C) wisdom is to owl
    (D) planet is to continents
    (E) gourd is to pumpkin

40. Adjust is to change as

    (A) benefit is to harm
    (B) observe is to ignore
    (C) cause is to effect
    (D) regard is to exhaust
    (E) doubt is to questioning

CONTINUE TO THE NEXT PAGE

41. Scout is to find as

   (A) emperor is to flee
   (B) porter is to carry
   (C) messenger is to obey
   (D) ranger is to call
   (E) burglar is to sell

42. Lunch is to dinner as

   (A) departure is to arrival
   (B) appeal is to request
   (C) delay is to correction
   (D) evening is to noon
   (E) district is to region

43. Pear is to fruit as

   (A) strings is to harp
   (B) reflection is to mirror
   (C) slipper is to shoe
   (D) ceiling is to wall
   (E) supplies is to container

44. Dentist is to teeth as

   (A) player is to jersey
   (B) nurse is to stethoscope
   (C) mechanic is to engine
   (D) banker is to money
   (E) driver is to automobile

45. Cloth is to fibers as

   (A) device is to switch
   (B) sidewalk is to cement
   (C) purchase is to sale
   (D) journal is to writing
   (E) fraction is to portion

46. Joint is to elbow as

   (A) knee is to leg
   (B) muscle is to heart
   (C) shoulder is to wrist
   (D) skin is to tissue
   (E) foot is to ankle

47. Dusty is to prairie as

   (A) sunny is to view
   (B) blustery is to tornado
   (C) humid is to jungle
   (D) frantic is to disaster
   (E) wet is to rain

48. Anxious is to terrified as

   (A) sincere is to frank
   (B) angry is to enraged
   (C) timid is to outgoing
   (D) beloved is to desperate
   (E) tame is to wild

49. Code is to mode as

   (A) fall is to tall
   (B) arrow is to target
   (C) litter is to latter
   (D) approach is to path
   (E) cub is to cup

50. Unique is to duplicate as

   (A) curious is to interest
   (B) pitiful is to sympathy
   (C) grumbling is to unhappiness
   (D) ordinary is to custom
   (E) clumsy is to coordination

51. Fair is to bias as

   (A) gradual is to relief
   (B) infinite is to end
   (C) obedient is to humor
   (D) innocent is to liberty
   (E) uneasy is to suspicion

52. Floor is to scrub as

   (A) tray is to lift
   (B) sleeve is to roll
   (C) mirror is to polish
   (D) flap is to secure
   (E) rack is to hang

CONTINUE TO THE NEXT PAGE

53. Wilted is to flower as

    (A) strong is to oak
    (B) limp is to plant
    (C) healthy is to leaf
    (D) lush is to grass
    (E) dormant is to winter

54. Extract is to remove as

    (A) apologize is to explain
    (B) disguise is to spy
    (C) leave is to vacate
    (D) hush is to silence
    (E) crush is to rumple

55. Doze is to sleep as

    (A) mumble is to speak
    (B) tangle is to straighten
    (C) confess is to investigate
    (D) demonstrate is to show
    (E) grab is to handle

56. Fin is to arm as

    (A) muzzle is to snout
    (B) grizzly is to bear
    (C) whale is to marine
    (D) scales is to skin
    (E) beak is to tongue

57. Dull is to luminous as

    (A) abrupt is to sudden
    (B) fresh is to ripe
    (C) essential is to distracted
    (D) social is to quiet
    (E) knit is to unravelled

58. Catalog is to inventory as

    (A) decoration is to adornment
    (B) missile is to jet
    (C) goods is to shelves
    (D) gravel is to rock
    (E) basin is to tap

59. Nautical is to sea as

    (A) tropical is to palms
    (B) civilized is to discussion
    (C) distressed is to house
    (D) trustworthy is to follower
    (E) terrestial is to land

60. Strength is to exercise as

    (A) clarity is to accuracy
    (B) intelligence is to nonsense
    (C) limp is to injury
    (D) flexibility is to endurance
    (E) mirth is to happiness

STOP

Section 4: Quantitative

25 questions
30 minutes

Directions: Each problem is followed by five answer choices. Solve each problem and then decide which answer choice is best.

1. In the sequence below, each term is nine more than the previous term. Which could be a number in this sequence?

   9, 18, 27, 36, …

   (A) 863
   (B) 899
   (C) 953
   (D) 962
   (E) 972

2. Which expression has the greatest value?

   (A) 6.2×100
   (B) $0.62 \times 10,000$
   (C) $0.62 \times 1,000$
   (D) 0.0062×10^5
   (E) 62×10

3. The first number in a sequence is 2, the second number is 3, the third number is 5, and each number is one less than twice the previous number. What is the 7th number in this sequence?

   (A) 9
   (B) 17
   (C) 33
   (D) 65
   (E) 66

CONTINUE TO THE NEXT PAGE

4.   Omar spends 35% of the hours in each day sleeping. Which circle graph best represents the amount of time Omar spends sleeping each day?

(A)

(B)
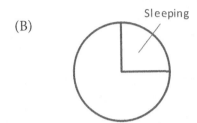

(C)
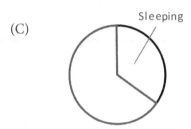

(D)
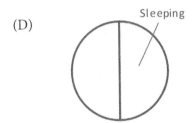

(E)

CONTINUE TO THE NEXT PAGE

5.   What is the value of 43 × 17 − 300?

(A)   431
(B)   444
(C)   452
(D)   737
(E)   1,031

6.   Luis, Carol, Forrest, Lindsay, and Randy were the only participants in a race. Carol finished before both Randy and Lindsay. Lindsay finished after Luis but before Forrest. If Randy finished before Lindsay, who finished in FOURTH place?

(A)   Randy
(B)   Lindsay
(C)   Forrest
(D)   Luis
(E)   cannot be determined from information given

7.   What fraction does the arrow point to on the number line?

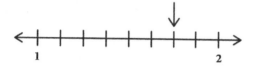

(A) $\dfrac{7}{8}$

(B) $\dfrac{3}{5}$

(C) $\dfrac{3}{4}$

(D) $\dfrac{13}{7}$

(E) $\dfrac{7}{4}$

CONTINUE TO THE NEXT PAGE

8.   If $x = 4$ and $y = 2$, then what is the value of $x^2 - y$?

(A)   2
(B)   6
(C)   8
(D)   10
(E)   14

9.   Which is the value of 199×306?

(A)   6,084
(B)   12,472
(C)   60,894
(D)   69,035
(E)   72,374

10.   What is the area, in square units, of the triangle shown below?

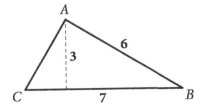

$$\left(A = \frac{1}{2}bh \right)$$

(A)   6
(B)   8
(C)   9
(D)   10.5
(E)   21

11.   Which ordered pair is found in the third quadrant?

(A) $(-5, -7)$
(B) $(-5, 6)$
(C) $(-7, 5)$
(D) $(6, -4)$
(E) $(3, 10)$

CONTINUE TO THE NEXT PAGE

12. Emma paid for six equally priced packages of candy with a $10 bill. She received $1.36 in change. How much did each package of candy cost?

   (A) $1.44
   (B) $1.66
   (C) $2.16
   (D) $1.89
   (E) $8.64

13. What is the value of 950 divided by 25?

   (A) 35
   (B) 38
   (C) 45
   (D) 48
   (E) 50

14. At a bakery, donuts cost $1.50 each and bagels cost $2 each. Carlos spent a total of $22.50 on donuts and bagels at this bakery. If Carlos bought 6 bagels, how many donuts did he buy?

   (A) 3
   (B) 4
   (C) 5
   (D) 6
   (E) 7

15. It took Casey 45 minutes to rake $\frac{3}{5}$ of the yard. If she continues raking at the same rate until the yard is completely raked, how long will it have taken her to rake the entire yard?

   (A) 1 hour
   (B) 1 hour 10 minutes
   (C) 1 hour 15 minutes
   (D) 1 hour 30 minutes
   (E) 1 hour 45 minutes

CONTINUE TO THE NEXT PAGE

16. In the problem shown, what is the value of $\Delta + \Diamond$?

$\Delta + \Diamond - 17 = -1$

(A) 4
(B) 5
(C) 8
(D) 13
(E) 16

17. Of 80 people in a room, $\dfrac{1}{5}$ of them are wearing boots. Of the people wearing boots, $\dfrac{1}{4}$ of them are wearing cowboy boots. How many people in the room are wearing cowboy boots?

(A) 4
(B) 16
(C) 32
(D) 64
(E) 72

18. What is the value of $\dfrac{5}{4}$ divided by 3?

(A) $\dfrac{1}{3}$

(B) $\dfrac{5}{12}$

(C) $\dfrac{15}{12}$

(D) $\dfrac{15}{4}$

(E) $\dfrac{15}{2}$

CONTINUE TO THE NEXT PAGE

19. Which expression is equivalent to $14b + 28w$?

   (A) $14(b + 14w)$

   (B) $7(2b + 28w)$

   (C) $7(2b + 3w)$

   (D) $\dfrac{1}{2}(7b + 14w)$

   (E) $\dfrac{1}{2}(28b + 56w)$

20. At a farm stand, for every 2 red peppers that were sold, 3 green peppers and 1 yellow pepper were sold. Which could be the total number of red, green, and yellow peppers sold?

   (A) 24

   (B) 25

   (C) 28

   (D) 32

   (E) 40

21. In the parallelogram below, what is the value of w?

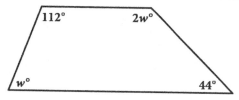

   (A) 32

   (B) 43

   (C) 54

   (D) 68

   (E) 195

CONTINUE TO THE NEXT PAGE

22. Jodi wants to paint a wall that is 12 feet wide and 9 feet tall. The paint is only sold in gallons, and one gallon of paint will cover 9 square yards. How many gallons of paint will she need to buy if she wants to cover the entire wall in one coat of paint?

    (A) 1
    (B) 2
    (C) 4
    (D) 12
    (E) 972

23. Balloons come in packages with 4 yellow balloons, 6 green balloons, and 8 red balloons. If Katya wants to create a bunch of balloons with 20 yellow balloons, 15 green balloons, and 15 red balloons, what is the minimum number of packages of balloons she must buy?

    (A) 2
    (B) 3
    (C) 5
    (D) 7
    (E) 8

24. If $25 - (-3m) = 16$, then what is the value of m?

    (A) −15
    (B) −13
    (C) −9
    (D) −3
    (E) 3

25. It took Kylie 3 days, 7 hours, and 14 minutes to complete a multi-day race. Lynnette completed the same race in 2 days, 23 hours, and 38 minutes. How much faster did Lynette complete the race than Kylie, in minutes?

    (A) 43
    (B) 138
    (C) 254
    (D) 315
    (E) 456

STOP

Section 1 – Quantitative

Correct Answer	Your Answer	Check (☑) if Answered Correctly	Check (☑) if Answered Incorrectly	Check (☑) if Omitted
1. A				
2. D				
3. D				
4. E				
5. C				
6. E				
7. A				
8. C				
9. B				
10. E				
11. C				
12. A				
13. E				
14. B				
15. C				
16. C				
17. A				
18. E				
19. B				
20. D				
21. E				
22. C				
23. A				
24. D				
25. B				
# of Checks (☑)	☒			☒

Enter and calculate: _____ – (_____ ÷ 4) = _____

Answered Correctly   # Answered Incorrectly   Your Raw Score

Section 2 - Reading Comprehension

Correct Answer	Your Answer	Check (☑) if Answered Correctly	Check (☑) if Answered Incorrectly	Check (☑) if Omitted
1. C				
2. E				
3. A				
4. B				
5. B				
6. D				
7. E				
8. B				
9. C				
10. E				
11. D				
12. A				
13. E				
14. A				
15. D				
16. C				
17. B				
18. C				
19. A				
20. E				
21. E				
22. A				
23. B				
24. D				
25. A				
26. D				
27. C				
28. B				
29. C				
30. C				
31. A				
32. E				
33. D				
34. D				

Correct Answer	Your Answer	Check (☑) if Answered Correctly	Check (☑) if Answered Incorrectly	Check (☑) if Omitted
35.E				
36.B				
37.A				
38.C				
39.E				
40.D				
# of Checks (☑)				

Enter and calculate: _____ – (_____ ÷ 4) = _____

Answered Correctly   # Answered Incorrectly   Your Raw Score

Section 3 – Verbal

Correct Answer	Your Answer	Check (☑) if Answered Correctly	Check (☑) if Answered Incorrectly	Check (☑) if Omitted
1. A				
2. E				
3. A				
4. B				
5. C				
6. D				
7. A				
8. D				
9. E				
10. B				
11. C				
12. E				
13. E				
14. B				
15. A				
16. C				
17. D				
18. B				
19. A				
20. A				
21. E				
22. D				
23. A				
24. C				
25. D				
26. C				
27. B				
28. C				
29. B				
30. C				
31. B				
32. D				
33. B				
34. D				

Correct Answer	Your Answer	Check (☑) if Answered Correctly	Check (☑) if Answered Incorrectly	Check (☑) if Omitted
35. A				
36. E				
37. A				
38. E				
39. B				
40. E				
41. B				
42. A				
43. C				
44. C				
45. B				
46. B				
47. C				
48. B				
49. A				
50. E				
51. B				
52. C				
53. B				
54. C				
55. A				
56. D				
57. E				
58. A				
59. E				
60. C				
# of Checks (☑)	✕			✕

Enter and calculate: _____ – (_____ ÷ 4) = _____

        # Answered Correctly   # Answered Incorrectly   Your Raw Score

Section 4 – Quantitative

Correct Answer	Your Answer	Check (☑) if Answered Correctly	Check (☑) if Answered Incorrectly	Check (☑) if Omitted
1. E				
2. B				
3. D				
4. C				
5. A				
6. B				
7. E				
8. E				
9. C				
10. D				
11. A				
12. A				
13. B				
14. E				
15. C				
16. E				
17. A				
18. B				
19. E				
20. A				
21. D				
22. B				
23. C				
24. D				
25. E				
# of Checks (☑)				

Enter and calculate: _____ – (_____ ÷ 4) = _____

                          # Answered Correctly   # Answered Incorrectly   Your Raw Score

Interpreting your scores

On the SSAT, your raw score is the number of questions that you answered correctly on each section minus the number of questions you answered incorrectly divided by 4. Nothing is added or subtracted for the questions that you omit. Your raw score is then converted into a scaled score. This scaled score is then converted into a percentile score. Remember that it is the percentile score that schools are looking at. Your percentile score compares you only to other students in your grade. Below is a chart that gives a very rough conversion between your raw score on the practice test and a percentile score.

PLEASE NOTE – The purpose of this chart is to let you see how the scoring works, not to give you an accurate percentile score. You will need to complete the practice test in *The Official Guide to the Middle Level SSAT* in order to get a more accurate percentile score.

Grade 5

	Section 1 + Section 4: Quantitative	Section 2: Reading comprehension	Section 3: Verbal
Approximate raw score for 75th percentile	28-29	22-23	28-29
Approximate raw score for 50th percentile	19-20	17-18	19-20
Approximate raw score for 25th percentile	11-12	11-12	12-13

Grade 6

	Section 1 + Section 4: Quantitative	Section 2: Reading comprehension	Section 3: Verbal
Approximate raw score for 75th percentile	35-36	27-28	36-37
Approximate raw score for 50th percentile	26-27	21-22	26-27
Approximate raw score for 25th percentile	16-17	14-15	17-18

Grade 7

	Section 1 + Section 4: Quantitative	Section 2: Reading comprehension	Section 3: Verbal
Approximate raw score for 75th percentile	39-40	29-30	42-43
Approximate raw score for 50th percentile	32-33	24-25	32-33
Approximate raw score for 25th percentile	22-23	17-18	23-24

Looking for more practice?

Check out our other book for the Middle Level SSAT:

The Best Unofficial Practice Tests for the Middle Level SSAT

✓ 2 full-length practice tests

Test Prep Works Catalog

	Content instruction	Test-taking strategies	Practice problems	Full-length practice tests
ISEE				
Lower Level (for students applying for admission to grades 5-6)				
Success on the Lower Level ISEE	✓	✓	✓	✓ (1)
30 Days to Acing the Lower Level ISEE		✓	✓	
The Best Unofficial Practice Tests for the Lower Level ISEE				✓ (2)
Middle Level (for students applying for admission to grades 7-8)				
Success on the Middle Level ISEE	✓	✓	✓	✓ (1)
The Best Unofficial Practice Tests for the Middle Level ISEE				✓ (2)
Upper Level (for students applying for admission to grades 9-12)				
Success on the Upper Level ISEE	✓	✓	✓	✓ (1)
The Best Unofficial Practice Tests for the Upper Level ISEE				✓ (2)
SSAT				
Middle Level (for students applying for admission to grades 6-8)				
Success on the Middle Level SSAT	✓	✓	✓	✓ (1)
The Best Unofficial Practice Tests for the Middle Level SSAT				✓ (2)
Upper Level (for students applying for admission to grades 9-12)				
Success on the Upper Level SSAT	✓	✓	✓	✓ (1)
30 Days to Acing the Upper Level SSAT		✓	✓	
30 More Days to Acing the Upper Level SSAT			✓	
The Best Unofficial Practice Tests for the Upper Level SSAT				✓ (2)

ABBOTT LEARNING LLC | TEST PREP WORKS

Made in the USA
Middletown, DE
30 November 2023